The Complete

Keto Diet

Cookbook

For Beginners

1600 Days of Easy, Low-Carb and Delicious Recipes for Ketogenic Living, With a 30-Day Meal Plan to Help You Manage Body Weight and Boost Energy Levels

Vincent M. Riehl

Table of Contents

Chapter 1

Introduction

Welcome to the wild and wonderful world of ketosis cuisine! Get ready to embark on a culinary adventure that will have your taste buds doing the happy dance while your body thanks you for the deliciously low-carb delights.

Now, before we dive headfirst into this cookbook, let's address the elephant in the room: the ketogenic diet. Yes, it's the diet that has everyone buzzing, and no, it's not a secret society of bacon worshipers (although we do love our bacon). It's a way of eating that's all about embracing healthy fats, moderate protein, and bidding farewell to those pesky carbs.

But fear not, dear reader, for this is no ordinary cookbook. No, we're not going to leave you dreaming of forbidden carbs while munching on lettuce leaves. Oh no! We've crafted a collection of keto recipes that will tickle your taste buds, make your tummy rumble with excitement, and prove once and for all that a low-carb lifestyle can be as delicious as it is nutritious.

So, whether you're a keto newbie, a seasoned keto warrior, or just someone looking to add some culinary pizzazz to your low-carb repertoire, you're in for a treat. From breakfast to dinner, snacks to desserts, we've got you covered with mouthwatering recipes that will make you forget all about those carb-loaded temptations lurking in the shadows.

But let's be real for a moment. We're all human, and we understand the occasional hankering for a slice of pizza or a gooey chocolate chip cookie. That's why we've included some clever keto hacks and inventive substitutions that will satisfy those cravings without derailing your progress. It's all about finding that delicate balance between indulgence and staying true to the keto way.

So, grab your apron, unleash your inner kitchen maestro, and get ready to create culinary masterpieces that will have your friends and family begging for seconds. With this Keto Diet Cookbook as your trusty guide, you'll discover that eating low-carb doesn't mean sacrificing flavor, fun, or foodie adventures.

Now, let's turn up the heat, fire up those taste buds, and let the ketogenic magic begin! Get ready to embark on a scrumptious journey that will have you saying, "Who needs carbs when you've got these ketolicious delights?" Let's dig in and savor every mouthwatering bite together. Bon appétit, keto warriors!

Explanation of the Keto Diet

The Keto Diet, short for ketogenic diet, is a low-carbohydrate, high-fat diet that has gained popularity in recent years. The main goal of the diet is to get your body into a state of ketosis, where it burns fat for energy instead of carbohydrates.

When you consume fewer carbohydrates, your body doesn't have enough glucose to use as fuel and starts breaking down stored fat for energy. This process produces molecules called ketones, which your body uses as an alternative source of energy.

The typical macronutrient breakdown for a keto diet is 70-80% fat, 20-25% protein, and 5-10% carbohydrates. This means that foods like meat, fish, eggs, cheese, nuts, seeds, and oils are encouraged, while high-carb foods like bread, pasta, rice, and sugary snacks are restricted.

While the keto diet has been shown to be effective for weight loss and improving certain health conditions such as epilepsy and type 2 diabetes, it may not be suitable for everyone. It's important to speak with a healthcare professional before starting any new diet or lifestyle change.

Benefits and Potential Challenges of Following a Keto Diet

Benefits of Following a Keto Diet:

1. Weight Loss: The keto diet can lead to significant weight loss due to the reduction in carbohydrates and increase in fat intake, which helps to suppress appetite and promote satiety.

2. Improved Blood Sugar Control: The keto diet may help to improve blood sugar control in people with type 2 diabetes by reducing insulin resistance and promoting better glucose utilization.

3. Reduced Inflammation: The keto diet has been shown to reduce inflammation in the body, which is linked to several chronic diseases such as heart disease, cancer, and Alzheimer's.

4. Increased Energy: When your body is in a state of ketosis, it uses stored fat for energy, which can lead to increased energy levels and improved mental clarity.

Potential Challenges of Following a Keto Diet:

1. Initial Side Effects: When transitioning to a keto diet, some people may experience side effects such as headaches, fatigue, and constipation, which usually resolve within a few days.

2. Limited Food Choices: The keto diet restricts high-carb foods such as bread, pasta, and fruit, which may make it challenging to follow for some people.

3. Nutrient Deficiencies: Since the keto diet limits certain food groups, it may be difficult to get all the necessary nutrients from food alone, so supplements may be necessary.

4. Difficulty Maintaining Long-Term: While the keto diet can be effective for short-term weight loss, it may be difficult to maintain long-term due to its restrictive nature.

Tips for Success on a Keto Diet

Here are some tips for success on a keto diet:

1. Plan Your Meals: Planning your meals in advance can help you stay on track and avoid making impulsive food choices. Make a weekly meal plan and grocery list to ensure you have everything you need.

2. Track Your Macros: Tracking your macronutrient intake (fat, protein, and carbohydrates) can help you stay within the recommended range for the keto diet. Use a food tracking app or website to make it easier.

3. Stay Hydrated: Drinking enough water is important for overall health and can also help prevent dehydration, which is common on the keto diet due to increased water loss.

4. Incorporate Healthy Fats: While the keto diet is high in fat, it's important to choose healthy sources such as avocados, nuts, seeds, olive oil, and fatty fish.

5. Don't Forget About Fiber: Since the keto diet limits carbohydrates, it's important to incorporate fiber-rich foods such as leafy greens, broccoli, cauliflower, and berries to help maintain digestive health.

6. Be Patient: It may take some time for your body to adjust to the keto diet and enter a state of ketosis. Be patient and stick with it, as the benefits can be significant.

7. Seek Support: Joining a support group or working with a healthcare professional who is knowledgeable about the keto diet can help you stay motivated and on track.

Chapter 2

Understanding the Keto Diet

Explanation of Ketosis and How It Affects the Body

Ketosis is a metabolic state in which the body uses stored fat for energy instead of carbohydrates. Normally, the body uses glucose (a type of sugar) from carbohydrates as its primary source of fuel. However, when carbohydrate intake is limited, such as on a ketogenic diet, the body starts to break down stored fat into molecules called ketones, which can be used for energy.

When the body enters a state of ketosis, several changes occur:

1. Increased Fat Burning: The body starts to burn more fat for energy, which can lead to weight loss.

2. Reduced Appetite: Ketones have been shown to suppress appetite, which can help with weight loss and calorie control.

3. Improved Blood Sugar Control: Ketones can also help improve blood sugar control by reducing insulin resistance and promoting better glucose utilization.

4. Mental Clarity: Some people report improved mental clarity and focus when in a state of ketosis.

However, it's important to note that ketosis can also have some potential side effects, such as bad breath, constipation, and fatigue. Additionally, people with certain medical conditions, such as liver or pancreatic disease, should not follow a ketogenic diet without first consulting with a healthcare professional.

Overall, ketosis can be a beneficial metabolic state for some people, particularly those looking to lose weight or improve blood sugar control. However, it's important to approach the keto diet with caution and seek guidance from a healthcare professional before starting.

Macronutrient Ratios and Food Composition on a Keto Diet

The macronutrient ratios on a keto diet typically involve high fat, moderate protein, and low carbohydrates. The recommended macronutrient breakdown for a keto diet is:

- 70-80% of calories from fat
- 20-25% of calories from protein
- 5-10% of calories from carbohydrates

In terms of food composition, the following foods are typically encouraged on a keto diet:

- Healthy fats: avocado, nuts, seeds, olive oil, coconut oil, butter, ghee, fatty fish, and cheese.
- Protein sources: meat, poultry, fish, eggs, and tofu.
- Low-carbohydrate vegetables: leafy greens, broccoli, cauliflower, zucchini, and asparagus.

- Berries: strawberries, raspberries, and blackberries.

High-carbohydrate foods such as grains, bread, pasta, rice, and sugary snacks are generally avoided or limited on a keto diet. It's important to note that some fruits and vegetables, such as bananas, potatoes, and corn, are also high in carbohydrates and may need to be avoided or limited on a keto diet.

It's important to work with a healthcare professional or registered dietitian when starting a keto diet to ensure that your nutrient needs are being met and to monitor for any potential side effects or complications.

Common Keto-Friendly Ingredients and Substitutions

Here are some common keto-friendly ingredients and substitutions that can be used on a keto diet:

1. Almond Flour: Almond flour is a low-carbohydrate alternative to wheat flour and can be used in baking and cooking.

2. Coconut Flour: Coconut flour is another low-carbohydrate alternative to wheat flour that is high in fiber and protein.

3. Cauliflower: Cauliflower is a versatile vegetable that can be used as a low-carbohydrate substitute for rice, potatoes, and even pizza crust.

4. Zucchini: Zucchini is another low-carbohydrate vegetable that can be used in place of pasta noodles or in casseroles.

5. Avocado: Avocado is a healthy source of fat that can be used in place of mayonnaise or as a topping for salads and sandwiches.

6. Nuts and Seeds: Nuts and seeds such as almonds, walnuts, chia seeds, and flax seeds are high in healthy fats and can be used as snacks or added to recipes for extra nutrition.

7. Coconut Oil: Coconut oil is a healthy source of fat that can be used in cooking and baking.

8. Greek Yogurt: Greek yogurt is high in protein and can be used as a substitute for sour cream or as a base for dips and dressings.

9. Stevia: Stevia is a natural sweetener that can be used in place of sugar in recipes.

10. Dark Chocolate: Dark chocolate with a high percentage of cocoa (70% or higher) is a keto-friendly treat that can satisfy a sweet tooth while still staying within the macronutrient ratios of a keto diet.

It's important to remember that portion control is still important on a keto diet, even with these keto-friendly ingredients and substitutions. It's also important to read food labels carefully and avoid hidden sources of carbohydrates.

Chapter 3

Meal Planning and Prepping

Tips for Successful Meal Planning on a Keto Diet

Here are some tips for successful meal planning on a keto diet:

1. Plan Ahead: Take time to plan your meals and snacks for the week ahead. This will help you stay on track and avoid making impulsive food choices.

2. Focus on Whole Foods: Choose whole foods that are high in healthy fats, moderate in protein, and low in carbohydrates. Examples include meat, fish, eggs, nuts, seeds, leafy greens, and non-starchy vegetables.

3. Batch Cook: Consider batch cooking meals and snacks in advance to save time during the week. For example, cook a large batch of chicken or beef and use it in different recipes throughout the week.

4. Keep It Simple: Don't feel like you need to make elaborate meals every day. Simple meals such as grilled chicken with roasted vegetables or a salad with avocado and nuts can be both delicious and nutritious.

5. Use Spices and Herbs: Using spices and herbs can add flavor and variety to your meals without adding extra calories or carbohydrates.

6. Meal Prep Containers: Invest in meal prep containers to make it easy to pack and store your meals and snacks for the week.

7. Snack Smart: Choose keto-friendly snacks such as nuts, seeds, cheese, and hard-boiled eggs to keep you satisfied between meals.

8. Read Food Labels: Be sure to read food labels carefully to avoid hidden sources of carbohydrates and to ensure that you're staying within your macronutrient ratios.

By following these tips, you can successfully plan and prepare meals on a keto diet, which can help you achieve your health and weight loss goals.

Meal Prepping

Here are some steps to prepare a keto diet recipe:

1. Choose your ingredients: The key to a successful keto recipe is choosing low-carb, high-fat ingredients. Examples include meats (such as beef, chicken, and pork), fish, eggs, non-starchy vegetables (such as spinach, broccoli, and cauliflower), nuts and seeds, and healthy fats (such as avocado, olive oil, and coconut oil).

2. Calculate your macros: To ensure that your recipe is keto-friendly, you'll need to calculate the macronutrient ratios. Generally, a keto diet consists of 70-75% fat, 20-25% protein, and 5-10% carbohydrates.

3. Plan your meal: Once you have chosen your ingredients and calculated your macros, plan out your meal. This can involve selecting a main dish (such as grilled salmon or roasted chicken), adding in some low-carb vegetables, and seasoning with herbs and spices.

4. Cook your meal: Prepare your ingredients according to your recipe instructions. For example, if you are making a keto-friendly lasagna, you may need to use zucchini instead of noodles and almond flour instead of wheat flour.

5. Track your macros: After you have prepared your meal, make sure to track your macros to ensure that you are staying within your daily limits. There are many apps and websites available that can help you track your macros and stay on track with your keto diet.

Remember to always consult with a healthcare professional before starting any new diet or exercise program.

Tips for Eating Out

Here are some tips for eating out on a keto diet:

1. Research the restaurant in advance: Check out the menu online before you go to see if there are any keto-friendly options available. Many restaurants now offer low-carb or gluten-free options that can be adapted to a keto diet.

2. Stick to simple dishes: When in doubt, stick to simple dishes that are easy to customize. For example, order a grilled chicken breast with a side of steamed vegetables and ask for extra butter or olive oil instead of sauce.

3. Avoid high-carb foods: Stay away from bread, pasta, rice, potatoes, and other high-carb foods. Instead, opt for salads, grilled meats, seafood, and low-carb vegetables.

4. Ask for substitutions: Don't be afraid to ask for substitutions or modifications to your meal. For example, ask for a lettuce wrap instead of a bun, or substitute a side salad for French fries.

5. Watch out for hidden carbs: Be aware of hidden carbs in sauces, dressings, and marinades. Ask for these on the side so you can control how much you consume.

6. Bring your own snacks: If you're worried about not finding keto-friendly options at a restaurant, bring your own snacks such as nuts, cheese, or beef jerky.

Remember, it's possible to eat out on a keto diet as long as you do your research and make smart choices. Don't be afraid to ask questions and customize your meal to fit your dietary needs.

Chapter 4

Start to Cook

Final Thoughts on the Keto Diet and Its Potential Benefits

The keto diet can be an effective way to lose weight and improve certain health markers, such as blood sugar control and cholesterol levels. By limiting carbohydrate intake and increasing fat consumption, the body enters a state of ketosis where it uses stored fat for energy instead of glucose.

However, it's important to approach the keto diet with caution and seek guidance from a healthcare professional before starting. The keto diet may not be appropriate for everyone, especially those with certain medical conditions or who are pregnant or breastfeeding.

Additionally, the keto diet can be challenging to maintain long-term and may require significant changes in eating habits and food choices. It's important to ensure that you're still meeting your nutrient needs and getting enough fiber while following a keto diet.

Overall, the keto diet can be a useful tool for weight loss and improving certain health markers, but it's important to approach it with caution and seek guidance from a healthcare professional to ensure that it's safe and appropriate for you.

Encouragement for Continued Success on a Keto Lifestyle

Congratulations on making the decision to adopt a keto lifestyle! It takes a lot of dedication and commitment to make changes to your diet and lifestyle, but the benefits can be significant. Here are some words of encouragement to help you continue on your journey:

1. Take it one day at a time: Remember that every small step you take towards your goal is progress. Don't get discouraged if you have setbacks or slip-ups along the way. Just focus on making healthy choices each day.

2. Celebrate your successes: Take time to celebrate your successes, no matter how small they may seem. Whether it's losing a few pounds or sticking to your meal plan for a week, acknowledge your accomplishments and give yourself credit for your hard work.

3. Surround yourself with support: Seek out friends, family members, or online communities who are also following a keto lifestyle. Having a support system can make all the difference in staying motivated and accountable.

4. Experiment with new recipes: Keep things interesting by trying out new keto-friendly recipes and ingredients. There are plenty of resources available online, including blogs, cookbooks, and social media groups.

5. Focus on the benefits: Remind yourself of the benefits of a keto lifestyle, such as improved energy levels, better blood sugar control, and weight loss. Keeping these benefits in mind can help you stay motivated and committed to your goals.

Remember, adopting a keto lifestyle is a journey, not a destination. Stay positive, stay focused, and keep pushing forward. You've got this!

30-Day Meal Plan

DAYS	BREAKFAST	LUNCH	DINNER	SNACK/DESSERT
1	Protein Waffles	Tilapia Bake	Chicken Kiev	Hummus Celery Boats
2	Easy Skillet Pancakes	Bacon Halibut Steak	Rotisserie Chicken	Thyme Sautéed Radishes
3	Bacon, Cheese, and Avocado Melt	Sweet Tilapia Fillets	Chicken Pesto Parmigiana	Garlic Herb Butter
4	Bacon Egg Cups	Tilapia with Pecans	Chicken Laksa	Buffalo Bill's Chicken Dip
5	Mocha Protein Keto Coffee	Coconut Milk-Braised Squid	Chicken Broth	Ketone Gummies
6	Jalapeño and Bacon Breakfast Pizza	Bacon-Wrapped Scallops	Chicken with Lettuce	Warm Herbed Olives
7	Indian Masala Omelet	Caprese Salmon	Poblano Chicken	Wedge Dippers
8	Kimchi Eggs	Tuna Avocado Bites	Chicken Tenders	Red Wine Mushrooms
9	Pulled Pork Hash	Spicy Shrimp Fried Rice	Classic Whole Chicken	Cheese Almond Crackers
10	Breakfast Pizza	Tuna Cakes	Thai Tacos with Peanut Sauce	Candied Georgia Pecans
11	Avocado Breakfast Sandwich	Taco Cheese Cups	Braised Pork Belly	Keto Asian Dumplings
12	Crunchy Vanilla Protein Bars	Rosemary Mint Marinated Lamb Chops	Mustard Lamb Chops	Asiago Shishito Peppers
13	Weekend Western Omelet	The Classic Juicy Lucy	Lamb Leg with Sun-Dried Tomato Pesto	Haystack Cookies
14	Jalapeño Popper Egg Cups	Baked Crustless Pizza	Homemade Classic Beef Burgers	Avocado Salsa
15	Skillet Pancake Puff	Low Carb Pork Tenderloin	Classic Pork and Cauliflower Keema	Tapenade
16	Everything Bagels	Stuffed Cabbage Rolls	Italian Beef Meatloaf	Vanilla Cream Pie
17	Dreamy Matcha Latte	Zucchini Rolls	Herb-Crusted Lamb Chops	Strawberry Panna Cotta

DAYS	BREAKFAST	LUNCH	DINNER	SNACK/DESSERT
18	Golden Pancakes	Braised Short Ribs	Bo Ssäm	Dark-Chocolate Strawberry Bark
19	Cheese Egg Muffins	Beef Barbacoa	London Broil with Herb Butter	Chocolate Chip Almond Cookies
20	Rocket Fuel Hot Chocolate	Garlic Balsamic London Broil	Thai Beef Lettuce Wraps	Chocolate Pecan Clusters
21	Chocolate Chip Waffle	Kung Pao Chicken	Cajun Cod Fillet	Pecan Brownies
22	Pumpkin Spice Smoothie	Chicken Fajitas	Tuna Casserole	Lemon Drops
23	Baked Eggs and Ham	Coconut Chicken	Salmon with Dill Butter	Lemon Vanilla Cheesecake
24	Pork and Quill Egg Cups	Caprese Chicken Skillet	Cod with Jalapeño	Fudgy Brownies
25	Double-Pork Frittata	Cheesy Chicken Bake with Zucchini	Lemon and Dill Salmon Kabobs	Orange–Olive Oil Cupcakes
26	Pepper Sausage Fry	Lemon Threaded Chicken Skewers	Clam Chowder	Fudge Pops
27	Cheese & Aioli Eggs	Italian Chicken with Sauce	Shrimp Ceviche Salad	Mixed Berry Cobbler
28	Savory Zucchini Cheddar Waffles	Blackened Cajun Chicken Tenders	Ginger Cod	Mini Cheesecake
29	Pizza Pâté	Peppercorn-Crusted Beef Tenderloin	Salmon Cakes	Lime Muffins
30	Overnight "Noats"	Beef and Butternut Squash Stew	Sole Meunière	Vanilla Flan with Mint

Chapter 5

Breakfasts

Protein Waffles

Prep time: 5 minutes | Cook time: 13 minutes | Makes 3 medium-sized waffles

Waffles:

4 large eggs

¼ cup natural peanut butter

¼ cup mascarpone cheese

¼ cup unsweetened almond

milk 1 scoop unflavored whey protein powder

2 tablespoons unsalted butter, melted

Toppings (Optional):

Sugar-free maple syrup

Natural peanut butter

Whipped cream

1. Preheat a waffle iron on the medium setting. 2. Put all the waffle ingredients in a large mixing bowl and combine using a whisk or an electric hand mixer. 3. Open the waffle iron and grease the top and bottom with coconut oil spray. 4. Using a ½-cup measuring cup, scoop up some of the batter and pour it into the center of the waffle iron. Close the lid and allow the waffle to cook for 4 to 4½ minutes, until golden brown. 5. Repeat with the remaining batter, making a total of 3 waffles. 6. Serve the waffles with maple syrup, peanut butter, and/or whipped cream, if desired.

Per Serving:

calories: 409 | fat: 33g | protein: 24g | carbs: 5g | net carbs: 3g | fiber: 2g

Prosciutto Baked Eggs with Spinach

Prep time: 5 minutes | Cook time: 20 minutes | Serves 6

1 (12 ounces / 340 g) bag frozen spinach, thawed and drained

6 ounces (170 g) prosciutto, very thinly sliced (about 12 large, ultra-thin slices)

1 tablespoon avocado oil

6 cloves garlic, minced

¼ cup finely chopped sun-dried tomatoes

⅛ teaspoon sea salt

Pinch of black pepper

12 large eggs

1. Preheat the oven to 350ºF (180ºC). 2. Place the thawed spinach into a kitchen towel and squeeze well over the sink, getting rid of as much liquid as possible. Set aside. 3. Line 12 cups of a muffin tin with a thin layer of prosciutto, overlapping the prosciutto pieces slightly if necessary. Wrap around the sides first, then patch any holes and the bottom. Set aside. 4. In a large skillet, heat the oil over medium-high heat. Add the minced garlic and sauté for about 30 seconds, until fragrant. Add the spinach and sun-dried tomatoes. Season with the sea salt and black pepper. Sauté for 5 minutes. 5. Divide the spinach mixture evenly among the prosciutto-lined muffin cups. Crack an egg into each muffin cup. 6. Transfer the pan to the oven and bake until the eggs are done to your liking, approximately as follows: a. Runny yolks: 13 to 15 minutes b. Semi-firm yolks: 16 to 18 minutes c. Firm yolks: 18 to 20 minutes 7. Allow the egg muffins to cool in the pan for a few minutes before removing.

Per Serving:

calories: 314 | fat: 22g | protein: 20g | carbs: 7g | net carbs: 5g | fiber: 2g

Easy Skillet Pancakes

Prep time: 5 minutes | Cook time: 5 minutes | Makes 8 pancakes

8 ounces (227 g) cream cheese

8 eggs

2 tablespoons coconut flour

2 teaspoons baking powder

1 teaspoon ground cinnamon

½ teaspoon vanilla extract

1 teaspoon liquid stevia or sweetener of choice (optional)

2 tablespoons butter

1. In a blender, combine the cream cheese, eggs, coconut flour, baking powder, cinnamon, vanilla, and stevia (if using). Blend until smooth. 2. In a large skillet over medium heat, melt the butter. 3. Use half the mixture to pour four evenly sized pancakes and cook for about a minute, until you see bubbles on top. Flip the pancakes and cook for another minute. Remove from the pan and add more butter or oil to the skillet if needed. Repeat with the remaining batter. 4. Top with butter and eat right away, or freeze the pancakes in a freezer-safe resealable bag with sheets of parchment in between, for up to 1 month.

Per Serving:

1 pancake: calories: 179 | fat: 15g | protein: 8g | carbs: 3g | net carbs: 2g | fiber: 1g

Traditional Eggs and Bacon Cooked in Butter

Prep time: 5 minutes | Cook time: 15 minutes | Serves 1

1 tablespoon grass-fed butter, divided

2 strips uncured bacon

2 eggs

Sea salt, for seasoning

Freshly ground black pepper, for seasoning

1. Cook the bacon. In a large skillet over medium-high heat, melt ½ tablespoon of butter. Add the bacon to the pan and fry until it is cooked through and crispy, turning once, about 10 minutes total. Transfer the bacon to paper towels to drain and wipe the skillet with more paper towels. 2. Cook the eggs. Turn the heat down to medium. Add the remaining ½ tablespoon of butter to the skillet. Carefully crack the eggs into the skillet and cook until the whites are completely set, about 3 minutes. 3. Serve. Carefully transfer the eggs and bacon to a plate and season the eggs with salt and pepper.

Per Serving:

calories: 322 | fat: 26g | protein: 19g | carbs: 3g | net carbs: 2g | fiber: 1g

Bacon, Cheese, and Avocado Melt

Prep time: 5 minutes | Cook time: 3 to 5 minutes | Serves 2

1 avocado	1 tablespoon heavy cream
4 slices cooked bacon, chopped	¼ cup shredded Cheddar
2 tablespoons salsa	cheese

1. Preheat the air fryer to 400ºF (204ºC). 2. Slice the avocado in half lengthwise and remove the stone. To ensure the avocado halves do not roll in the basket, slice a thin piece of skin off the base. 3. In a small bowl, combine the bacon, salsa, and cream. Divide the mixture between the avocado halves and top with the cheese. 4. Place the avocado halves in the air fryer basket and air fry for 3 to 5 minutes until the cheese has melted and begins to brown. Serve warm.

Per Serving:

calories: 357 | fat: 30g | protein: 14g | carbs: 11g | net carbs: 4g | fiber: 7g

Nori Rolls with Almond Dipping Sauce

Prep time: 30 minutes | Cook time: 5 minutes | Serves 8

Nori Rolls:

8 nori sheets	3 tablespoons roasted sesame
2 large Hass avocados,	seeds
skinned, cored, and sliced	½ packed cup (35 g) fresh
(about 12 ounces/340 g flesh)	cilantro leaves, roughly
½ English cucumber, sliced	chopped
thin	

Almond Dipping Sauce:

1 teaspoon toasted sesame oil	1 tablespoon fish sauce
2 small cloves garlic, minced	2 teaspoons coconut aminos
½ cup (140 g) unsweetened	1 teaspoon Sriracha sauce
smooth almond butter	2 drops liquid stevia
⅓ cup (80 ml) MCT oil	1 tablespoon apple cider
1 tablespoon fresh lime juice	vinegar

1. Place a nori sheet on a sushi mat and, using your finger dabbed in water, lightly dampen the bottom three-quarters of the sheet. Stack the nori roll ingredients along the bottom of the sheet, 1 inch (2. 5 cm) from the end, placing one-eighth of the avocado, then one-eighth of the cucumber, followed by a sprinkle of sesame seeds and chopped cilantro. 2. Pick up the edge of the sushi mat and roll it into itself, over the fillings, being careful not to push the ingredients up the nori sheet. Continue to roll until you get to the last one-quarter section that isn't damp yet. Dampen that area, then roll onto it, pressing down to seal. Rotate the roll in the mat for a couple of seconds to secure the sheet. Remove the roll from the sushi mat and place on a clean plate. If you find that the roll is a bit dry, dampen it all over with additional water. 3. Repeat with the remaining nori roll ingredients. Once complete, use a sharp knife to cut each roll into 6 pieces. Set on a clean plate. 4. Prepare the almond sauce: Place the sesame oil and minced garlic in a small saucepan. Heat on low just until fragrant, about 2 minutes. 5. Add the almond butter, MCT oil, lime juice, fish sauce, aminos, Sriracha, and stevia. Cook, whisking occasionally, until the mixture is smooth and only lightly simmering. 6. Stir in the vinegar and let the sauce sit for 2 minutes before using. Drizzle the sauce over the rolls and serve extra on the side for dipping.

Per Serving:

calories: 321 | fat: 29g | protein: 6g | carbs: 9g | net carbs: 3g | fiber: 6g

Bacon Egg Cups

Prep time: 5 minutes | Cook time: 7 minutes | Serves 4

6 large eggs	¼ teaspoon sea salt
2 strips cooked bacon, sliced	¼ teaspoon black pepper
in ¼-inch wide pieces	1 cup water
½ cup Cheddar cheese,	1 tablespoon chopped fresh
divided	flat leaf parsley

1. In a small bowl, beat the eggs. Stir in the cooked bacon, ¼ cup of the cheese, sea salt and pepper. Divide the egg mixture equally among four ramekins and loosely cover with aluminum foil. 2. Pour the water and place the trivet in the Instant Pot. Place two ramekins on the trivet and stack the other two on the top. 3. Lock the lid. Select the Manual mode and set the cooking time for 7 minutes at High Pressure. When the timer goes off, use a natural pressure release for 10 minutes, then release any remaining pressure. Carefully open the lid. 4. Top each ramekin with the remaining ¼ cup of the cheese. Lock the lid and melt the cheese for 2 minutes. Garnish with the chopped parsley and serve immediately.

Per Serving:

calories: 168 | fat: 12g | protein: 13g | carbs: 1g | net carbs: 1g | fiber: 0g

Mocha Protein Keto Coffee

Prep time: 5 minutes | Cook time: 1 minutes | Serves 1

12 ounces hot brewed coffee	1 scoop chocolate-flavored
2 tablespoons heavy whipping	protein powder
cream	1 scoop unflavored collagen
1 tablespoon unsalted butter	peptides
1 tablespoon cocoa powder	10 drops of liquid stevia

1. Place all the ingredients in a blender and blend until smooth and frothy. Pour into a 16-ounce mug and serve immediately, or pour it into a Thermos and take it on the go!

Per Serving:

calories: 361 | fat: 24g | protein: 37g | carbs: 4g | net carbs: 2g | fiber: 2g

Jalapeño and Bacon Breakfast Pizza

Prep time: 5 minutes | Cook time: 10 minutes | Serves 2

1 cup shredded Mozzarella cheese	bacon, chopped
1 ounce (28 g) cream cheese, broken into small pieces	¼ cup chopped pickled jalapeños
4 slices cooked sugar-free	1 large egg, whisked
	¼ teaspoon salt

1. Place Mozzarella in a single layer on the bottom of an ungreased round nonstick baking dish. Scatter cream cheese pieces, bacon, and jalapeños over Mozzarella, then pour egg evenly around baking dish. 2. Sprinkle with salt and place into air fryer basket. Adjust the temperature to 330ºF (166ºC) and bake for 10 minutes. When cheese is brown and egg is set, pizza will be done. 3. Let cool on a large plate 5 minutes before serving.

Per Serving:
calories: 486 | fat: 37g | protein: 29g | carbs: 5g | net carbs: 3g | fiber: 1g

Everything Bagels

Prep time: 15 minutes | Cook time: 14 minutes | Makes 6 bagels

1¾ cups shredded Mozzarella cheese or goat cheese Mozzarella	vinegar
2 tablespoons unsalted butter or coconut oil	1 cup blanched almond flour
	1 tablespoon baking powder
1 large egg, beaten	⅛ teaspoon fine sea salt
1 tablespoon apple cider	1½ teaspoons everything bagel seasoning

Make the dough: Put the Mozzarella and butter in a large microwave-safe bowl and microwave for 1 to 2 minutes, until the cheese is entirely melted. Stir well. Add the egg and vinegar. Using a hand mixer on medium, combine well. Add the almond flour, baking powder, and salt and, using the mixer, combine well. 2. Lay a piece of parchment paper on the countertop and place the dough on it. Knead it for about 3 minutes. The dough should be a little sticky but pliable. (If the dough is too sticky, chill it in the refrigerator for an hour or overnight.) 3. Preheat the air fryer to 350ºF (177ºC). Spray a baking sheet or pie pan that will fit into your air fryer with avocado oil. 4. Divide the dough into 6 equal portions. Roll 1 portion into a log that is 6 inches long and about ½ inch thick. Form the log into a circle and seal the edges together, making a bagel shape. Repeat with the remaining portions of dough, making 6 bagels. 5. Place the bagels on the greased baking sheet. Spray the bagels with avocado oil and top with everything bagel seasoning, pressing the seasoning into the dough with your hands. 6. Place the bagels in the air fryer and bake for 14 minutes, or until cooked through and golden brown, flipping after 6 minutes. 7. Remove the bagels from the air fryer

and allow them to cool slightly before slicing them in half and serving. Store leftovers in an airtight container in the fridge for up to 4 days or in the freezer for up to a month.

Per Serving:
calories: 290 | fat: 25g | protein: 13g | carbs: 7g | net carbs: 4g | fiber: 3g

Indian Masala Omelet

Prep time: 8 minutes | Cook time: 25 minutes | Makes 1 large omelet

3 tablespoons avocado oil, coconut oil, or ghee	and finely diced
	1½ teaspoons curry powder
¼ cup (20 g) sliced green onions	½ teaspoon garam masala
1 clove garlic, minced	6 large eggs, beaten
1 small tomato, diced	¼ cup (15 g) chopped fresh cilantro leaves and stems
1 green chili pepper, seeded	

1. Heat the oil in a large frying pan over medium heat until it shimmers. When the oil is shimmering, add the green onions, garlic, tomato, and chili pepper. Cook for 10 minutes, or until the liquid from the tomatoes has evaporated. 2. Reduce the heat to low and sprinkle the tomato mixture with the curry powder and garam masala. Stir to incorporate, then drizzle the beaten eggs over the top. 3. Cover and cook for 5 minutes, or until the edges are cooked through. 4. Sprinkle with the cilantro, fold one side over the other, cover, and cook for another 10 minutes. 5. Remove from the heat, cut in half, and serve.

Per Serving:
calories: 438 | fat: 36g | protein: 20g | carbs: 8g | net carbs: 6g | fiber: 2g

Kimchi Eggs

Prep time: 4 minutes | Cook time: 5 minutes | Serves 2

1 tablespoon Paleo fat	ground black pepper, to taste
4 large eggs	1 cup kimchi
Fine sea salt and freshly	
For Garnish (optional):	
Sliced green onions	Red pepper flakes

1. Heat the fat in a cast-iron skillet over low heat. Crack the eggs into the skillet. Season with salt and pepper. Cover with a lid and cook until the whites are cooked through on top and the yolks are still runny, about 4 minutes. 2. Meanwhile, divide the kimchi between two serving bowls. When the eggs are done, remove them from the heat and place 2 eggs into each bowl. Garnish with green onions and red pepper flakes, if desired.

Per Serving:
calories: 240 | fat: 16g | protein: 16g | carbs: 8g | net carbs: 5g | fiber: 3g

Sausage, Egg, and Cheese Breakfast Bake

Prep time: 15 minutes | Cook time: 35 minutes | Serves 6

1 tablespoon unsalted butter
⅓ cup chopped yellow onions
1 pound bulk breakfast sausage
8 large eggs
⅓ cup heavy whipping cream
1 clove garlic, pressed
1 teaspoon salt
½ teaspoon ground black pepper
1 cup shredded cheddar cheese

1. Preheat the oven to 350°F. Lightly coat an 8-inch deep-dish pie dish or baking dish with coconut oil or nonstick cooking spray. 2. Heat the butter in a large skillet over medium heat. Add the onions and sauté until soft, 3 to 4 minutes. 3. Add the sausage and cook until evenly browned, 4 to 5 minutes. Drain and set aside. 4. In a large bowl, whisk the eggs, cream, garlic, salt, and pepper. 5. Spread the sausage evenly on the bottom of the prepared dish and top with the cheese. Pour the egg mixture over the cheese. 6. Bake for 35 minutes, until the eggs are set and the top is lightly golden brown. 7. Allow to cool for 3 to 5 minutes before serving. Leftovers can be covered and stored in the refrigerator for up to 4 days.

Per Serving:
calories: 394 | fat: 33g | protein: 22g | carbs: 3g | net carbs: 3g | fiber: 0g

Breakfast Pizza

Prep time: 5 minutes | Cook time: 8 minutes | Serves 1

2 large eggs
¼ cup unsweetened, unflavored almond milk (or unflavored hemp milk for nut-free)
¼ teaspoon fine sea salt
⅛ teaspoon ground black pepper
¼ cup diced onions
¼ cup shredded Parmesan cheese (omit for dairy-free)
6 pepperoni slices (omit for vegetarian)
¼ teaspoon dried oregano leaves
¼ cup pizza sauce, warmed, for serving

1. Preheat the air fryer to 350ºF (177ºC). Grease a cake pan. 2. In a small bowl, use a fork to whisk together the eggs, almond milk, salt, and pepper. Add the onions and stir to mix. Pour the mixture into the greased pan. Top with the cheese (if using), pepperoni slices (if using), and oregano. 3. Place the pan in the air fryer and bake for 8 minutes, or until the eggs are cooked to your liking. 4. Loosen the eggs from the sides of the pan with a spatula and place them on a serving plate. Drizzle the pizza sauce on top. Best served fresh.

Per Serving:
calories: 406 | fat: 31g | protein: 24g | carbs: 8g | net carbs: 6g | fiber: 2g

Cheese Egg Muffins

Prep time: 5 minutes | Cook time: 10 minutes | Serves 6

4 eggs
2 tablespoons heavy cream
¼ teaspoon salt
⅛ teaspoon pepper
⅓ cup shredded Cheddar cheese
1 cup water

1. In a large bowl, whisk eggs and heavy cream. Add salt and pepper. 2. Pour mixture into 6 silicone cupcake baking molds. Sprinkle cheese into each cup. 3. Pour water into Instant Pot and place steam rack in bottom of pot. Carefully set filled silicone molds steadily on steam rack. If all do not fit, separate into two batches. 4. Click lid closed. Press the Manual button and adjust time for 10 minutes. When timer beeps, allow a quick release and remove lid. Egg bites will look puffy at first, but will become smaller once they begin to cool. Serve warm.

Per Serving:
calories: 90 | fat: 6g | protein: 6g | carbs: 1g | net carbs: 1g | fiber: 0g

Crunchy Vanilla Protein Bars

Prep time: 10 minutes | Cook time: 5 minutes | Serves 8

Topping:
½ cup flaked coconut
2 tablespoons raw cacao nibs

Bars:
1½ cups almond flour
1 cup collagen powder
2 tablespoons ground or whole chia seeds
1 teaspoon vanilla powder or 1 tablespoon unsweetened vanilla extract
¼ cup virgin coconut oil
½ cup coconut milk
1½ teaspoons fresh lemon zest
⅓ cup macadamia nuts, halved
Optional: low-carb sweetener, to taste

1. Preheat the oven to 350°F (180ºC) fan assisted or 380°F (193ºC) conventional. 2. To make the topping: Place the coconut flakes on a baking tray and bake for 2 to 3 minutes, until lightly golden. Set aside to cool. 3. To make the bars: In a bowl, combine all of the ingredients for the bars. Line a small baking tray with parchment paper or use a silicone baking tray. A square 8 × 8–inch (20 × 20 cm) or a rectangular tray of similar size will work best. 4. Press the dough into the pan and sprinkle with the cacao nibs, pressing them into the bars with your fingers. Add the toasted coconut and lightly press the flakes into the dough. Refrigerate until set, for about 1 hour. Slice to serve. Store in the refrigerator for up to 1 week.

Per Serving:
calories: 510 | fat: 41g | protein: 32g | carbs: 10g | net carbs: 6g | fiber: 4g

Weekend Western Omelet

Prep time: 10 minutes | Cook time: 39 minutes | Serves 4

8 large eggs	1 small green bell pepper, seeded and chopped
10 ounces smoked ham, finely chopped	8 tablespoons unsalted butter, divided
4 tablespoons heavy whipping cream	1 cup shredded Cheddar cheese, divided
1 small yellow onion, peeled and chopped	

1 In a large bowl, whisk eggs and mix in the ham and cream. 2 In a medium microwave-safe bowl, microwave the onion and pepper for 3 minutes. 3 In a medium skillet over medium-low heat, melt 2 tablespoons butter and quickly pour one-quarter of the egg mixture into skillet before it separates. 4 After 4–5 minutes, when entire bottom of egg mixture has cooked, add one-quarter of onion and pepper to center of omelet. 5 Use spatula to fold egg mixture in half onto itself. Let omelet finish cooking another 3–4 minutes. 6 Slide the fully cooked omelet onto a warmed plate. Top with one-quarter of shredded cheese. 7 Repeat process three more times for the remaining three omelets.

Per Serving:

calories: 676 | fat: 57g | protein: 36g | carbs: 5g | net carbs: 4g | fiber: 1g

Golden Pancakes

Prep time: 5 minutes | Cook time: 20 minutes | Serves 4

⅔ cup almond flour	¼ to ½ cup coconut milk
⅓ cup coconut flour	3 tablespoons coconut oil
1 tablespoon monk fruit sweetener, powder form (optional)	1 teaspoon pure vanilla extract
	Grass-fed butter, for cooking the pancakes
1 teaspoon baking powder	½ cup sugar-free syrup (optional)
¼ teaspoon ground nutmeg	
3 eggs	

1. Mix the dry ingredients. In a large bowl, stir together the almond flour, coconut flour, monk fruit sweetener (if using), baking powder, and nutmeg until everything is well blended. 2. Add the wet ingredients. In a small bowl, whisk together the eggs, ¼ cup of the coconut milk, and the coconut oil and vanilla. Add the wet ingredients to the dry ingredients and whisk until the batter is smooth. If the batter is too thick, add more coconut milk. 3. Cook the pancakes. In a large skillet over medium heat, melt the butter. Drop the pancake batter by tablespoons, about 3 per pancake, and spread it out to form circles. You should be able to cook about four pancakes per batch. Cook until bubbles form on the pancakes and burst, about 2 minutes. Flip the pancakes and cook until browned and cooked through, about 2 more minutes. Transfer the pancakes to a plate and set it aside. Repeat with the remaining batter until it's all used up. 4. Serve. Divide the pancakes between four plates and top with your favorite accompaniments.

Per Serving:

calories: 389 | fat: 33g | protein: 10g | carbs: 14g | net carbs: 4g | fiber: 8g

Chocolate Chip Waffle

Prep time: 5 minutes | Cook time: 5 minutes | Serves 1

⅓ cup blanched almond flour	chocolate chips
½ tablespoon coconut flour	For Topping (Optional)
¼ teaspoon baking powder	Swerve confectioners'-style sweetener
2 large eggs	Sugar-free syrup
¼ teaspoon vanilla extract	Salted butter
4 drops liquid stevia	
1 tablespoon stevia-sweetened	

1 Preheat a waffle maker to medium-high heat. 2 Place all the ingredients except the chocolate chips in a large bowl and blend until smooth. Fold in the chocolate chips. 3 Spray the hot waffle maker with nonstick cooking spray. 4 Pour the batter into the hot waffle iron and cook for 3 to 5 minutes, until light golden brown. 5 Serve dusted with Swerve confectioners'-style sweetener and topped with sugar-free syrup and butter, if desired.

Per Serving:

1 waffle: calories: 398 | fat: 31g | protein: 23g | carbs: 14g | net carbs: 6g | fiber: 8g

Skillet Pancake Puff

Prep time: 5 minutes | Cook time: 20 minutes | serves 4

2 tablespoons salted butter	2 tablespoons granular erythritol
4 large eggs	½ teaspoon vanilla extract
¼ cup water	¼ teaspoon salt
¼ cup heavy whipping cream	
2 tablespoons coconut flour	
For garnish (optional):	
Fresh blueberries	Confectioners'-style erythritol

1. Preheat the oven to 425°F. 2. Put the butter in a 10-inch cast-iron skillet or other ovenproof skillet and place it in the oven to melt the butter. When the butter is melted, remove the skillet from the oven. 3. In a medium-sized bowl, whisk the eggs. Using a spoon, mix in the water, cream, coconut flour, erythritol, vanilla extract, and salt. Continue stirring until the batter is well blended. 4. Pour the batter into the hot skillet and bake for 18 to 20 minutes, until the pancake is puffed and golden. Slice into quarters and garnish with blueberries and confectioners'-style erythritol, if desired.

Per Serving:

calories: 164 | fat: 14g | protein: 7g | carbs: 2g | net carbs: 1g | fiber: 1g

Dreamy Matcha Latte

Prep time: 2 minutes | Cook time: 0 minutes | Serves 1

1 cup hot water
⅓ cup full-fat coconut, nut, or dairy milk
1 tablespoon cacao butter
1 scoop grass-fed collagen

peptides
½ to 1 teaspoon matcha powder
2 or 3 drops stevia extract (optional)

1. Place all the ingredients in a blender and blend until smooth.

Per Serving:

calories: 261 | fat: 23g | protein: 13g | carbs: 2g | net carbs: 2g | fiber: 0g

Pulled Pork Hash

Prep time: 10 minutes | Cook time: 15 minutes | Serves 4

4 eggs
10 ounces (283 g) pulled pork, shredded
1 teaspoon coconut oil
1 teaspoon red pepper

1 teaspoon chopped fresh cilantro
1 tomato, chopped
¼ cup water

1. Melt the coconut oil in the instant pot on Sauté mode. 2. Then add pulled pork, red pepper, cilantro, water, and chopped tomato. 3. Cook the ingredients for 5 minutes. 4. Then stir it well with the help of the spatula and crack the eggs over it. 5. Close the lid. 6. Cook the meal on Manual mode (High Pressure) for 7 minutes. Then make a quick pressure release.

Per Serving:

calories: 275 | fat: 18g | protein: 22g | carbs: 6g | net carbs: 5g | fiber: 1g

Avocado Breakfast Sandwich

Prep time: 5 minutes | Cook time: 15 minutes | Serves 1

2 slices bacon
2 eggs

1 avocado

1. Press the Sauté button. Press the Adjust button to set heat to Low. Add bacon to Instant Pot and cook until crispy. Remove and set aside. 2. Crack egg over Instant Pot slowly, into bacon grease. Repeat with second egg. When edges become golden, after 2 to 3 minutes, flip. Press the Cancel button. 3. Cut avocado in half and scoop out half without seed. Place in small bowl and mash with fork. Spread on one egg. Place bacon on top and top with second egg. Let cool 5 minutes before eating.

Per Serving:

calories: 489 | fat: 39g | protein: 21g | carbs: 7g | net carbs: 2g | fiber: 5g

Rocket Fuel Hot Chocolate

Prep time: 5 minutes | Cook time: 0 minutes | Makes 2

2 cups (475 ml) milk (nondairy or regular), hot
2 tablespoons cocoa powder
2 tablespoons collagen peptides or protein powder
2 tablespoons coconut oil, MCT oil, unflavored MCT oil

powder, or ghee
1 tablespoon coconut butter
1 tablespoon erythritol, or 4 drops liquid stevia
Pinch of ground cinnamon (optional)

1. Place all the ingredients in a blender and blend for 10 seconds, or until the ingredients are fully incorporated. 2. Divide between 2 mugs, sprinkle with cinnamon if you'd like, and enjoy!

Per Serving:

calories: 357 | fat: 29g | protein: 13g | carbs: 11g | net carbs: 7g | fiber: 4g

Kale Frittata with Crispy Pancetta Salad

Prep time: 20 minutes | Cook time: 15 minutes | Serves 4

6 slices pancetta
4 tomatoes, cut into 1-inch chunks
1 large cucumber, seeded and sliced
1 small red onion, sliced
¼ cup balsamic vinegar
Salt and black pepper to taste
8 eggs

1 bunch kale, chopped
Salt and black pepper to taste
6 tablespoons grated Parmesan cheese
4 tablespoons olive oil
1 large white onion, sliced
3 ounces beef salami, thinly sliced
1 clove garlic, minced

1Place the pancetta in a skillet and fry over medium heat until crispy, about 4 minutes. Remove to a cutting board and chop. 2Then, in a small bowl, whisk the vinegar, 2 tablespoons of olive oil, salt, and pepper to make the dressing. 3Next, combine the tomatoes, red onion, and cucumber in a salad bowl, drizzle with the dressing and toss the veggies. Sprinkle with the pancetta and set aside. 4Reheat the broiler to 400°F. 5Crack the eggs into a bowl and whisk together with half of the Parmesan, salt, and pepper. Set aside. 6Next, heat the remaining olive oil in the cast iron pan over medium heat. Sauté the onion and garlic for 3 minutes. Add the kale to the skillet, season with salt and pepper, and cook for 2 minutes. Top with the salami, stir and cook further for 1 minute. Pour the egg mixture all over the kale, reduce the heat to medium-low, cover, and cook the ingredients for 4 minutes. 7Sprinkle the remaining cheese on top and transfer the pan to the oven. Broil to brown on top for 1 minute. When ready, remove the pan and run a spatula around the edges of the frittata; slide it onto a warm platter. Cut the frittata into wedges and serve with the pancetta salad.

Per Serving:

calories: 584 | fat: 44g | protein: 30g | carbs: 15g | net carbs: 12g | fiber: 3g

Pumpkin Spice Smoothie

Prep time: 5 minutes | Cook time: 0 minutes | Serves 2

1 cup full-fat coconut, nut, or dairy milk
¾ cup canned pumpkin
½ cup frozen riced cauliflower
1 cup water
1 teaspoon ground cinnamon, plus extra for garnish if desired
1 teaspoon pumpkin pie spice

1 teaspoon pure vanilla extract
Small handful of ice (optional)
2 scoops collagen peptides
⅛ teaspoon green stevia, or 2 or 3 drops stevia extract (optional)
1 tablespoon coconut chips, for garnish (optional)

1. Place all the ingredients except the coconut chips in a blender and blend until smooth. If you prefer a thinner smoothie, add more water or milk to your liking. 2. Garnish with ground cinnamon and coconut chips before serving, if desired.

Per Serving:

calories: 302 | fat: 24g | protein: 13g | carbs: 12g | net carbs: 9g | fiber: 3g

Not Your Average Boiled Eggs

Prep time: 10 minutes | Cook time: 10 minutes | Serves 5

Boiled Eggs:
10 eggs
1 tablespoon coconut vinegar
Sauce:
1½ cups water
2 tablespoons liquid aminos or tamari
2 tablespoons coconut aminos
2 tablespoons coconut vinegar or apple cider vinegar
1 teaspoon minced fresh garlic

or apple cider vinegar

or garlic powder
1 teaspoon minced fresh ginger or ground ginger
1 teaspoon sea salt
½ teaspoon freshly ground black pepper

Make the Boiled Eggs: 1. Place the eggs in a medium pot and add enough cold water to cover them. Add a splash of vinegar (this makes the eggs easier to peel) and bring to a boil. When the water boils, remove the pot from the heat, cover, and let sit for 10 minutes. 2. Meanwhile, fill a large bowl with water and ice. When the eggs are done, transfer them to the ice bath for another 10 minutes. 3. Peel the eggs and set them aside. Make the Sauce: 4. In a large storage bowl with a lid, whisk together the water, liquid aminos, coconut aminos, vinegar, garlic, ginger, salt, and pepper. Alternatively, you can divide the ingredients in half and add to two large mason jars with lids. 5. Place the peeled eggs in the sauce. Cover and refrigerate. The longer the eggs soak up the sauce, the more flavorful they will be.

Per Serving:

2 eggs: calories: 144 | fat: 10g | protein: 12g | carbs: 2g | net carbs: 2g | fiber: 0g

Turmeric Scrambled Eggs

Prep time: 5 minutes | Cook time: 5 minutes | Serves 2

3 large eggs
2 tablespoons heavy cream (optional)
1 teaspoon ground turmeric

Salt, to taste
Freshly ground black pepper, to taste
1 tablespoon butter

1. In a small bowl, lightly beat the eggs with the cream. Add the turmeric, salt, and pepper. 2. Melt the butter in a skillet over medium heat. When it just starts to bubble, gently pour in the egg mixture. Stir frequently as eggs begin to set, and cook for 2 to 3 minutes. 3. Remove from the heat, taste and add more pepper and salt if needed, and serve.

Per Serving:

calories: 213 | fat: 18g | protein: 10g | carbs: 2g | net carbs: 2g | fiber: 0g

Baked Eggs and Ham

Prep time: 5 minutes | Cook time: 5 minutes | Serves 2

4 large eggs, beaten
4 slices ham, diced
½ cup shredded Cheddar cheese

½ cup heavy cream
½ teaspoon sea salt
Pinch ground black pepper

1. Grease two ramekins. 2. In a large bowl, whisk together all the ingredients. Divide the egg mixture equally between the ramekins. 3. Set a trivet in the Instant Pot and pour in 1 cup water. Place the ramekins on the trivet. 4. Lock the lid. Select the Manual mode and set the cooking time for 5 minutes on High Pressure. When the timer goes off, perform a quick pressure release. Carefully open the lid. 5. Remove the ramekins from the Instant Pot. 6. Serve immediately.

Per Serving:

calories: 591 | fat: 51g | protein: 33g | carbs: 3g | net carbs: 3g | fiber: 0g

Heart-Healthy Hazelnut-Collagen Shake

Prep time: 5 minutes | Cook time: 0 minutes | Serves 1

1½ cups unsweetened almond milk
2 tablespoons hazelnut butter
2 tablespoons grass-fed collagen powder
½–1 teaspoon cinnamon

⅛ teaspoon LoSalt or pink Himalayan salt
⅛ teaspoon sugar-free almond extract
1 tablespoon macadamia oil or hazelnut oil

1. Place all of the ingredients in a blender and pulse until smooth and frothy. Serve immediately.

Per Serving:

calories: 345 | fat: 32g | protein: 13g | carbs: 8g | net carbs: 3g | fiber: 5g

Pork and Quill Egg Cups

Prep time: 15 minutes | Cook time: 15 minutes | Serves 4

10 ounces (283 g) ground pork	1 teaspoon dried dill
1 jalapeño pepper, chopped	½ teaspoon salt
1 tablespoon butter, softened	1 cup water
	4 quill eggs

1. In a bowl, stir together all the ingredients, except for the quill eggs and water. Transfer the meat mixture to the silicone muffin molds and press the surface gently. 2. Pour the water and insert the trivet in the Instant Pot. Put the meat cups on the trivet. 3. Crack the eggs over the meat mixture. 4. Set the lid in place. Select the Manual mode and set the cooking time for 15 minutes on High Pressure. When the timer goes off, do a quick pressure release. Carefully open the lid. 5. Serve warm.

Per Serving:

calories: 142 | fat: 6g | protein: 20g | carbs: 0g | net carbs: 0g | fiber: 0g

Gyro Breakfast Patties with Tzatziki

Prep time: 10 minutes | Cook time: 20 minutes per batch | Makes 16 patties

Patties:

2 pounds (907 g) ground lamb or beef	1 teaspoon dried oregano leaves
½ cup diced red onions	1 teaspoon Greek seasoning
¼ cup sliced black olives	2 cloves garlic, minced
2 tablespoons tomato sauce	1 teaspoon fine sea salt

Tzatziki:

1 cup full-fat sour cream	1 clove garlic, minced
1 small cucumber, chopped	¼ teaspoon dried dill weed, or 1 teaspoon finely chopped fresh dill
½ teaspoon fine sea salt	
½ teaspoon garlic powder, or	

For Garnish/Serving:

½ cup crumbled feta cheese (about 2 ounces / 57 g)	Sliced black olives
Diced red onions	Sliced cucumbers

1. Preheat the air fryer to 350ºF (177ºC). 2. Place the ground lamb, onions, olives, tomato sauce, oregano, Greek seasoning, garlic, and salt in a large bowl. Mix well to combine the ingredients. 3. Using your hands, form the mixture into sixteen 3-inch patties. Place about 5 of the patties in the air fryer and air fry for 20 minutes, flipping halfway through. Remove the patties and place them on a serving platter. Repeat with the remaining patties. 4. While the patties cook, make the tzatziki: Place all the ingredients in a small bowl and stir well. Cover and store in the fridge until ready to serve. Garnish with ground black pepper before serving. 5. Serve the patties with a dollop of tzatziki, a sprinkle of crumbled feta cheese, diced red onions, sliced black olives, and sliced cucumbers. 6. Store leftovers in an airtight container in the refrigerator for up to 5 days or in the freezer for up to a month. Reheat the patties in a preheated 390ºF (199ºC) air fryer for a few minutes, until warmed through.

Per Serving:

calories: 149 | fat: 10g | protein: 13g | carbs: 2g | net carbs: 2g | fiber: 0g

Mexican Breakfast Beef Chili

Prep time: 5 minutes | Cook time: 45 minutes | Serves 4

2 tablespoons coconut oil	1 teaspoon hot sauce
1 pound (454 g) ground grass-fed beef	½ teaspoon chili powder
1 (14 ounces / 397 g) can sugar-free or low-sugar diced tomatoes	½ teaspoon crushed red pepper
	½ teaspoon ground cumin
½ cup shredded full-fat Cheddar cheese (optional)	½ teaspoon kosher salt
	½ teaspoon freshly ground black pepper

1. Set the Instant Pot to Sauté and melt the oil. 2. Pour in ½ cup of filtered water, then add the beef, tomatoes, cheese, hot sauce, chili powder, red pepper, cumin, salt, and black pepper to the Instant Pot, stirring thoroughly. 3. Close the lid, set the pressure release to Sealing, and hit Cancel to stop the current program. Select Manual, set the Instant Pot to 45 minutes on High Pressure and let cook. 4. Once cooked, let the pressure naturally disperse from the Instant Pot for about 10 minutes, then carefully switch the pressure release to Venting. 5. Open the Instant Pot, serve, and enjoy!

Per Serving:

calories: 351 | fat: 19g | protein: 39g | carbs: 6g | net carbs: 4g | fiber: 2g

Cinnamon Roll Fat Bombs

Prep time: 5 minutes | Cook time: 5 minutes | Serves 5 to 6

2 tablespoons coconut oil	½ cup Swerve, or more to taste
2 cups raw coconut butter	
1 cup sugar-free chocolate chips	½ teaspoon ground cinnamon, or more to taste
1 cup heavy whipping cream	½ teaspoon vanilla extract

1. Set the Instant Pot to Sauté and melt the oil. 2. Add the butter, chocolate chips, whipping cream, Swerve, cinnamon, and vanilla to the Instant Pot and cook. Stir occasionally until the mixture reaches a smooth consistency. 3. Pour mixture into a silicone mini-muffin mold. 4. Freeze until firm. Serve, and enjoy!

Per Serving:

calories: 372 | fat: 32g | protein: 4g | carbs: 15g | net carbs: 8g | fiber: 7g

Double-Pork Frittata

Prep time: 5 minutes | Cook time: 25 minutes | Serves 4

1 tablespoon butter or pork lard	4 ounces pancetta, chopped
8 large eggs	2 ounces prosciutto, thinly
1 cup heavy (whipping) cream	sliced
Pink Himalayan salt	1 tablespoon chopped fresh
Freshly ground black pepper	dill

1. Preheat the oven to 375°F. Coat a 9-by-13-inch baking pan with the butter. 2. In a large bowl, whisk the eggs and cream together. Season with pink Himalayan salt and pepper, and whisk to blend. 3. Pour the egg mixture into the prepared pan. Sprinkle the pancetta in and distribute evenly throughout. 4. Tear off pieces of the prosciutto and place on top, then sprinkle with the dill. 5. Bake for about 25 minutes, or until the edges are golden and the eggs are just set. 6. Transfer to a rack to cool for 5 minutes. 7. Cut into 4 portions and serve hot.

Per Serving:

calories: 437 | fat: 39g | protein: 21g | carbs: 3g | net carbs: 3g | fiber: 0g

No-Bake Keto Power Bars

Prep time: 10 minutes | Cook time: 0 minutes | Makes 12 bars

½ cup pili nuts	vanilla collagen and 1 scoop
½ cup whole hazelnuts	Perfect Keto unflavored
½ cup walnut halves	collagen powder)
¼ cup hulled sunflower seeds	½ teaspoon ground cinnamon
¼ cup unsweetened coconut	½ teaspoon sea salt
flakes or chips	¼ cup coconut oil, melted
¼ cup hulled hemp seeds	1 teaspoon vanilla extract
2 tablespoons unsweetened	Stevia or monk fruit to
cacao nibs	sweeten (optional if you are
2 scoops collagen powder	using unflavored collagen
(I use 1 scoop Perfect Keto	powder)

1. Line a 9-inch square baking pan with parchment paper. 2. In a food processor or blender, combine the pili nuts, hazelnuts, walnuts, sunflower seeds, coconut, hemp seeds, cacao nibs, collagen powder, cinnamon, and salt and pulse a few times. 3. Add the coconut oil, vanilla extract, and sweetener (if using). Pulse again until the ingredients are combined. Do not over pulse or it will turn to mush. You want the nuts and seeds to still have some texture. 4. Pour the mixture into the prepared pan and press it into an even layer. Cover with another piece of parchment (or fold over extra from the first piece) and place a heavy pan or dish on top to help press the bars together. 5. Refrigerate overnight and then cut into 12 bars. Store the bars in individual storage bags in the refrigerator for a quick grab-and-go breakfast.

Per Serving:

calories: 242 | fat: 22g | protein: 6g | carbs: 4g | net carbs: 2g | fiber: 2g

Jalapeño Popper Egg Cups

Prep time: 10 minutes | Cook time: 10 minutes | Serves 2

4 large eggs	cheese
¼ cup chopped pickled	½ cup shredded sharp
jalapeños	Cheddar cheese
2 ounces (57 g) full-fat cream	

1. In a medium bowl, beat the eggs, then pour into four silicone muffin cups. 2. In a large microwave-safe bowl, place jalapeños, cream cheese, and Cheddar. Microwave for 30 seconds and stir. Take a spoonful, approximately ¼ of the mixture, and place it in the center of one of the egg cups. Repeat with remaining mixture. 3. Place egg cups into the air fryer basket. 4. Adjust the temperature to 320ºF (160ºC) and bake for 10 minutes. 5. Serve warm.

Per Serving:

calories: 373 | fat: 30g | protein: 20g | carbs: 3g | net carbs: 2g | fiber: 1g

Savory Zucchini Cheddar Waffles

Prep time: 10 minutes | Cook time: 18 minutes | Makes 4 medium-sized waffles

Waffles:

2 large zucchini	2 tablespoons coconut flour
2 large eggs	½ teaspoon garlic powder
⅔ cup shredded cheddar	½ teaspoon red pepper flakes
cheese (about 2⅔ ounces)	¼ teaspoon pink Himalayan salt

For Garnish (optional):

Sour cream	Minced fresh chives
Shredded cheddar cheese	

1. Preheat a waffle iron on the medium setting. 2. Using a vegetable or cheese grater, grate the zucchini into a large colander set inside of a bowl. Squeeze the excess water out of the grated zucchini using your hands and drain. 3. Add the eggs and cheese to the drained zucchini and combine with a fork. Add the coconut flour, garlic powder, red pepper flakes, and salt and use the fork to combine once more. 4. Open the waffle iron and grease the top and bottom with coconut oil spray. 5. Using a ⅓-cup measuring cup, scoop out some of the batter, place it in the center of the waffle iron, and close the lid. Cook the waffle for 4 to 4½ minutes, until golden brown and fully cooked through. Use a fork to lift it off the iron and set on a plate. 6. Repeat with the remaining batter, making a total of 4 waffles. Garnish with sour cream, shredded cheddar cheese, and/or minced chives, if desired.

Per Serving:

calories: 292 | fat: 19g | protein: 20g | carbs: 14g | net carbs: 9g | fiber: 5g

Pepper Sausage Fry

Prep time: 5 minutes | Cook time: 20 minutes | Serves 4

¼ cup (60 ml) avocado oil, or ¼ cup (55 g) coconut oil

12 ounces (340 g) smoked sausages, thinly sliced

1 small green bell pepper, thinly sliced

1 small red bell pepper, thinly sliced

1½ teaspoons garlic powder

1 teaspoon dried oregano leaves

1 teaspoon paprika

¼ teaspoon finely ground sea salt

¼ teaspoon ground black pepper

¼ cup (17 g) chopped fresh parsley

1. Heat the oil in a large frying pan over medium-low heat until it shimmers. 2. When the oil is shimmering, add the rest of the ingredients, except the parsley. Cover and cook for 15 minutes, until the bell peppers are fork-tender. 3. Remove the lid and continue to cook for 5 to 6 minutes, until the liquid evaporates. 4. Remove from the heat, stir in the parsley, and serve.

Per Serving:

calories: 411 | fat: 38g | protein: 11g | carbs: 6g | net carbs: 5g | fiber: 2g

Jelly-Filled Breakfast Strudels

Prep time: 10 minutes | Cook time: 25 minutes | Serves 2

Pastry:

¾ cup shredded low-moisture mozzarella cheese

2 ounces (57 g) full-fat cream cheese, at room temperature

Frosting:

¼ cup powdered erythritol

2 ounces (57 g) full-fat cream cheese, at room temperature

1 tablespoon butter, at room

1 cup almond flour

1 large egg

4 tablespoons stevia-sweetened jelly

temperature

2 teaspoons heavy (whipping) cream

¼ teaspoon vanilla extract

1. Preheat the oven to 325ºF (163ºC). Have a silicone-lined baking sheet nearby. 2. To make the dough: In a large, microwave-safe bowl, combine the mozzarella and cream cheese. 3. Microwave for 1 minute, until the cheese is melted. Then stir to combine. 4. Add the almond flour and egg to the melted cheese. Combine using a rubber scraper, working quickly so the cheese does not cool and harden. (If it starts to harden, reheat in the microwave for 20 seconds, being careful not to cook the egg.) 5. Roll out the dough between 2 pieces of parchment paper to a large rectangle that is between ¼ and ⅛ inch thick. 6. Make 3 even cuts widthwise to form 4 long rectangles of dough. 7. Place 1 tablespoon of jelly in the top half of each rectangle, leaving a little room on the sides. 8. Puncture the non-jellied bottom of each rectangle with a fork. Then, fold this bottom half over the top jellied half. 9. Seal the edges all the way around the square by pressing down with a fork.

Transfer the squares to the baking sheet. 10. Bake for 20 to 25 minutes, until the pastry is golden brown. 11. Remove from the oven, and allow to cool for 10 minutes. 12. To make the frosting: In a small bowl, combine the erythritol, cream cheese, butter, cream, and vanilla and mix until smooth. 13. With a knife or the back of a spoon, coat the strudels with frosting and enjoy.

Per Serving:

calories: 702 | fat: 61g | protein: 27g | carbs: 16g | net carbs: 10g | fiber: 6g

Egg Muffins in Ham Cups

Prep time: 5 minutes | Cook time: 18 minutes | Serves 6

1 tablespoon coconut oil, melted

6 slices ham (thin-sliced is better)

6 large eggs

Salt and pepper, to taste

3 tablespoons shredded Cheddar cheese (optional)

1. Preheat the oven to 400ºF (205ºC). Brush six cups of a muffin tin with the melted coconut oil. 2. Line each cup with 1 slice of ham. Crack 1 egg into each cup. Season with salt and pepper, then sprinkle ½ tablespoon of Cheddar cheese on each egg. 3. Bake for 13 to 18 minutes depending on how you like your egg yolks set. 4. Remove from the oven and let cool for a few minutes before carefully removing the "muffins." Refrigerate in a glass or plastic container so they don't get smushed or dried out.

Per Serving:

calories: 178 | fat: 13g | protein: 14g | carbs: 1g | net carbs: 1g | fiber: 0g

Eggs & Crabmeat with Creme Fraiche Salsa

Prep time: 10 minutes | Cook time: 10 minutes | Serves 3

1 tablespoon olive oil

6 eggs, whisked

1 (6 ounces) can crabmeat,

For The Salsa:

¾ cup crème fraiche

½ cup scallions, chopped

½ teaspoon garlic powder

flaked

Salt and black pepper to taste

Salt and black pepper to taste

½ teaspoon fresh dill, chopped

Set a sauté pan over medium heat and warm olive oil. Crack in eggs and scramble them. Stir in crabmeat and season with salt and black pepper; cook until cooked thoroughly. 2. In a mixing dish, combine all salsa ingredients. Equally, split the egg/crabmeat mixture among serving plates; serve alongside the scallions and salsa to the side.

Per Serving:

calories: 364 | fat: 26g | protein: 25g | carbs: 5g | net carbs: 5g | fiber: 0g

Cheese Stuffed Avocados

Prep time: 10 minutes | Cook time: 17 minutes | Serves 4

3 avocados, halved and pitted, skin on	2 eggs, beaten
½ cup feta cheese, crumbled	Salt and black pepper, to taste
½ cup cheddar cheese, grated	1 tablespoon fresh basil, chopped

1. Set oven to 360°F and lay the avocado halves in an ovenproof dish. 2. In a mixing dish, mix both types of cheeses, black pepper, eggs, and salt. 3. Split the mixture equally into the avocado halves. 4. Bake thoroughly for 15 to 17 minutes. 5. Decorate with fresh basil before serving.

Per Serving:

calories: 365 | fat: 32g | protein: 12g | carbs: 13g | net carbs: 5g | fiber: 10g

Cheese & Aioli Eggs

Prep time: 15 minutes | Cook time: 0 minutes | Serves 8

8 eggs, hard-boiled, chopped	½ cup green onions, finely chopped
28 ounces tuna in brine, drained	½ cup feta cheese, crumbled
½ cup lettuces, torn into pieces	⅓ cup sour cream
For Aioli:	½ tbsp mustard
1cup mayonnaise	1 tablespoon lemon juice
2cloves garlic, minced	Salt and black pepper, to taste

1Set the eggs in a serving bowl. Place in tuna, onion, mustard, cheese, lettuce, and sour cream. 2To prepare aioli, mix in a bowl mayonnaise, lemon juice, and garlic. Add in black pepper and salt. Stir in the prepared aioli to the bowl to incorporate everything. Serve with pickles.

Per Serving:

calories: 471 | fat: 32g | protein: 40g | carbs: 5g | net carbs: 5g | fiber: 1g

Pizza Pâté

Prep time: 10 minutes | Cook time: 0 minutes | Makes 2½ cups

1 cup (190 g) chopped pepperoni	2 teaspoons apple cider vinegar
¾ cup (120 g) raw almonds, soaked for 12 hours, then drained and rinsed ½ cup (120 ml) melted coconut oil	2 teaspoons onion powder
	1 teaspoon garlic powder
	¼ teaspoon finely ground gray sea salt
⅓ cup (80 ml) tomato sauce	1 tablespoon finely chopped fresh basil
¼ cup (17 g) nutritional yeast	

1. Place all the ingredients except the basil in a high-powered blender or food processor. Blend or pulse until smooth, about 1 minute. 2. Add the basil and pulse until just mixed in.

Per Serving:

calories: 144 | fat: 13g | protein: 5g | carbs: 3g | net carbs: 1g | fiber: 1g

Broccoli-Mushroom Frittata

Prep time: 10 minutes | Cook time: 20 minutes | Serves 2

1 tablespoon olive oil	½ teaspoon salt
1½ cups broccoli florets, finely chopped	¼ teaspoon freshly ground black pepper
½ cup sliced brown mushrooms	6 eggs
¼ cup finely chopped onion	¼ cup Parmesan cheese

1. In a nonstick cake pan, combine the olive oil, broccoli, mushrooms, onion, salt, and pepper. Stir until the vegetables are thoroughly coated with oil. Place the cake pan in the air fryer basket and set the air fryer to 400°F (204°C). Air fry for 5 minutes until the vegetables soften. 2. Meanwhile, in a medium bowl, whisk the eggs and Parmesan until thoroughly combined. Pour the egg mixture into the pan and shake gently to distribute the vegetables. Air fry for another 15 minutes until the eggs are set. 3. Remove from the air fryer and let sit for 5 minutes to cool slightly. Use a silicone spatula to gently lift the frittata onto a plate before serving.

Per Serving:

calories: 345 | fat: 24g | protein: 23g | carbs: 8g | net carbs: 6g | fiber: 2g

PB&J Overnight Hemp

Prep time: 5 minutes | Cook time: 0 minutes | serves 6

3 cups unsweetened almond milk, plus more for serving	1½ cups hemp hearts
	2 tablespoons chia seeds
1 tablespoon sugar-free peanut butter	¼ cup cacao nibs
	⅛ cup unsweetened coconut flakes
4 drops liquid stevia or sugar-free sweetener of choice	¼ cup freeze-dried raspberries

1. In a large mixing bowl, whisk together the almond milk, peanut butter, and stevia. 2. Once well combined, add the hemp hearts, chia seeds, cacao nibs, coconut, and raspberries, and stir together. 3. Pour the mixture into a lidded storage container and place in the refrigerator for at least 8 hours. 4. Divide the mixture among 6 small serving bowls and top with a splash of almond milk.

Per Serving:

calories: 324 | fat: 24g | protein: 16g | carbs: 10g | net carbs: 2g | fiber: 8g

Overnight "Noats"

Prep time: 5 minutes | Cook time: 0 minutes | Serves 1

2 tablespoons hulled hemp seeds
1 tablespoon chia seeds
½ scoop collagen powder

½ cup unsweetened nut or seed milk (hemp, almond, coconut, cashew)

1. In a small mason jar or glass container, combine the hemp seeds, chia seeds, collagen, and milk. 2. Secure tightly with a lid, shake well, and refrigerate overnight.

Per Serving:

calories: 263 | fat: 19g | protein: 16g | carbs: 7g | net carbs: 2g | fiber: 5g

Egg Omelet Roll with Cream Cheese & Salmon

Prep time: 15 minutes | Cook time: 5 minutes | Serves 1

½ avocado, sliced
2 tablespoons chopped chives
½ package smoked salmon, cut into strips
1 spring onions, sliced

3 eggs
2 tablespoons cream cheese
1 tablespoon butter
Salt and black pepper, to taste

In a small bowl, combine the chives and cream cheese; set aside. Beat the eggs in a large bowl and season with salt and black pepper. 2. Melt the butter in a pan over medium heat. Add the eggs to the pan and cook for about 3 minutes. Flip the omelet over and continue cooking for another 2 minutes until golden. 3. Remove the omelet to a plate and spread the chive mixture over. Arrange the salmon, avocado, and onion slices. Wrap the omelet and serve immediately.

Per Serving:

calories: 646 | fat: 53g | protein: 28g | carbs: 12g | net carbs: 7g | fiber: 5g

Broccoli & Colby Cheese Frittata

Prep time: 15 minutes | Cook time: 20 minutes | Serves 4

3tbsp olive oil
½ cup onions, chopped
1 cup broccoli, chopped
8 eggs, beaten

½ teaspoon jalapeño pepper, minced
Salt and red pepper, to taste
¾ cup colby cheese, grated
¼ cup fresh cilantro, to serve

1Set an ovenproof frying pan over medium heat and warm the oil. Add onions and sauté until caramelized. Place in the broccoli and cook until tender. Add in jalapeno pepper and eggs; season with red pepper and salt. Cook until the eggs are set. 2Scatter colby cheese over the frittata. Set oven to 370°F and cook for approximately 12 minutes, until frittata is set in the middle. Slice into wedges and decorate with fresh cilantro before serving.

Per Serving:

calories: 426 | fat: 34g | protein: 23g | carbs: 8g | net carbs: 6g | fiber: 2g

Chapter 6

Snacks and Appetizers

Hummus Celery Boats

Prep time: 5 minutes | Cook time: 0 minutes | Serves 10

1 cup (160 g) raw macadamia nuts	Pinch of cayenne pepper
3 tablespoons fresh lemon juice	Pinch of finely ground sea salt
2 cloves garlic	Pinch of ground black pepper
2 tablespoons olive oil	1 bunch celery, stalks cut crosswise into 2-inch (5-cm) pieces
2 tablespoons tahini	

1. Place the macadamia nuts in a large bowl and cover with water. Cover the bowl and place in the fridge to soak for 24 hours. 2. After 24 hours, drain and rinse the macadamia nuts. Transfer to a food processor or blender. Add the lemon juice, garlic, olive oil, tahini, cayenne, salt, and pepper and blend until smooth. 3. Spread the hummus on the celery pieces and place on a plate for serving.

Per Serving:

calories: 171 | fat: 16g | protein: 2g | carbs: 5g | net carbs: 3g | fiber: 3g

Thyme Sautéed Radishes

Prep time: 5 minutes | Cook time: 15 minutes | Serves 4

1 pound (454 g) radishes, quartered (remove leaves and ends)	¼ teaspoon minced garlic
	⅛ teaspoon salt
	⅛ teaspoon garlic powder
2 tablespoons butter	⅛ teaspoon dried rosemary
¼ teaspoon dried thyme	

1. Press the Sauté button and then press the Adjust button to lower heat to Less. 2. Place radishes into Instant Pot with butter and seasoning. 3. Sauté, stirring occasionally until tender, about 10 to 15 minutes. Add a couple of teaspoons of water if radishes begin to stick.

Per Serving:

calories: 62 | fat: 5g | protein: 1g | carbs: 3g | net carbs: 2g | fiber: 1g

Almond and Chocolate Chia Pudding

Prep time: 10 minutes | Cook time: 0 minutes | Serves 4

1 (14 ounces / 397 g) can full-fat coconut milk	2 to 3 teaspoons granulated sugar-free sweetener of choice (optional)
⅓ cup chia seeds	
1 tablespoon unsweetened cocoa powder	½ teaspoon vanilla extract
2 tablespoons unsweetened almond butter	½ teaspoon almond extract (optional)

1. Combine all the ingredients in a small bowl, whisking well to fully incorporate the almond butter. 2. Divide the mixture between four ramekins or small glass jars. 3. Cover and refrigerate for at least 6 hours, preferably overnight. Serve cold.

Per Serving:

calories: 335 | fat: 31g | protein: 7g | carbs: 13g | net carbs: 6g | fiber: 7g

Lemon-Cheese Cauliflower Bites

Prep time: 5 minutes | Cook time: 8 minutes | Serves 6

1 cup water	2 tablespoons extra-virgin olive oil
1 pound (454 g) cauliflower, broken into florets	
	2 tablespoons lemon juice
Sea salt and ground black pepper, to taste	1 cup grated Cheddar cheese

1. Pour the water into the Instant Pot and insert a steamer basket. Place the cauliflower florets in the basket. 2. Lock the lid. Select the Manual mode and set the cooking time for 3 minutes at Low Pressure. 3. When the timer beeps, perform a quick pressure release. Carefully remove the lid. 4. Season the cauliflower with salt and pepper. Drizzle with olive oil and lemon juice. Sprinkle the grated cheese all over the cauliflower. 5. Press the Sauté button to heat the Instant Pot. Allow to cook for about 5 minutes, or until the cheese melts. Serve warm.

Per Serving:

calories: 136 | fat: 10g | protein: 7g | carbs: 5g | net carbs: 3g | fiber: 2g

Buffalo Bill's Chicken Dip

Prep time: 15 minutes | Cook time: 30 minutes | Serves 10

2 (4.2 ounces) chicken breasts from cooked rotisserie chicken	powder seasoning mix
	1 cup full-fat mayonnaise
	1 cup full-fat sour cream
1 (8 ounces) package full-fat cream cheese, softened	½ cup finely chopped green onion
2 cups shredded whole milk mozzarella cheese	¼ cup buffalo wing sauce
	1 teaspoon garlic powder
1 cup shredded Cheddar cheese	½ pound no-sugar-added bacon, cooked and crumbled
1 (1 ounce) package ranch	

1. Preheat oven to 350°F. Grease a 2-quart (8" × 8") baking dish. 2. In a small bowl, finely shred chicken. 3. Combine chicken with remaining ingredients, except bacon, in baking dish, stirring to mix well. 4. Bake 25–30 minutes; stop when bubbling and browned on top. 5. Take out of the oven and stir again to mix all the melted ingredients. Top with the crumbled bacon. Serve immediately.

Per Serving:

calories: 539| fat: 43g | protein: 25g | carbs: 5g | net carbs: 5g | fiber: 0g

Burrata Caprese Stack

Prep time: 5 minutes | Cook time: 0 minutes | Serves 4

1 large organic tomato, preferably heirloom
½ teaspoon salt
¼ teaspoon freshly ground black pepper
1 (4 ounces / 113 g) ball burrata cheese

8 fresh basil leaves, thinly sliced
2 tablespoons extra-virgin olive oil
1 tablespoon red wine or balsamic vinegar

1. Slice the tomato into 4 thick slices, removing any tough center core and sprinkle with salt and pepper. Place the tomatoes, seasoned-side up, on a plate. 2. On a separate rimmed plate, slice the burrata into 4 thick slices and place one slice on top of each tomato slice. Top each with one-quarter of the basil and pour any reserved burrata cream from the rimmed plate over top. 3. Drizzle with olive oil and vinegar and serve with a fork and knife.

Per Serving:

calories: 118 | fat: 11g | protein: 4g | carbs: 4g | net carbs: 4g | fiber: 1g

Manchego Crackers

Prep time: 15 minutes | Cook time: 15 minutes | Makes 40 crackers

4 tablespoons butter, at room temperature
1 cup finely shredded Manchego cheese
1 cup almond flour

1 teaspoon salt, divided
¼ teaspoon freshly ground black pepper
1 large egg

1. Using an electric mixer, cream together the butter and shredded cheese until well combined and smooth. 2. In a small bowl, combine the almond flour with ½ teaspoon salt and pepper. Slowly add the almond flour mixture to the cheese, mixing constantly until the dough just comes together to form a ball. 3. Transfer to a piece of parchment or plastic wrap and roll into a cylinder log about 1½ inches thick. Wrap tightly and refrigerate for at least 1 hour. 4. Preheat the oven to 350°F(180°C). Line two baking sheets with parchment paper or silicone baking mats. 5. To make the egg wash, in a small bowl, whisk together the egg and remaining ½ teaspoon salt. 6. Slice the refrigerated dough into small rounds, about ¼ inch thick, and place on the lined baking sheets. 7. Brush the tops of the crackers with egg wash and bake until the crackers are golden and crispy, 12 to 15 minutes. Remove from the oven and allow to cool on a wire rack. 8. Serve warm or, once fully cooled, store in an airtight container in the refrigerator for up to 1 week.

Per Serving:

2 crackers: calories: 100 | fat: 9g | protein: 3g | carbs: 2g | net carbs: 1g | fiber: 1g

Ketone Gummies

Prep time: 10 minutes | Cook time: 5 minutes | Makes 8 gummies

½ cup (120 ml) lemon juice
8 hulled strawberries (fresh or frozen and defrosted)
2 tablespoons unflavored gelatin

2 teaspoons exogenous ketones
Special Equipment (optional):
Silicone mold with eight 2-tablespoon or larger cavities

1. Have on hand your favorite silicone mold. I like to use a large silicone ice cube tray and spoon 2 tablespoons of the mixture into each cavity, If you do not have a silicone mold, you can use an 8-inch (20 cm) square silicone or metal baking pan; if using a metal pan, line it with parchment paper, draping some over the sides for easy removal. 2. Place the lemon juice, strawberries, and gelatin in a blender or food processor and pulse until smooth. Transfer the mixture to a small saucepan and set over low heat for 5 minutes, or until it becomes very liquid-y and begins to simmer. 3. Remove from the heat and stir in the exogenous ketones. 4. Divide the mixture evenly among 8 cavities of the mold or pour into the baking pan. Transfer to the fridge and allow to set for 30 minutes. If using a baking pan, cut into 8 squares.

Per Serving:

calories: 19 | fat: 0g | protein: 3g | carbs: 1g | net carbs: 1g | fiber: 0g

Antipasto Skewers

Prep time: 10 minutes | Cook time: 0 minutes | Makes 8 skewers

8 ounces (227 g) fresh whole Mozzarella
16 fresh basil leaves
16 slices salami (4 ounces / 113 g)
16 slices coppa or other cured meat like prosciutto (4 ounces / 113 g)
8 artichoke hearts, packed in water (8 ounces / 227 g)
¼ cup vinaigrette made with olive oil or avocado oil and apple cider vinegar
Flaky salt and freshly ground black pepper, to taste

1. Cut the Mozzarella into 16 small chunks. 2. Skewer 2 pieces each of the Mozzarella, basil leaves, salami slices, and coppa slices, along with one artichoke heart, on each skewer. You'll probably want to fold the basil leaves in half and the salami and coppa in fourths (or more depending on size) before skewering. 3. Place the skewers in a small shallow dish and drizzle with the dressing, turning to coat. If possible, let them marinate for 30 minutes or more. Sprinkle lightly with flaky salt and the pepper before serving.

Per Serving:

calories: 200 | fat: 15g | protein: 11g | carbs: 4g | net carbs: 4g | fiber: 0g

Warm Herbed Olives

Prep time: 5 minutes | Cook time: 4 minutes | Serves 4

¼ cup good-quality olive oil
4 ounces green olives
4 ounces Kalamata olives
½ teaspoon dried thyme
¼ teaspoon fennel seeds
Pinch red pepper flakes

1. Sauté the olives. In a large skillet over medium heat, warm the olive oil. Sauté the olives, thyme, fennel seeds, and red pepper flakes until the olives start to brown, 3 to 4 minutes. 2. Serve. Put the olives into a bowl and serve them warm.
Per Serving:
calories: 165 | fat: 17g | protein: 1g | carbs: 3g | net carbs: 2g | fiber: 1g

Garlic Herb Butter

Prep time: 10 minutes | Cook time: 8 minutes | Serves 4

⅓ cup butter
1 teaspoon dried parsley
1 tablespoon dried dill
½ teaspoon minced garlic
¼ teaspoon dried thyme

1. Preheat the instant pot on Sauté mode. 2. Then add butter and melt it. 3. Add dried parsley, dill, minced garlic, and thyme. Stir the butter mixture well. 4. Transfer it in the butter mold and refrigerate until it is solid.
Per Serving:
calories: 138 | fat: 15g | protein: 0g | carbs: 1g | net carbs: 1g | fiber: 0g

Asparagus with Creamy Dip

Prep time: 5 minutes | Cook time: 1 minute | Serves 6

1 cup water
1½ pounds (680 g) asparagus
Dipping Sauce:
½ cup mayonnaise
½ cup sour cream
2 tablespoons chopped scallions
spears, trimmed

2 tablespoons fresh chervil
1 teaspoon minced garlic
Salt, to taste

1. Pour the water into the Instant Pot and insert a steamer basket. Place the asparagus in the basket. 2. Lock the lid. Select the Manual mode and set the cooking time for 1 minute at High Pressure. 3. When the timer beeps, perform a quick pressure release. Carefully remove the lid. Transfer the asparagus to a plate. 4. Whisk together the remaining ingredients to make your dipping sauce. Serve the asparagus with the dipping sauce on the side.
Per Serving:
calories: 119 | fat: 9g | protein: 5g | carbs: 7g | net carbs: 4g | fiber: 3g

Wedge Dippers

Prep time: 5 minutes | Cook time: 0 minutes | Serves 4

1 medium head iceberg lettuce (about 6 in/15 cm in diameter)
½ cup (120 ml) ranch dressing

1. Cut the head of lettuce in half, then lay the halves cut side down. Cut each half into 8 wedges, like a pie, for a total of 16 wedges. 2. Serve with the ranch dressing.
Per Serving:
calories: 132 | fat: 12g | protein: 1g | carbs: 5g | net carbs: 4g | fiber: 1g

Red Wine Mushrooms

Prep time: 5 minutes | Cook time: 15 minutes | Serves 2

8 ounces (227 g) sliced mushrooms
¼ cup dry red wine
2 tablespoons beef broth
½ teaspoon garlic powder
¼ teaspoon Worcestershire sauce
Pinch of salt
Pinch of black pepper
¼ teaspoon xanthan gum

1. Add the mushrooms, wine, broth, garlic powder, Worcestershire sauce, salt, and pepper to the pot. 2. Close the lid and seal the vent. Cook on High Pressure for 13 minutes. Quick release the steam. Press Cancel. 3. Turn the pot to Sauté mode. Add the xanthan gum and whisk until the juices have thickened, 1 to 2 minutes.
Per Serving:
calories: 94 | fat: 1g | protein: 4g | carbs: 8g | net carbs: 6g | fiber: 2g

English Cucumber Tea Sandwiches

Prep time: 10 minutes | Cook time: 0 minutes | Makes 12 snacks

1 large cucumber, peeled (approximately 10 ounces / 283 g)
4 ounces (113 g) cream cheese, softened
2 tablespoons finely chopped fresh dill
Freshly ground black pepper, to taste

1. Slice the cucumbers into 24 rounds approximately ¼ inch (6 mm) thick. Place in a single layer between two kitchen towels. Put a cutting board on top. Allow to sit about 5 minutes. 2. Mix the cream cheese and dill. 3. Spread 2 teaspoons cream cheese on half the cucumber slices. Grind black pepper over the cheese. Place another slice of cucumber on top of each and secure with a toothpick, if desired.
Per Serving:
calories: 96 | fat: 8g | protein: 3g | carbs: 3g | net carbs: 1g | fiber: 2g

Cheese Almond Crackers

Prep time: 10 minutes | Cook time: 20 minutes | Serves 4

Olive oil cooking spray	¼ teaspoon garlic powder
1 cup almond flour	¼ teaspoon sea salt
½ cup finely shredded	1 egg
Cheddar cheese	2 teaspoons good-quality
1 tablespoon nutritional yeast	olive oil
¼ teaspoon baking soda	

1. Preheat the oven. Set the oven temperature to 350°F. Line a baking sheet with parchment paper and set it aside. Lightly grease two sheets of parchment paper with olive oil cooking spray and set them aside. 2. Mix the dry ingredients. In a large bowl, stir together the almond flour, Cheddar, nutritional yeast, baking soda, garlic powder, and salt until everything is well blended. 3. Mix the wet ingredients. In a small bowl, whisk together the egg and olive oil. Using a wooden spoon, mix the wet ingredients into the dry until the dough sticks together to form a ball. Gather the ball together using your hands, and knead it firmly a few times. 4. Roll out the dough. Place the ball on one of the lightly greased parchment paper pieces and press it down to form a disk. Place the other piece of greased parchment paper on top and use a rolling pin to roll the dough into a 9-by-12-inch rectangle about ⅛ inch thick. 5. Cut the dough. Use a pizza cutter and a ruler to cut the edges of the dough into an even rectangle and cut the dough into 1½-by-1½-inch columns and rows. Transfer the crackers to the baking sheet. 6. Bake. Bake the crackers for 15 to 20 minutes until they're crisp. Transfer them to a wire rack and let them cool completely. 7. Serve. Eat the crackers immediately or store them in an airtight container in the refrigerator for up to one week.
Per Serving:
calories: 146 | fat: 12g | protein: 7g | carbs: 1g | net carbs: 0g | fiber: 1g

Candied Georgia Pecans

Prep time: 10 minutes | Cook time: 1 hour | Serves 12

12 ounces raw pecan halves	liquid stevia
1 large egg white	1 teaspoon ground cinnamon
1 teaspoon water	1 teaspoon pink Himalayan
2 teaspoons vanilla extract	salt
½ teaspoon plus 10 drops of	

1. Preheat the oven to 250°F. Line a rimmed baking sheet with parchment paper. 2. Spread the pecan halves on the prepared baking sheet in an even layer. 3. In a small bowl, whisk together the egg white, water, vanilla extract, stevia, cinnamon, and salt until combined. Pour the mixture over the pecans and toss with your hands or a spoon until the pecans are evenly coated. 4. Flatten out the pecans into a single layer and bake for 45 to 60 minutes, tossing every 15 minutes. The pecans are done when they have

fully dried out and browned.
Per Serving:
calories: 202 | fat: 24g | protein: 3g | carbs: 4g | net carbs: 3g | fiber: 3g

Spinach-Artichoke-Jalapeño Dip

Prep time: 5 minutes | Cook time: 15 minutes | Serves 4

¼ cup cooked fresh spinach or thawed frozen	1 jalapeño pepper, seeded and finely chopped
½ cup grated Parmesan cheese	1 garlic clove, minced
3 ounces (85 g) full-fat cream cheese	½ teaspoon pink Himalayan sea salt
⅓ cup canned artichoke hearts	½ teaspoon freshly ground black pepper
2 tablespoons sour cream	
2 tablespoons mayonnaise	

1. Preheat the oven to 350ºF (180ºC). 2. In a medium bowl, combine the spinach, Parmesan, cream cheese, artichoke hearts, sour cream, mayonnaise, jalapeño, garlic, salt, and pepper and mix to combine. 3. Transfer the mixture to a ramekin or other small baking dish. Bake for 15 minutes, then serve.
Per Serving:
calories: 196 | fat: 17g | protein: 6g | carbs: 5g | net carbs: 3g | fiber: 2g

Haystack Cookies

Prep time: 10 minutes | Cook time: 5 minutes | Makes 20 cookies

½ cup (95 g) erythritol	¼ cup (20 g) cocoa powder
¼ cup (60 ml) full-fat coconut milk	⅓ cup (30 g) unflavored MCT oil powder (optional)
3 tablespoons coconut oil, ghee, or cacao butter	2 cups (200 g) unsweetened shredded coconut

1. Line a rimmed baking sheet or large plate with parchment paper or a silicone baking mat. 2. Place the erythritol, coconut milk, and oil in a large frying pan. Slowly bring to a simmer over medium-low heat, whisking periodically to prevent burning; this should take about 5 minutes. 3. When the mixture reaches a simmer, remove from the heat and stir in the cocoa powder. Once fully combined, stir in the MCT oil powder, if using, and then the shredded coconut. 4. Using a 1-tablespoon measuring spoon, carefully scoop out a portion of the mixture and press it into the spoon. Place the haystack on the lined baking sheet and repeat, making a total of 20 cookies. 5. Refrigerate for 30 to 45 minutes before enjoying.
Per Serving:
calories: 122 | fat: 11g | protein: 1g | carbs: 4g | net carbs: 2g | fiber: 2g

Keto Asian Dumplings

Prep time: 20 minutes | Cook time: 20 minutes | Serves 4

Dipping Sauce:

¼ cup gluten-free soy sauce	1 tablespoon rice vinegar
2 tablespoons sesame oil	1 teaspoon chili garlic sauce

Filling:

1 tablespoon sesame oil	2 tablespoons gluten-free soy
2 garlic cloves	sauce
1 teaspoon grated fresh ginger	½ teaspoon fish sauce
1 celery stalk, minced	Salt and freshly ground black
½ onion, minced	pepper, to taste
1 carrot, minced	3 scallions, green parts only,
8 ounces (227 g) ground pork	chopped
8 ounces (227 g) shrimp,	1 head napa cabbage, rinsed,
peeled, deveined, and finely	leaves separated (about 12
chopped	leaves)

Make the Dipping Sauce 1. In a small bowl, whisk together the soy sauce, sesame oil, vinegar, and chili garlic sauce. Set aside. Make the Filling 2. In a large skillet over medium heat, heat the sesame oil. 3. Add the garlic, ginger, celery, onion, and carrot. Sauté for 5 to 7 minutes until softened. 4. Add the pork. Cook for 5 to 6 minutes, breaking it up with a spoon, until it starts to brown. 5. Add the shrimp and stir everything together well. 6. Stir in the soy sauce and fish sauce. Season with a little salt and pepper. Give it a stir and add the scallions. Keep it warm over low heat until ready to fill the dumplings. 7. Steam the cabbage leaves: Place the leaves in a large saucepan with just 1 to 2 inches of boiling water. Cook for about 5 minutes or until the leaves become tender. Remove from the water and set aside to drain. 8. Lay each leaf out flat. Put about 2 tablespoons of filling in the center of one leaf. Wrap the leaf over itself, tucking the sides in so the whole thing is tightly wrapped. Secure with a toothpick. Continue with the remaining leaves and filling. Serve with the dipping sauce. Refrigerate leftovers in an airtight container for up to 3 days.

Per Serving:

3 dumplings: calories: 305 | fat: 17g | protein: 27g | carbs: 11g | net carbs: 8g | fiber: 3g

Fried Prosciutto-Wrapped Deviled Eggs

Prep time: 10 minutes | Cook time: 10 minutes | Makes 12 deviled eggs

1 cup coconut oil	homemade or store-bought
6 slices prosciutto	1 teaspoon prepared yellow
6 hard-boiled eggs, peeled	mustard
1 small red onion or 2	½ teaspoon fine sea salt,
shallots, thinly sliced	divided
(optional)	¾ teaspoon smoked paprika,
½ cup mayonnaise,	for garnish

1. Preheat the oil to 350°F (180°C) in a deep-fryer or a 4-inch-deep (or deeper) cast-iron skillet over medium heat. The oil should be at least 3 inches deep; add more oil if needed. 2. While the oil is heating, wrap 1 slice of prosciutto around each hard-boiled egg. 3. When the oil is hot, fry the wrapped eggs, three or four at a time, in the hot oil for about 2 minutes, or until crispy on the outside. Remove from the oil with a slotted spoon onto a paper towel. 4. Fry the onion, if using, in the hot oil until golden brown, about 1 minute. Remove from the oil with a slotted spoon, place on a paper towel, and dust lightly with salt while still hot. Go easy on the salt since prosciutto can be salty. 5. Slice the eggs in half and scoop the yolks into a small bowl. Set the whites aside on a serving platter. 6. Smash the yolks with the back of a fork until very crumbly. Add the mayonnaise, mustard, and salt and stir until smooth and creamy. 7. Spoon or pipe about 1 rounded tablespoon of the filling into each egg white half. If desired, top each deviled egg with some fried onion. Dust with smoked paprika. 8. These are best served immediately for maximum crispiness. Store extras in an airtight container for up to 3 days. Reheating is not recommended.

Per Serving:

calories: 232 | fat: 21g | protein: 10g | carbs: 1g | net carbs: 1g | fiber: 0g

Bacon-Stuffed Mushrooms

Prep time: 20 minutes | Cook time: 40 minutes | Makes 16 stuffed mushrooms

16 large white mushrooms	1 clove garlic, minced
(1½ to 2 inches in diameter)	1 (8 ounces) package cream
1 tablespoon avocado oil	cheese, cubed
8 slices bacon, diced	Sliced green onions, for
¼ cup finely chopped green	garnish (optional)
onions	

1. Preheat the oven to 350°F. Line a sheet pan with parchment paper. 2. Clean the mushrooms and pat them dry. Remove the stems and chop them; set aside. Set the mushroom caps on the lined sheet pan, stem side up. 3. Heat the oil in a medium-sized skillet over medium heat. Add the bacon, chopped mushroom stems, green onions, and garlic and cook until the bacon is crispy and the mushroom stems are tender. Reduce the heat to low. 4. Add the cream cheese to the skillet and stir until melted and well incorporated into the other ingredients. Remove the skillet from the heat. 5. Fill each mushroom with a spoonful of the cream cheese mixture and place on the lined sheet pan. 6. Bake the stuffed mushrooms for 30 minutes, or until tender and slightly browned on top. This could take less time depending on how large your mushrooms are. Garnish with sliced green onions before serving, if desired.

Per Serving:

calories: 305 | fat: 25g | protein: 14g | carbs: 5g | net carbs: 4g | fiber: 1g

Asiago Shishito Peppers

Prep time: 5 minutes | Cook time: 10 minutes | Serves 4

Oil, for spraying
6 ounces (170 g) shishito peppers
1 tablespoon olive oil

½ teaspoon salt
½ teaspoon lemon pepper
⅓ cup grated Asiago cheese, divided

1. Line the air fryer basket with parchment and spray lightly with oil. 2. Rinse the shishitos and pat dry with paper towels. 3. In a large bowl, mix together the shishitos, olive oil, salt, and lemon pepper. Place the shishitos in the prepared basket. 4. Roast at 350ºF (177ºC) for 10 minutes, or until blistered but not burned. 5. Sprinkle with half of the cheese and cook for 1 more minute. 6. Transfer to a serving plate. Immediately sprinkle with the remaining cheese and serve.

Per Serving:

calories: 90 | fat: 6g | protein: 3g | carbs: 7g | net carbs: 6g | fiber: 1g

Avocado Salsa

Prep time: 10 minutes | Cook time: 0 minutes | Serves 4

2 or 3 avocados, peeled, pitted, and diced
¼ red onion, diced
1 garlic clove, minced
Zest of ½ lime

Juice of 1 lime
¼ cup olive oil
Salt and freshly ground black pepper, to taste
¼ cup chopped fresh cilantro

1. In a large bowl, gently toss together the diced avocados, onion, garlic, lime zest and juice, and olive oil. Season with salt and pepper. Cover and refrigerate in an airtight container for up to 4 days. Top with the cilantro before serving.

Per Serving:

calories: 450 | fat: 42g | protein: 3g | carbs: 15g | net carbs: 5g | fiber: 10g

Tapenade

Prep time: 5 minutes | Cook time: 0 minutes | Serves 2

1 cup pitted black olives
1 cup pitted green olives
¼ cup sun-dried tomatoes in oil, drained
6 fresh basil leaves
1 tablespoon capers
1 tablespoon fresh parsley leaves
2 teaspoons fresh thyme

leaves
Leaves from 1 sprig fresh oregano
1 clove garlic
1 anchovy fillet
¼ cup olive oil
6 medium celery stalks, cut into sticks, for serving

1. Place all the ingredients, except the olive oil and celery sticks, in a blender or food processor. Pulse until roughly chopped. 2.

Add the olive oil and pulse a couple more times, just to combine. 3. Transfer to a 16-ounce (475-ml) or larger serving dish and enjoy with celery sticks. Store it: :Keep in an airtight container in the fridge for up to 5 days.

Per Serving:

calories: 167 | fat: 16g | protein: 1g | carbs: 4g | net carbs: 3g | fiber: 1g

Cheddar Cauliflower Rice

Prep time: 3 minutes | Cook time: 1 minute | Serves 4

1 head fresh cauliflower, chopped into florets
1 cup water
3 tablespoons butter
1 tablespoon heavy cream

1 cup shredded sharp Cheddar cheese
½ teaspoon salt
¼ teaspoon pepper
¼ teaspoon garlic powder

1. Place cauliflower in steamer basket. Pour water into Instant Pot and lower steamer rack into pot. Click lid closed. Press the Steam button and adjust time for 1 minute. When timer beeps, quick-release the pressure. 2. Remove steamer basket and place cauliflower in food processor. Pulse until cauliflower is broken into small pearls. Place cauliflower into large bowl, and add remaining ingredients. Gently fold until fully combined.

Per Serving:

calories: 241 | fat: 18g | protein: 10g | carbs: 8g | net carbs: 5g | fiber: 3g

Fried Cabbage Wedges

Prep time: 5 minutes | Cook time: 15 minutes | Serves 6

1 large head green or red cabbage (about 2½ pounds/1.2 kg)
2 tablespoons coconut oil or avocado oil
2 teaspoons garlic powder
½ teaspoon finely ground sea

salt
¾ cup (180 ml) green goddess dressing
Special Equipment:
12 (4-in/10-cm) bamboo skewers

1. Cut the cabbage in half through the core, from top to bottom. Working with each half separately, remove the core by cutting a triangle around it and pulling it out. Then lay the half cut side down and cut into 6 wedges. Press a bamboo skewer into each wedge to secure the leaves. Repeat with the other half. 2. Heat the oil in a large frying pan over medium-low heat. 3. Place the cabbage wedges in the frying pan and sprinkle with the garlic powder and salt. Cook for 10 minutes on one side, or until lightly browned, then cook for 5 minutes on the other side. Serve with the dressing on the side.

Per Serving:

calories: 252 | fat: 20g | protein: 3g | carbs: 12g | net carbs: 7g | fiber: 5g

Superpower Fat Bombs

Prep time: 10 minutes | Cook time: 0 minutes | Makes 8 bombs

⅔ cup (145 g) coconut oil, cacao butter, or ghee, melted

¼ cup (40 g) collagen peptides or protein powder

¼ cup (25 g) unflavored MCT oil powder

2 tablespoons cocoa powder

2 tablespoons roughly ground flax seeds

1 tablespoon cacao nibs

1 teaspoon instant coffee granules

4 drops liquid stevia, or 1 tablespoon plus 1 teaspoon confectioners'-style erythritol

Pinch of finely ground sea salt

Special Equipment (Optional): Silicone mold with eight 2-tablespoon or larger cavities

1. Have on hand your favorite silicone mold. I like to use a large silicone ice cube tray and spoon 2 tablespoons of the mixture into each well, If you do not have a silicone mold, making this into a bark works well, too. Simply use an 8-inch (20-cm) square silicone or metal baking pan; if using a metal pan, line it with parchment paper, draping some over the sides for easy removal. 2. Place all the ingredients in a medium-sized bowl and stir until well mixed and smooth. 3. Divide the mixture evenly among 8 cavities in the silicone mold or pour into the baking pan. Transfer to the fridge and allow to set for 15 minutes if using cacao butter or 30 minutes if using ghee or coconut oil. If using a baking pan, break the bark into 8 pieces for serving.

Per Serving:

calories: 136 | fat: 12g | protein: 6g | carbs: 3g | net carbs: 1g | fiber: 2g

Creamed Onion Spinach

Prep time: 3 minutes | Cook time: 5 minutes | Serves 6

4 tablespoons butter

¼ cup diced onion

8 ounces (227 g) cream cheese

1 (12 ounces / 340 g) bag

frozen spinach

½ cup chicken broth

1 cup shredded whole-milk Mozzarella cheese

1. Press the Sauté button and add butter. Once butter is melted, add onion to Instant Pot and sauté for 2 minutes or until onion begins to turn translucent. 2. Break cream cheese into pieces and add to Instant Pot. Press the Cancel button. Add frozen spinach and broth. Click lid closed. Press the Manual button and adjust time for 5 minutes. When timer beeps, quick-release the pressure and stir in shredded Mozzarella. If mixture is too watery, press the Sauté button and reduce for additional 5 minutes, stirring constantly.

Per Serving:

calories: 273 | fat: 24g | protein: 9g | carbs: 5g | net carbs: 3g | fiber: 2g

Cheese Stuffed Mushrooms

Prep time: 15 minutes | Cook time: 8 minutes | Serves 4

1 cup cremini mushroom caps

1 tablespoon chopped scallions

1 tablespoon chopped chives

1 teaspoon cream cheese

1 teaspoon sour cream

1 ounce (28 g) Monterey Jack cheese, shredded

1 teaspoon butter, softened

½ teaspoon smoked paprika

1 cup water, for cooking

1. Trim the mushroom caps if needed and wash them well. 2. After this, in the mixing bowl, mix up scallions, chives, cream cheese, sour cream, butter, and smoked paprika. 3. Then fill the mushroom caps with the cream cheese mixture and top with shredded Monterey Jack cheese. 4. Pour water and insert the trivet in the instant pot. 5. Arrange the stuffed mushrooms caps on the trivet and close the lid. 6. Cook the meal on Manual (High Pressure) for 8 minutes. 7. Then make a quick pressure release.

Per Serving:

calories: 45 | fat: 4g | protein: 3g | carbs: 1g | net carbs: 1g | fiber: 0g

Breaded Mushroom Nuggets

Prep time: 15 minutes | Cook time: 50 minutes | Serves 4

24 cremini mushrooms (about 1 pound/455 g)

2 large eggs

½ cup (55 g) blanched almond flour

1 teaspoon garlic powder

1 teaspoon paprika

½ teaspoon finely ground sea

salt

2 tablespoons avocado oil

½ cup (120 ml) honey mustard dressing, for serving (optional)

Special Equipment (optional): Toothpicks

1. Preheat the oven to 350°F (177°C). Line a rimmed baking sheet with parchment paper or a silicone baking mat. 2. Break the stems off the mushrooms or cut them short so that the stems are level with the caps. 3. Crack the eggs into a small bowl and whisk. 4. Place the almond flour, garlic powder, paprika, and salt in a medium-sized bowl and whisk to combine. 5. Dip one mushroom at a time into the eggs, then use the same hand to drop it into the flour mixture, being careful not to get the flour mixture on that hand. Rotate the mushroom in the flour mixture with a fork to coat on all sides, then transfer it to the lined baking sheet. Repeat with the remaining mushrooms. 6. Drizzle the coated mushrooms with the oil. Bake for 50 minutes, or until the tops begin to turn golden. 7. Remove from the oven and serve with the dressing, if using. If serving to friends and family, provide toothpicks.

Per Serving:

calories: 332 | fat: 29g | protein: 8g | carbs: 9g | net carbs: 7g | fiber: 2g

Peanut Butter Keto Fudge

Prep time: 5 minutes | Cook time: 10 minutes | Serves 12

½ cup (1 stick) butter	1 teaspoon vanilla extract (or
8 ounces (227 g) cream cheese	the seeds from 1 vanilla bean)
1 cup unsweetened peanut	1 teaspoon liquid stevia
butter	(optional)

1. Line an 8 or 9-inch square or 9-by-13-inch rectangular baking dish with parchment paper. Set aside. 2. In a saucepan over medium heat, melt the butter and cream cheese together, stirring frequently, for about 5 minutes. 3. Add the peanut butter and continue to stir until smooth. Remove from the heat. 4. Stir in the vanilla and stevia (if using). Pour the mixture into the prepared dish and spread into an even layer. Refrigerate for about 1 hour until thickened and set enough to cut and handle. Cut into small squares and enjoy! Refrigerate, covered, for up to 1 week.

Per Serving:
1 fudge square: calories: 261 | fat: 24g | protein: 8g | carbs: 5g | net carbs: 4g | fiber: 1g

Smoked Salmon Cream Cheese Rollups with Arugula and Truffle Oil Drizzle

Prep time: 10 minutes | Cook time: 0 minutes | Serves 4

½ cup cream cheese	12 slices (½ pound) smoked
¼ cup plain Greek-style	salmon
yogurt	¾ cup arugula
2 teaspoons chopped fresh dill	Truffle oil, for garnish

1. Mix the filling. In a small bowl, blend together the cream cheese, yogurt, and dill until the mixture is smooth. 2. Make the rollups. Spread the cream cheese mixture onto the smoked salmon slices, dividing it evenly. Place several arugula leaves at one end of each slice and roll them up. Secure them with a toothpick if they're starting to unroll. 3. Serve. Drizzle the rolls with truffle oil and place three rolls on each of four plates.

Per Serving:
calories: 234 | fat: 20g | protein: 13g | carbs: 2g | net carbs: 2g | fiber: 0g

Easy Baked Zucchini Chips

Prep time: 5 minutes | Cook time: 2½ hours | Serves 4

2 medium zucchini (10 ounces	avocado oil
/ 283 g total)	½ teaspoon sea salt
1 tablespoon olive oil or	

1. Preheat the oven to 200°F (93°C). 2. Use a mandoline or a sharp knife to slice the zucchini into ⅛-inch-thick slices. 3. Place the zucchini in a large bowl. Add the olive oil and toss to thoroughly coat. Sprinkle lightly with sea salt. Toss to coat again. 4. Place ovenproof wire cooling racks on top of two baking sheets, then top those with parchment paper. (The cooling rack method allows for better air circulation.) Arrange the zucchini slices in a single layer. It's fine if they touch, but make sure they don't overlap. 5. Bake side by side for about 2½ hours, rotating the pans front to back halfway through, until the chips are golden and just starting to get crispy. 6. Allow the chips to cool in the oven with the heat off and the door propped slightly open. This is a crucial step, as they will be soft initially and crisp up when they cool using this method.

Per Serving:
calories: 46 | fat: 4g | protein: 2g | carbs: 4g | net carbs: 2g | fiber: 2g

Cauliflower Patties

Prep time: 10 minutes | Cook time: 10 minutes | Makes 10 patties

1 medium head cauliflower	1 teaspoon finely ground sea
(about 1½ pounds/680 g),	salt
or 3 cups (375 g) pre-riced	1 teaspoon garlic powder
cauliflower	½ teaspoon turmeric powder
2 large eggs	¼ teaspoon ground black
⅔ cup (75 g) blanched almond	pepper
flour	3 tablespoons coconut oil or
¼ cup (17 g) nutritional yeast	ghee, for the pan
1 tablespoon dried chives	

1. If you're using pre-riced cauliflower, skip ahead to Step 2. Otherwise, cut the base off the head of cauliflower and remove the florets. Transfer the florets to a food processor or blender and pulse 3 or 4 times to break them up into small (¼-inch/6-mm) pieces. 2. Transfer the riced cauliflower to a medium-sized saucepan and add enough water to the pan to completely cover the cauliflower. Cover with the lid and bring to a boil over medium heat. Boil, covered, for 3½ minutes. 3. Meanwhile, place a fine-mesh strainer over a bowl. 4. Pour the hot cauliflower into the strainer, allowing the bowl to catch the boiling water. With a spoon, press down on the cauliflower to remove as much water as possible. 5. Discard the cooking water and place the cauliflower in the bowl, then add the eggs, almond flour, nutritional yeast, chives, salt, and spices. Stir until everything is incorporated. 6. Heat a large frying pan over medium-low heat. Add the oil and allow to melt completely. 7. Using a ¼-cup (60-ml) scoop, scoop up a portion of the mixture and roll between your hands to form a ball about 1¾ inches (4.5 cm) in diameter. Place in the hot oil and flatten the ball with the back of a fork until it is a patty about ½ inch (1.25 cm) thick. Repeat with the remaining cauliflower mixture, making a total of 10 patties. 8. Cook the patties for 5 minutes per side, or until golden brown. Transfer to a serving plate and enjoy!

Per Serving:
calories: 164 | fat: 12g | protein: 7g | carbs: 7g | net carbs: 3g | fiber: 4g

Chicharrón

Prep time: 5 minutes | Cook time: 2 hours | Serves 4

2 teaspoons baking soda
1 teaspoon fine sea salt
1 pound (454 g) fresh pork belly, skin on
Fine sea salt and freshly

ground black pepper, to taste
Cajun seasoning or other spices of choice, such as ground cumin

1. Rub the baking soda and salt over the surface of the pork skin, taking care to distribute the powder evenly. Set the pork belly on a rack and place it, uncovered, in the refrigerator for at least an hour but preferably overnight and up to a full day. 2. Remove the pork belly from the refrigerator. Rinse well under running water and pat dry with paper towels. 3. Slice the pork belly into chip-sized pieces, about 2 inches square and ⅓ inch thick. 4. Place the pork chips in a pot and add enough water to cover all the pieces. 5. Heat on low for 2 hours, flipping the chips every 30 minutes, until the water has evaporated and the fat is rendered. Depending on how much moisture is in the pork belly, this process could take up to 3 hours. 6. When all the water has evaporated and there is liquid lard in the bottom of the pot, turn the heat to high to start the frying process—this happens quickly, so don't walk away from the pot! 7. Fry the chips in the rendered lard for 4 to 5 minutes, until they are golden brown. Using a slotted spoon, remove the chicharrónes to a plate lined with paper towels to drain. Sprinkle with salt and any other desired seasonings. 8. Store extras in an airtight container in the fridge for up to 1 week.

Per Serving:

calories: 320 | fat: 28g | protein: 17g | carbs: 0g | net carbs: 0g | fiber: 0g

Smoky "Hummus" and Veggies

Prep time: 15 minutes | Cook time: 20 minutes | serves 6

Nonstick coconut oil cooking spray
1 cauliflower head, cut into florets
¼ cup tahini
¼ cup cold-pressed olive oil, plus extra for drizzling
Juice of 1 lemon
1 tablespoon ground paprika

1 teaspoon sea salt
¼ cup chopped fresh parsley, for garnish
2 tablespoons pine nuts (optional)
Flax crackers, for serving
Sliced cucumbers, for serving
Celery pieces, for serving

1. Preheat the oven to 400°F and grease a baking sheet with cooking spray. 2. Spread the cauliflower florets out on the prepared baking sheet and bake for 20 minutes. 3. Remove the cauliflower from the oven and allow it to cool for 10 minutes. 4. In a food processor or high-powered blender, combine the cauliflower with the tahini, olive oil, lemon juice, paprika, and salt. Blend on high until a fluffy, creamy texture is achieved. If the mixture seems

too thick, slowly add a few tablespoons of water until smooth. 5. Scoop the "hummus" into an airtight container and chill in the refrigerator for about 20 minutes. 6. Transfer the "hummus" to a serving bowl and drizzle with olive oil. Garnish with the parsley and pine nuts (if using). 7. Serve with your favorite flax crackers and sliced cucumbers and celery.

Per Serving:

calories: 169 | fat: 15g | protein: 4g | carbs: 9g | net carbs: 5g | fiber: 4g

Charlie's Energy Balls

Prep time: 10 minutes | Cook time: 20 minutes | Makes 20 balls

½ cup natural almond butter, room temperature
¼ cup coconut oil, melted
1 large egg
½ cup coconut flour

2 tablespoons unflavored beef gelatin powder
1 scoop chocolate-flavored whey protein powder

1. Preheat the oven to 350°F and grease a rimmed baking sheet with coconut oil spray. 2. In a large mixing bowl, mix together the almond butter, coconut oil, and egg using a fork. In a small bowl, whisk together the coconut flour, gelatin, and protein powder. 3. Pour the dry ingredients into the wet mixture and mash with a fork until you have a cohesive dough. It should not be too sticky. Note: If the dough doesn't come together well or is very sticky, add a little coconut flour until it combines well. 4. Using your hands, form the dough into 20 even-sized balls, about 1½ inches in diameter, and put them on the prepared baking sheet. 5. Bake for 20 minutes, until slightly browned and hardened. Allow to cool on the baking sheet for 10 minutes prior to serving. 6. Store in a zip-top plastic bag in the refrigerator for up to a week.

Per Serving:

calories: 91 | fat: 7g | protein: 4g | carbs: 3g | net carbs: 2g | fiber: 1g

Lemon-Butter Mushrooms

Prep time: 10 minutes | Cook time: 4 minutes | Serves 2

1 cup cremini mushrooms, sliced
½ cup water
1 tablespoon lemon juice

1 teaspoon almond butter
1 teaspoon grated lemon zest
½ teaspoon salt
½ teaspoon dried thyme

1. Combine all the ingredients in the Instant Pot. 2. Secure the lid. Select the Manual mode and set the cooking time for 4 minutes at High Pressure. 3. Once cooking is complete, do a natural pressure release for 5 minutes, then release any remaining pressure. Carefully open the lid. 4. Serve warm.

Per Serving:

calories: 63 | fat: 5g | protein: 3g | carbs: 3g | net carbs: 2g | fiber: 1g

Sweet and Spicy Beef Jerky

Prep time: 15 minutes | Cook time: 4 to 6 hours | Serves 16

3 pounds flat-iron steak	2 teaspoons ground black
Marinade:	pepper
½ cup soy sauce	1½ teaspoons garlic powder
½ cup apple cider vinegar	1 teaspoon onion powder
¼ cup Frank's RedHot sauce	Special equipment:
½ teaspoon liquid stevia	10 (12-inch) bamboo skewers
2 teaspoons liquid smoke	

1. Marinate the steak: Slice the steak into thin jerky-sized strips, about ¼ inch thick, and put them in a gallon-sized ziptop plastic bag. Add the marinade ingredients, seal the bag, and shake to fully coat the meat. 2. Seal the bag tightly (removing any excess air) and place it in a bowl to catch any leakage. Place the bowl in the refrigerator for at least 4 hours or up to 24 hours. 3. Make the jerky: Adjust the racks in your oven so that one is in the highest position and one is in the lowest position. Preheat the oven to 190°F. 4. Remove the steak strips from the marinade and pat them as dry as possible using paper towels; discard the remaining marinade. 5. Using bamboo skewers, pierce the tip of each meat strip so that there are anywhere from 5 to 7 strips hanging on each skewer. Be sure to leave space between the strips so that air can circulate around them. Hang the skewers from the top oven rack and place a rimmed baking sheet on the lowest rack to catch any drippings. 6. Bake for 4 to 6 hours, until the jerky is dry to the touch. 7. Store in a zip-top plastic bag in the refrigerator for up to 10 days.

Per Serving:

calories: 150 | fat: 10g | protein: 16g | carbs: 1g | net carbs: 1g | fiber: 0g

Keto Antipasto

Prep time: 20 minutes | Cook time: 0 minutes | Serves 12

8 ounces (227 g) soppressata salami, diced	medium), pitted and chopped
5 ounces (142 g) Calabrese salami, diced	10 pepperoncini peppers, diced
4 ounces (113 g) sharp provolone or white Cheddar cheese, diced	¼ cup fresh basil, chopped
	1 tablespoon Italian seasoning
4 ounces (113 g) Mozzarella, diced	2 tablespoons olive oil
	2 tablespoons red wine vinegar
4 celery stalks, diced	1 teaspoon balsamic vinegar
¼ medium red onion, finely chopped (about ½ cup)	1 teaspoon Dijon mustard
	Sea salt and freshly ground black pepper, to taste
24 large green olives (or 35	

1. In a large bowl, combine the soppressata, Calabrese, provolone, Mozzarella, celery, onion, olives, peppers, basil, and Italian seasoning. Mix until well combined. 2. In a small bowl, whisk together the olive oil, red wine vinegar, balsamic vinegar, and mustard. Add salt and pepper. 3. Pour the dressing over the meat and cheese mixture and stir well. 4. Serve immediately or transfer to an airtight container and store in the refrigerator for up to 1 week or in the freezer for up to 3 months.

Per Serving:

⅓ cup: calories: 206 | fat: 16g | protein: 12g | carbs: 3g | net carbs: 3g | fiber: 0g

Bacon-Pepper Fat Bombs

Prep time: 10 minutes | Cook time: 0 minutes | Makes 12 fat bombs

2 ounces goat cheese, at room temperature	temperature
	8 bacon slices, cooked and chopped
2 ounces cream cheese, at room temperature	Pinch freshly ground black pepper
¼ cup butter, at room	

1. Line a small baking sheet with parchment paper and set aside. 2. In a medium bowl, stir together the goat cheese, cream cheese, butter, bacon, and pepper until well combined. 3. Use a tablespoon to drop mounds of the bomb mixture on the baking sheet and place the sheet in the freezer until the fat bombs are very firm but not frozen, about 1 hour. 4. Store the fat bombs in a sealed container in the refrigerator for up to 2 weeks.

Per Serving:

1 fat bomb: calories: 89 | fat: 8g | protein: 3g | carbs: 0g | net carbs: 0g | fiber: 0g

Crispy Parmesan Crackers

Prep time: 10 minutes | Cook time: 5 minutes | Makes 8 crackers

1 teaspoon butter

8 ounces full-fat Parmesan cheese, shredded or freshly grated

1. Preheat the oven to 400°F. 2. Line a baking sheet with parchment paper and lightly grease the paper with the butter. 3. Spoon the Parmesan cheese onto the baking sheet in mounds, spread evenly apart. 4. Spread out the mounds with the back of a spoon until they are flat. 5. Bake the crackers until the edges are browned and the centers are still pale, about 5 minutes. 6. Remove the sheet from the oven, and remove the crackers with a spatula to paper towels. Lightly blot the tops with additional paper towels and let them completely cool. 7. Store in a sealed container in the refrigerator for up to 4 days.

Per Serving:

1 cracker : calories: 133 | fat: 11g | protein: 11g | carbs: 1g | net carbs: 1g | fiber: 0g

Zucchini Chips

Prep time: 10 minutes | Cook time: 2 hours | serves 6

1 large zucchini, cut into thin disks

1 teaspoon sea salt

2 tablespoons coconut oil

1 teaspoon dried dill

1 tablespoon freshly ground black pepper

1. Preheat the oven to 225°F. 2. Line a baking sheet with parchment paper. If you don't have parchment paper, use aluminum foil or a greased pan. 3. Sprinkle the zucchini slices with the salt and spread them out on paper towels. 4. With a separate paper towel, firmly press the zucchini slices and pat them dry (the dryer the better). 5. Toss the zucchini slices in the coconut oil, dill, and pepper, then spread them out on the prepared baking sheet. 6. Bake for 2 hours, or until they are golden and crisp. Check every 30 minutes or so for burn marks. If you begin to see them burn, remove the chips immediately. 7. Remove the chips from the oven and cool. 8. Once the chips have cooled, transfer them to a serving bowl or store in an airtight container for up to 3 days.

Per Serving:

calories: 52 | fat: 5g | protein: 1g | carbs: 3g | net carbs: 1g | fiber: 1g

Macadamia Nut Cream Cheese Log

Prep time: 10 minutes | Cook time: 0 minutes | Serves 8

1 (8 ounces / 227 g) brick cream cheese, cold

1 cup finely chopped macadamia nuts

1. Place the cream cheese on a piece of parchment paper or wax paper. 2. Roll the paper around the cream cheese, then roll the wrapped cream cheese with the palm of your hands lengthwise on the cream cheese, using the paper to help you roll the cream cheese into an 8-inch log. 3. Open the paper and sprinkle the macadamia nuts all over the top and sides of the cream cheese until the log is entirely covered in nuts. 4. Chill in the refrigerator for 30 minutes before serving. 5. Serve on a small plate, cut into 8 even slices.

Per Serving:

calories: 285 | fat: 29g | protein: 4g | carbs: 4g | net carbs: 3g | fiber: 1g

Sautéed Asparagus with Lemon-Tahini Sauce

Prep time: 5 minutes | Cook time: 10 minutes | Serves 4

16 asparagus spears, woody ends snapped off

2 tablespoons avocado oil

Lemon-Tahini Sauce:

2 tablespoons tahini

1 tablespoon avocado oil

2½ teaspoons lemon juice

1 small clove garlic, minced

1/16 teaspoon finely ground sea salt

Pinch of ground black pepper

1 to 1½ tablespoons water

1. Place the asparagus and oil in a large frying pan over medium heat. Cook, tossing the spears in the oil every once in a while, until the spears begin to brown slightly, about 10 minutes. 2. Meanwhile, make the sauce: Place the tahini, oil, lemon juice, garlic, salt, pepper, and 1 tablespoon of water in a medium-sized bowl. Whisk until incorporated. If the dressing is too thick, add the additional ½ tablespoon of water and whisk again. 3. Place the cooked asparagus on a serving plate and drizzle with the lemon tahini sauce.

Per Serving:

calories: 106 | fat: 8g | protein: 4g | carbs: 6g | net carbs: 3g | fiber: 3g

Prosciutto-Wrapped Asparagus

Prep time: 5 minutes | Cook time: 12 minutes | Serves 6

18 asparagus spears, ends trimmed

2 tablespoons coconut oil,

melted

6 slices prosciutto

1 teaspoon garlic powder

1 Preheat the oven to 400°F. Line a rimmed baking sheet with parchment paper. 2 Place the asparagus and coconut oil in a large zip-top plastic bag. Seal and toss until the asparagus is evenly coated. 3 Wrap a slice of prosciutto around 3 grouped asparagus spears. Repeat with the remaining prosciutto and asparagus, making a total of 6 bundles. Arrange the bundles in a single layer on the lined baking sheet. Sprinkle the garlic powder over the bundles. 4 Bake for 8 to 12 minutes, until the asparagus is tender.

Per Serving:

calories: 122 | fat: 10g | protein: 8g | carbs: 3g | net carbs: 2g | fiber: 1g

Mayo Chicken Celery

Prep time: 15 minutes | Cook time: 15 minutes | Serves 4

14 ounces (397 g) chicken breast, skinless, boneless

1 cup water

4 celery stalks

1 teaspoon salt

½ teaspoon onion powder

1 teaspoon mayonnaise

1. Combine all the ingredients except the mayo in the Instant Pot. 2. Secure the lid. Select the Manual mode and set the cooking time for 15 minutes at High Pressure. 3. Once cooking is complete, do a natural pressure release for 6 minutes, then release any remaining pressure. Carefully open the lid. 4. Remove the chicken and shred with two forks, then return to the Instant Pot. 5. Add the mayo and stir well. Serve immediately.

Per Serving:

calories: 119 | fat: 3g | protein: 21g | carbs: 1g | net carbs: 1g | fiber: 0g

Salami, Pepperoncini, and Cream Cheese Pinwheels

Prep time: 20 minutes | Cook time: 0 minutes | Serves 2

8 ounces cream cheese, at room temperature

¼ pound salami, thinly sliced

2 tablespoons sliced pepperoncini (I use Mezzetta)

1. Lay out a sheet of plastic wrap on a large cutting board or counter. 2. Place the cream cheese in the center of the plastic wrap, and then add another layer of plastic wrap on top. Using a rolling pin, roll the cream cheese until it is even and about ¼ inch thick. Try to make the shape somewhat resemble a rectangle. 3. Pull off the top layer of plastic wrap. 4. Place the salami slices so they overlap to completely cover the cream-cheese layer. 5. Place a new piece of plastic wrap on top of the salami layer so that you can flip over your cream cheese–salami rectangle. Flip the layer so the cream cheese side is up. 6. Remove the plastic wrap and add the sliced pepperoncini in a layer on top. 7. Roll the layered ingredients into a tight log, pressing the meat and cream cheese together. (You want it as tight as possible.) Then wrap the roll with plastic wrap and refrigerate for at least 6 hours so it will set. 8. Use a sharp knife to cut the log into slices and serve.

Per Serving:

calories: 583 | fat: 54g | protein: 19g | carbs: 7g | net carbs: 7g | fiber: 0g

Hushpuppies

Prep time: 10 minutes | Cook time: 15 minutes | Makes 10 hushpuppies

High-quality oil, for frying

1 cup finely ground blanched almond flour

1 tablespoon coconut flour

1 teaspoon baking powder

½ teaspoon salt

¼ cup finely chopped onions

¼ cup heavy whipping cream

1 large egg, beaten

1. Attach a candy thermometer to a Dutch oven or other large heavy pot, then pour in 3 inches of oil and set over medium-high heat. Heat the oil to 375°F. 2. In a medium-sized bowl, stir together the almond flour, coconut flour, baking powder, and salt. Stir in the rest of the ingredients and mix until blended. Do not overmix. 3. Use a tablespoon-sized cookie scoop to gently drop the batter into the hot oil. Don't overcrowd the hushpuppies; cook them in two batches. Fry for 3 minutes, then use a mesh skimmer or slotted spoon to turn and fry them for 3 more minutes or until golden brown on all sides. 4. Use the skimmer or slotted spoon to remove the hushpuppies from the oil and place on a paper towel–lined plate to drain. They are best served immediately.

Per Serving:

calories: 172 | fat: 14g | protein: 6g | carbs: 5g | net carbs: 3g | fiber: 3g

Loaded Bacon and Cheddar Cheese Balls

Prep time: 10 minutes | Cook time: 0 minutes | Makes 16 balls

7 bacon slices, cooked until crisp, cooled, and crumbled

1 tablespoon chopped chives

8 ounces (227 g) cream cheese

1½ cups finely shredded Cheddar cheese

½ teaspoon smoked paprika

1 teaspoon onion powder

½ teaspoon sea salt

Olive oil or butter, for greasing

1. Line a plate or storage container with parchment paper. 2. In a small bowl, toss together the crumbled bacon and chives and set aside. 3. In a food processor or blender, mix together the cream cheese, Cheddar, paprika, onion powder, and salt. 4. Grease your hands with olive oil or butter to avoid sticking, and form 16 balls of cheese. Roll each ball in the bacon and chive "batter" as you go, and set them on the prepared plate or storage container. 5. Serve right away, or store in an airtight container in the refrigerator for up to 5 days.

Per Serving:

2 cheese balls: calories: 228 | fat: 20g | protein: 10g | carbs: 2g | net carbs: 2g | fiber: 0g

Baked Crab Dip

Prep time: 15 minutes | Cook time: 25 minutes | Serves 4 to 6

4 ounces cream cheese, softened

½ cup shredded Parmesan cheese, plus ½ cup extra for topping (optional) ⅓ cup mayonnaise

¼ cup sour cream

1 tablespoon chopped fresh parsley

2 teaspoons fresh lemon juice

1½ teaspoons Sriracha sauce

½ teaspoon garlic powder

8 ounces fresh lump crabmeat

Salt and pepper

1. Preheat the oven to 375°F. 2. Combine all the ingredients except for the crabmeat in a mixing bowl and use a hand mixer to blend until smooth. 3. Put the crabmeat in a separate bowl, check for shells, and rinse with cold water, if needed. Pat dry or allow to rest in a strainer until most of the water has drained. 4. Add the crabmeat to the bowl with the cream cheese mixture and gently fold to combine. Taste for seasoning and add salt and pepper to taste, if needed. Pour into an 8-inch round or square baking dish and bake for 25 minutes, until the cheese has melted and the dip is warm throughout. 5. If desired, top the dip with another ½ cup of Parmesan cheese and broil for 2 to 3 minutes, until the cheese has melted and browned slightly.

Per Serving:

calories: 275 | fat: 23g | protein: 16g | carbs: 1g | net carbs: 1g | fiber: 0g

Sausage Balls

Prep time: 5 minutes | Cook time: 25 minutes | Makes 2 dozen

1 pound (454 g) bulk Italian sausage (not sweet)	2 teaspoons baking powder
1 cup almond flour	1 teaspoon onion powder
1½ cups finely shredded Cheddar cheese	1 teaspoon fennel seed (optional)
1 large egg	½ teaspoon cayenne pepper (optional)

1. Preheat the oven to 350ºF (180ºC) and line a rimmed baking sheet with aluminum foil. 2. In a large bowl, combine all the ingredients. Use a fork to mix until well blended. 3. Form the sausage mixture into 1½-inch balls and place 1 inch apart on the prepared baking sheet. 4. Bake for 20 to 25 minutes, or until browned and cooked through.

Per Serving:

calories: 241 | fat: 21g | protein: 11g | carbs: 3g | net carbs: 2g | fiber: 1g

Citrus-Marinated Olives

Prep time: 10 minutes | Cook time: 0 minutes | Makes 2 cups

2 cups mixed green olives with pits	clementines or 1 large orange
¼ cup red wine vinegar	1 teaspoon red pepper flakes
¼ cup extra-virgin olive oil	2 bay leaves
4 garlic cloves, finely minced	½ teaspoon ground cumin
Zest and juice of 2	½ teaspoon ground allspice

1. In a large glass bowl or jar, combine the olives, vinegar, oil, garlic, orange zest and juice, red pepper flakes, bay leaves, cumin, and allspice and mix well. Cover and refrigerate for at least 4 hours or up to a week to allow the olives to marinate, tossing again before serving.

Per Serving:

¼ cup: calories: 100 | fat: 10g | protein: 1g | carbs: 3g | net carbs: 2g | fiber: 1g

90-Second Bread

Prep time: 5 minutes | Cook time: 90 seconds | Serves 1

1 heaping tablespoon coconut flour	1 large egg
½ teaspoon baking powder	1½ tablespoons butter, melted
	Pinch salt

1. In a small, 3- to 4-inch diameter, microwave-safe bowl, combine the coconut flour, baking powder, egg, butter, and salt, and mix until well combined. 2. Place the bowl in the microwave and cook on high for 90 seconds. 3. Dump the bread from the bowl and allow to cool for a couple of minutes. 4. With a serrated knife, cut the bread in half horizontally to make two halves, if desired.

Per Serving:

calories: 204 | fat: 17g | protein: 8g | carbs: 5g | net carbs: 2g | fiber: 3g

Keto Crackers-Two Ways

Prep time: 15 minutes | Cook time: 6 minutes | Serves 2

Simple Keto Crackers	Crackers
½ cup shredded mozzarella cheese	½ cup shredded cheddar cheese
⅓ cup blanched almond flour	⅓ cup blanched almond flour
⅛ teaspoon garlic powder	⅛ teaspoon garlic powder
Dash of salt	Dash of salt
1 large egg yolk	1 large egg yolk
Keto Cheddar Cheese	

1. Preheat the oven to 425°F. 2. In a microwave-safe bowl, combine the cheese, almond flour, garlic powder, and salt. Microwave for 30 seconds. 3. Use your hands to knead the dough until fully mixed. Add the egg yolk and knead until it's blended into the dough. 4. Lay a piece of parchment paper on a flat surface, place the dough on top, and place another piece of parchment on top of the dough. Press down and spread the dough (with your hands or a rolling pin) into a very thin, even rectangle. 5. Using a fork, gently poke holes in the dough to prevent it from bubbling while baking. (Don't skip this step!) 6. Use a knife to cut the dough into 1-inch squares. 7. Line a baking sheet with parchment paper and lay the squares on the parchment with a bit of space between them. Bake for 5 to 6 minutes, until golden brown. 8. For extra-crunchy crackers, flip them over and bake for an additional 2 to 4 minutes, watching closely to ensure that they don't burn!

Per Serving:

calories: 234 | fat: 20g | protein: 12g | carbs: 5g | net carbs: 3g | fiber: 2g

Buttered Cabbage

Prep time: 5 minutes | Cook time: 5 minutes | Serves 4

1 medium head white cabbage, sliced into strips	½ teaspoon salt
4 tablespoons butter	¼ teaspoon pepper
	1 cup water

1. Place cabbage in 7-cup glass bowl with butter, salt, and pepper. 2. Pour water into Instant Pot and place steam rack on bottom. Place bowl on steam rack. Click lid closed. Press the Manual button and adjust time for 5 minutes. When timer beeps, quick-release the pressure.

Per Serving:

calories: 158 | fat: 10g | protein: 3g | carbs: 13g | net carbs: 8g | fiber: 5g

Bacon-Wrapped Avocado Fries

Prep time: 10 minutes | Cook time: 18 minutes | Serves 4

2 medium Hass avocados, peeled and pitted (about 8 oz/220 g of flesh)

16 strips bacon (about 1 pound/455 g), cut in half lengthwise

1. Cut each avocado into 8 fry-shaped pieces, making a total of 16 fries. 2. Wrap each avocado fry in 2 half-strips of bacon. Once complete, place in a large frying pan. 3. Set the pan over medium heat and cover with a splash guard. Fry for 6 minutes on each side and on the bottom, or until crispy, for a total of 18 minutes. 4. Remove from the heat and enjoy immediately!

Per Serving:
calories: 723 | fat: 58g | protein: 43g | carbs: 6g | net carbs: 3g | fiber: 4g

Chicken Tinga Wings

Prep time: 10 minutes | Cook time: 30 minutes | Serves 6

1 to 2 cups coconut oil, for frying

1 pound (454 g) chicken wings (about 12 wings)

Fine sea salt and freshly ground black pepper, to taste

Tinga Sauce:

1 pound (454 g) Mexican-style fresh (raw) chorizo

½ large white onion, chopped

1 clove garlic, minced

3 cups chopped tomatoes

1 cup chopped husked tomatillos

2 tablespoons puréed chipotles in adobo sauce

1½ teaspoons fine sea salt

1 teaspoon freshly ground black pepper

½ teaspoon dried oregano leaves

1 sprig fresh thyme

½ cup chicken bone broth, homemade or store-bought

1. Preheat the oil to 350°F (180°C) in a deep-fryer or a 4-inch-deep (or deeper) cast-iron skillet over medium heat. The oil should be at least 3 inches deep; add more oil if needed. 2. While the oil heats, make the sauce: Cook the chorizo, onion, and garlic in a large cast-iron skillet over medium heat until the meat is crumbled and cooked through, about 5 minutes. Add the tomatoes, tomatillos, chipotles, salt, pepper, and herbs and stir to combine. Continue cooking for 5 minutes. Add the chicken broth and cook for 5 more minutes. Remove the thyme sprig and set the sauce aside. 3. Fry about six wings at a time until golden brown on all sides and cooked through, about 8 minutes. Remove from the oil and sprinkle with salt and pepper. Repeat with the remaining wings. 4. Place the wings on a serving platter and serve with the sauce, or toss the wings in the sauce before serving. They are best served fresh. Store extra wings and sauce separately in airtight containers in the fridge for up to 3 days. To reheat, place the chicken wings on a rimmed baking sheet and heat in a preheated 400°F (205°C) oven for 4 minutes, or until warmed. Heat the sauce in a saucepan over medium-low heat until warmed.

Per Serving:
calories: 247 | fat: 17g | protein: 19g | carbs: 5g | net carbs: 3g | fiber: 2g

Pecan Sandy Fat Bombs

Prep time: 15 minutes | Cook time: 0 minutes | Makes 8 fat bombs

½ cup (1 stick) unsalted butter, room temperature

¼ cup granulated sugar-free sweetener

½ teaspoon vanilla extract

1 cup almond flour

¾ cup chopped roasted unsalted pecans, divided

1. In a large bowl, use an electric mixer on medium speed to cream together the butter and sweetener until smooth. Add the vanilla and beat well. 2. Add the almond flour and ½ cup of chopped pecans, and stir until well incorporated. Place the mixture in the refrigerator for 30 minutes, or until slightly hardened. Meanwhile, very finely chop the remaining ¼ cup of pecans. 3. Using a spoon or your hands, form the chilled mixture into 8 (1-inch) round balls and place on a baking sheet lined with parchment paper. Roll each ball in the finely chopped pecans, and refrigerate for at least 30 minutes before serving. Store in an airtight container in the refrigerator for up to 1 week or in the freezer for up to 2 months.

Per Serving:
calories: 242 | fat: 25g | protein: 4g | carbs: 4g | net carbs: 1g | fiber: 3g

Pimento Cheese

Prep time: 20 minutes | Cook time: 0 minutes | serves 8

1 (8 ounces) block sharp cheddar cheese

1 (8 ounces) block mild cheddar cheese

1 cup mayonnaise

1 (4 ounces) jar diced pimentos, drained

3 ounces cream cheese (6

Serving Suggestions:

Sliced bell peppers or celery

tablespoons), softened

1 tablespoon finely chopped onions

1 tablespoon dill relish

½ teaspoon onion powder

¼ teaspoon garlic powder

¼ teaspoon ground black pepper

Pork rinds

1. Using the large holes on the side of a box grater, shred the cheeses into a large bowl. 2. Add the rest of the ingredients to the bowl with the shredded cheese and mix with a spoon until well combined. Refrigerate for at least 1 hour before serving. Leftovers can be stored in an airtight container in the refrigerator for up to a week.

Per Serving:
calories: 464 | fat: 46g | protein: 14g | carbs: 3g | net carbs: 3g | fiber: 0g

Creamy Scallion Dip

Prep time: 10 minutes | Cook time: 11 minutes | Serves 4

5 ounces (142 g) scallions, diced	1 teaspoon garlic powder
4 tablespoons cream cheese	2 tablespoons coconut cream
1 tablespoon chopped fresh parsley	½ teaspoon salt
	1 teaspoon coconut oil

1. Heat up the instant pot on Sauté mode. 2. Then add coconut oil and melt it. 3. Add diced scallions and sauté it for 6 to 7 minutes or until it is light brown. 4. Add cream cheese, parsley, garlic powder, salt, and coconut cream. 5. Close the instant pot lid and cook the scallions dip for 5 minutes on Manual mode (High Pressure). 6. Make a quick pressure release. Blend the dip will it is smooth if desired.

Per Serving:

calories: 76 | fat: 6g | protein: 2g | carbs: 4g | net carbs: 3g | fiber: 1g

Cheese and Charcuterie Board

Prep time: 15 minutes | Cook time: 0 minutes | Serves 7

4 ounces prosciutto, sliced	cheese
4 ounces Calabrese salami, sliced	7 ounces Brie cheese
4 ounces capicola, sliced	½ cup roasted almonds
7 ounces Parrano Gouda cheese	½ cup mixed olives
7 ounces aged Manchego	12 cornichons (small, tart pickles)

1. sprig fresh rosemary or other herbs of choice, for garnish Arrange the meats, cheeses, and almonds on a large wooden cutting board. Place the olives and pickles in separate bowls and set them on or alongside the cutting board. Garnish with a spring of rosemary or other fresh herbs of your choice.

Per Serving:

calories: 445 | fat: 35g | protein: 31g | carbs: 3g | net carbs: 2g | fiber: 1g

Bacon-Studded Pimento Cheese

Prep time: 10 minutes | Cook time: 5 minutes | Serves 6

2 ounces (57 g) bacon (about 4 thick slices)	¼ teaspoon cayenne pepper (optional)
4 ounces (113 g) cream cheese, room temperature	1 cup thick-shredded extra-sharp Cheddar cheese
¼ cup mayonnaise	2 ounces (57 g) jarred diced pimentos, drained
¼ teaspoon onion powder	

1. Chop the raw bacon into ½-inch-thick pieces. Cook in a small skillet over medium heat until crispy, 3 to 4 minutes. Use a slotted spoon to transfer the bacon onto a layer of paper towels. Reserve the rendered fat. 2. In a large bowl, combine the cream cheese, mayonnaise, onion powder, and cayenne (if using), and beat with an electric mixer or by hand until smooth and creamy. 3. Add the rendered bacon fat, Cheddar cheese, and pimentos and mix until well combined. 4. Refrigerate for at least 30 minutes before serving to allow flavors to blend. Serve cold with raw veggies.

Per Serving:

calories: 216 | fat: 20g | protein: 8g | carbs: 2g | net carbs: 0g | fiber: 2

Chicken-Pecan Salad Cucumber Bites

Prep time: 15 minutes | Cook time: 0 minutes | Serves 2

1 cup diced cooked chicken breast	Pink Himalayan salt
2 tablespoons mayonnaise	Freshly ground black pepper
¼ cup chopped pecans	1 cucumber, peeled and cut into ¼-inch slices
¼ cup diced celery	

1. In a medium bowl, mix together the chicken, mayonnaise, pecans, and celery. Season with pink Himalayan salt and pepper. 2. Lay the cucumber slices out on a plate, and add a pinch of pink Himalayan salt to each. 3. Top each cucumber slice with a spoonful of the chicken-salad mixture and serve.

Per Serving:

calories: 323 | fat: 24g | protein: 23g | carbs: 6g | net carbs: 4g | fiber: 3g

Bacon Ranch Dip

Prep time: 10 minutes | Cook time: 10 minutes | Serves 10

1 (8 ounces / 227 g) package full-fat cream cheese, at room temperature	½ teaspoon dried dill
	½ teaspoon celery seed
1 cup full-fat sour cream	½ teaspoon garlic powder
8 bacon slices, cooked and crumbled	½ teaspoon onion powder
	Salt and freshly ground black pepper, to taste
1½ teaspoons dried chives	¼ cup sliced scallion, or fresh chives, for garnish
1 teaspoon dry mustard	

1. In a medium bowl, stir the cream cheese until it becomes fluffy and smooth. Add the sour cream and gently fold to combine. 2. Add the bacon, chives, mustard, dill, celery seed, garlic powder, and onion powder. Season with salt and pepper and stir to combine. Top with the scallion and serve immediately, or refrigerate in an airtight container for up to 1 week.

Per Serving:

calories: 211 | fat: 19g | protein: 8g | carbs: 2g | net carbs: 2g | fiber: 0g

Dairy-Free Queso

Prep time: 10 minutes | Cook time: 10 minutes | Serves 5

1 cup (130 g) raw cashews	1 teaspoon ground cumin
½ cup (120 ml) nondairy milk	¾ teaspoon garlic powder
¼ cup (17 g) nutritional yeast	¼ teaspoon onion powder
½ teaspoon finely ground sea salt	½ teaspoon dried oregano leaves
¼ cup (60 ml) avocado oil	⅛ teaspoon paprika
1 medium yellow onion, sliced	⅛ teaspoon cayenne pepper
2 cloves garlic, roughly chopped	3½ ounces (100 g) pork rinds, or 2 medium zucchinis, cut into sticks, for serving (optional)
1 tablespoon chili powder	

1. Place the cashews in a 12-ounce (350-ml) or larger sealable container. Cover with water. Seal and place in the fridge to soak for 12 hours. 2. After 12 hours, drain and rinse the cashews, then place them in a food processor or blender along with the milk, nutritional yeast, and salt. Set aside. 3. Heat the oil in a medium-sized frying pan over medium-low heat until shimmering. Add the onion, garlic, and spices and toss to coat the onion with the seasonings. Stir the mixture every couple of minutes until the onion begins to soften, about 10 minutes. 4. Transfer the onion mixture to the food processor or blender. Cover and blend until smooth. 5. Enjoy the queso with pork rinds or zucchini sticks, if desired.

Per Serving:
calories: 300 | fat: 24g | protein: 7g | carbs: 14g | net carbs: 11g | fiber: 3g

Jelly Cups

Prep time: 10 minutes | Cook time: 10 minutes | Makes 16 jelly cups

Butter Base:
⅔ cup (170 g) coconut butter or smooth unsweetened nut or seed butter
⅔ cup (145 g) coconut oil, ghee, or cacao butter, melted
2 teaspoons vanilla extract
7 drops liquid stevia, or 2 teaspoons confectioners'-style erythritol

Jelly Filling:
½ cup (70 g) fresh raspberries
¼ cup (60 ml) water
3 drops liquid stevia, or 1 teaspoon confectioners'-style erythritol
1½ teaspoons unflavored gelatin

Special Equipment:
16 mini muffin cup liners, or 1 silicone mini muffin pan

1. Set 16 mini muffin cup liners on a tray or have on hand a silicone mini muffin pan. 2. Make the base: Place the coconut butter, melted oil, vanilla, and sweetener in a medium-sized bowl and stir to combine. 3. Take half of the base mixture and divide it equally among the 16 mini muffin cup liners or 16 wells of the mini muffin pan, filling each about one-quarter full. Place the muffin cup liners (or muffin pan) in the fridge. Set the remaining half of the base mixture aside. 4. Make the jelly filling: Place the raspberries, water, and sweetener in a small saucepan and bring to a simmer over medium heat. Simmer for 5 minutes, then sprinkle with the gelatin and mash with a fork. Transfer to the fridge to set for 15 minutes. 5. Pull the muffin cup liners and jelly filling out of the fridge. Using a ½-teaspoon measuring spoon, scoop out a portion of the jelly and roll it into a ball between your palms, then flatten it into a disc about 1 inch (2.5 cm) in diameter (or in a diameter to fit the size of the liners you're using). Press into a chilled butter base cup. Repeat with the remaining jelly filling and cups. Then spoon the remaining butter base mixture over the tops. 6. Place in the fridge for another 15 minutes before serving.

Per Serving:
calories: 151 | fat: 15g | protein: 1g | carbs: 3g | net carbs: 1g | fiber: 2g

Salami Chips with Pesto

Prep time: 10 minutes | Cook time: 12 minutes | Serves 6

Chips:
6 ounces sliced Genoa salami

Pesto:

1 cup fresh basil leaves	salt
3 cloves garlic	¼ teaspoon ground black pepper
¼ cup grated Parmesan cheese	
¼ cup raw walnuts	½ cup extra-virgin olive oil
¼ teaspoon pink Himalayan	

1. Make the chips: Preheat the oven to 375°F and line 2 rimmed baking sheets with parchment paper. 2. Arrange the salami in a single layer on the lined baking sheets. Bake for 10 to 12 minutes, until crisp. Transfer to a paper towel–lined plate to absorb the excess oil. Allow to cool and crisp up further. 3. Make the pesto: Put all the pesto ingredients, except for the olive oil, in a food processor and pulse until everything is roughly chopped and a coarse paste has formed. 4. With the food processor running, slowly pour in the olive oil. Process until all of the oil has been added and the ingredients are fully incorporated. Taste and season with additional salt and pepper, if desired. 5. Pour the pesto into a small serving bowl and serve the salami chips alongside. Store leftover pesto in a sealed container in the refrigerator for up to 2 weeks; store the chips in a zip-top plastic bag in the refrigerator for up to 5 days.

Per Serving:
calories: 202 | fat: 9g | protein: 8g | carbs: 1g | net carbs: 1g | fiber: 0g

Quick Salsa

Prep time: 5 minutes | Cook time: 0 minutes | Makes about 3 cups

¼ cup fresh cilantro, stems and leaves, finely chopped
1 small red onion, finely chopped
8 roma tomatoes or other small to medium tomatoes, finely chopped
1 small jalapeño pepper, minced, seeded if desired for less heat (optional)
Juice of 1 to 2 limes
Sea salt and ground black pepper, to taste

1. Toss together all the ingredients in a large mixing bowl. Alternatively, place all the ingredients in a food processor and pulse until the desired consistency is reached. 2. Season with salt and pepper to taste. 3. Store in an airtight container in the refrigerator for up to 5 days.

Per Serving:

calories: 12 | fat: 3g | protein: 1g | carbs: 3g | net carbs: 2g | fiber 1g

Sweet Pepper Poppers

Prep time: 10 minutes | Cook time: 20 minutes | serves 4

12 mini sweet peppers	crumbled
1 (8 ounces) package cream cheese, softened	1 green onion, thinly sliced
5 slices bacon, cooked and	¼ teaspoon ground black pepper

1. Preheat the oven to 400°F. Line a sheet pan with parchment paper. 2. Cut each sweet pepper in half lengthwise, then remove and discard the seeds; set the peppers aside. 3. In a small bowl, mix together the cream cheese, bacon, green onion (reserve some of the slices for garnish, if desired), and black pepper. Spoon the mixture into the sweet pepper halves. 4. Place the stuffed peppers on the lined sheet pan and bake for 20 minutes, until the peppers are tender and the tops are starting to brown. Garnish with the reserved green onion slices, if desired.

Per Serving:

calories: 163 | fat: 12g | protein: 7g | carbs: 5g | net carbs: 4g | fiber: 1g

Cheese Stuffed Bell Peppers

Prep time: 10 minutes | Cook time: 5 minutes | Serves 5

1 cup water	scallions
10 baby bell peppers, seeded and sliced lengthwise	1 tablespoon olive oil
4 ounces (113 g) Monterey Jack cheese, shredded	1 teaspoon minced garlic
4 ounces (113 g) cream cheese	½ teaspoon cayenne pepper
2 tablespoons chopped	¼ teaspoon ground black pepper, or more to taste

1. Pour the water into the Instant Pot and insert a steamer basket. 2. Stir together the remaining ingredients except the bell peppers in a mixing bowl until combined. Stuff the peppers evenly with the mixture. Arrange the stuffed peppers in the basket. 3. Lock the lid. Select the Manual mode and set the cooking time for 5 minutes at High Pressure. 4. When the timer beeps, perform a quick pressure release. Carefully remove the lid. 5. Cool for 5 minutes and serve.

Per Serving:

calories: 226 | fat: 18g | protein: 9g | carbs: 9g | net carbs: 7g | fiber: 2g

Pancetta Pizza Dip

Prep time: 10 minutes | Cook time: 4 minutes | Serves 10

10 ounces (283 g) Pepper Jack cheese	1 cup green olives, pitted and halved
10 ounces (283 g) cream cheese	1 teaspoon dried oregano
10 ounces (283 g) pancetta, chopped	½ teaspoon garlic powder
	1 cup chicken broth
1 pound (454 g) tomatoes, puréed	4 ounces (113 g) Mozzarella cheese, thinly sliced

1. Mix together the Pepper Jack cheese, cream cheese, pancetta, tomatoes, olives, oregano, and garlic powder in the Instant Pot. Pour in the chicken broth. 2. Lock the lid. Select the Manual mode and set the cooking time for 4 minutes at High Pressure. 3. When the timer beeps, perform a quick pressure release. Carefully remove the lid. 4. Scatter the Mozzarella cheese on top. Cover and allow to sit in the residual heat. Serve warm.

Per Serving:

calories: 287 | fat: 21g | protein: 21g | carbs: 3g | net carbs: 2g | fiber: 1g

Creamy Spinach

Prep time: 5 minutes | Cook time: 4 minutes | Serves 4

2 cups chopped spinach	1 tablespoon butter
2 ounces (57 g) Monterey Jack cheese, shredded	1 teaspoon minced garlic
1 cup almond milk	½ teaspoon salt

1. Combine all the ingredients in the Instant Pot. 2. Secure the lid. Select the Manual mode and set the cooking time for 4 minutes at High Pressure. 3. Once cooking is complete, do a quick pressure release. Carefully open the lid. 4. Give the mixture a good stir and serve warm.

Per Serving:

calories: 101 | fat: 8g | protein: 4g | carbs: 3g | net carbs: 3g | fiber: 0g

Bacon-Wrapped Avocados

Prep time: 10 minutes | Cook time: 15 minutes | Serves 4

8 bacon slices

1 ripe avocado, peeled and cut into 8 wedges

Salt and freshly ground black

pepper, to taste

1 or 2 lime wedges

Ground cayenne pepper

1. Wrap 1 bacon slice around each avocado wedge. If needed, use a toothpick to secure them. 2. Heat a nonstick skillet over medium-high heat. Evenly space the bacon-wrapped wedges around the skillet. If you aren't using a toothpick, place the loose end of the bacon facing down to create a seal as it cooks. Cook for 6 to 8 minutes, turning every couple of minutes until the bacon is cooked. 3. Remove from the heat and finish with a sprinkle of salt, pepper, lime juice, and cayenne. Serve warm.

Per Serving:

calories: 314 | fat: 26g | protein: 15g | carbs: 5g | net carbs: 2g | fiber: 3g

Smoked Salmon Fat Bombs

Prep time: 10 minutes | Cook time: 0 minutes | Makes 12 fat bombs

½ cup goat cheese, at room temperature

½ cup butter, at room temperature

2 ounces smoked salmon

2 teaspoons freshly squeezed lemon juice

Pinch freshly ground black pepper

1. Line a baking sheet with parchment paper and set aside. 2. In a medium bowl, stir together the goat cheese, butter, smoked salmon, lemon juice, and pepper until very well blended. 3. Use a tablespoon to scoop the salmon mixture onto the baking sheet until you have 12 even mounds. 4. Place the baking sheet in the refrigerator until the fat bombs are firm, 2 to 3 hours. 5. Store the fat bombs in a sealed container in the refrigerator for up to 1 week.

Per Serving:

2 fat bomb: calories: 193 | fat: 18g | protein: 8g | carbs: 0g | net carbs: 0g | fiber: 0g

Cabbage and Broccoli Slaw

Prep time: 5 minutes | Cook time: 10 minutes | Serves 6

2 cups broccoli slaw

½ head cabbage, thinly sliced

¼ cup chopped kale

4 tablespoons butter

1 teaspoon salt

¼ teaspoon pepper

1. Press the Sauté button and add all ingredients to Instant Pot. Stir-fry for 7 to 10 minutes until cabbage softens. Serve warm.

Per Serving:

calories: 97 | fat: 7g | protein: 2g | carbs: 6g | net carbs: 3g | fiber: 3g

Herbed Cashew Cheese

Prep time: 10 minutes | Cook time: 0 minutes | Makes 1½ cups

1 cup raw cashews

1 cup warm water

¼ cup extra-virgin olive oil

¼ cup water

2 tablespoons fresh lemon juice

1 clove garlic, minced or grated

2 tablespoons minced fresh chives

Sea salt and ground black pepper, to taste

1. Place the cashews in a small container and add the warm water. (If it doesn't cover the cashews completely, just add more warm water.) Soak for 1 to 4 hours unrefrigerated or up to overnight in the refrigerator. 2. Drain and rinse the cashews, then place them in a blender or food processor. Add the olive oil, the ¼ cup water, the lemon juice, and the garlic. Process until smooth and creamy, stopping occasionally to scrape down the sides of the processor, about 5 minutes total. Mix in the chives and add salt and pepper to taste. 3. If you'd like a lighter texture, add warm water, 1 tablespoon at a time, until you achieve the desired consistency.

Per Serving:

calories: 288 | fat: 25g | protein: 7g | carbs: 13g | net carbs: 12g | fiber: 1g

Gourmet "Cheese" Balls

Prep time: 1 hour 20 minutes | Cook time: 0 minutes | serves 6

1 cup raw hazelnuts, soaked overnight

¼ cup water

2 tablespoons nutritional yeast

1 teaspoon apple cider vinegar

1 teaspoon miso paste

1 teaspoon mustard

½ cup almond flour

1 cup slivered almonds

1 teaspoon dried oregano

1. In a high-powered blender, combine the hazelnuts, water, nutritional yeast, vinegar, miso paste, and mustard, and blend until well combined, thick, and creamy. 2. Transfer the mixture to a medium bowl. 3. Slowly stir in the almond flour until the mixture forms a dough-like consistency. Set aside. 4. In a separate, small bowl, toss the almonds and oregano together and set aside. 5. Using a soup spoon or tablespoon, scoop some mixture into your hand and shape it into a bite-size ball. Place the ball on a baking sheet. Repeat until you have used all the mixture (about 2 dozen balls). 6. One by one, roll the hazelnut balls in the almond and oregano mixture until thoroughly coated, placing each coated ball back on the baking sheet. 7. Place the sheet in the refrigerator for 1 hour to allow the balls to set.

Per Serving:

calories: 308 | fat: 27g | protein: 10g | carbs: 11g | net carbs: 5g | fiber: 6g

Chapter 7

Fish and Seafood

Tilapia Bake

Prep time: 5 minutes | Cook time: 30 minutes | Serves 4

3 medium or 4 small tilapia fillets (approximately 1 pound / 454 g total)	thinly sliced (¾ cup)
	10 ounces (283 g) baby spinach
1 teaspoon kosher salt	¼ cup heavy cream
1 teaspoon black pepper	½ teaspoon dried parsley
2 tablespoons plus 1 teaspoon butter	½ teaspoon dried oregano
	¼ teaspoon red pepper flakes
1 medium leek, white part	1 cup crumbled feta cheese

1. Preheat the oven to 425ºF (220ºC). Season the tilapia fillets with ½ teaspoon each of the salt and pepper. 2. In a large skillet, melt 2 tablespoons of the butter over medium-high heat. Add the leeks and sauté a few minutes, until soft but not brown. Add the spinach a handful at a time; the spinach will reduce in volume by a lot. Add the cream and the parsley, oregano, and red pepper flakes, as well as the remaining ½ teaspoon each salt and pepper. Reduce the heat to medium low and simmer, stirring frequently, until the mixture thickens a bit. 3. Use the remaining 1 teaspoon butter to lightly grease a small glass baking dish. Transfer three-fourths of the spinach mixture to the baking dish and arrange the fish in a single layer on top. Layer the rest of the spinach on top. Sprinkle the feta evenly over and bake for 20 to 25 minutes, or until the fish is cooked through.

Per Serving:

calories: 318 | fat: 20g | protein: 27g | carbs: 5g | net carbs: 3g | fiber: 2g

Caprese Salmon

Prep time: 10 minutes | Cook time: 15 minutes | Serves 2

10 ounces (283 g) salmon fillet (2 fillets)	½ teaspoon ground black pepper
4 ounces (113 g) Mozzarella, sliced	1 tablespoon apple cider vinegar
4 cherry tomatoes, sliced	1 tablespoon butter
1 teaspoon erythritol	1 cup water, for cooking
1 teaspoon dried basil	

1. Grease the mold with butter and put the salmon inside. 2. Sprinkle the fish with erythritol, dried basil, ground black pepper, and apple cider vinegar. 3. Then top the salmon with tomatoes and Mozzarella. 4. Pour water and insert the steamer rack in the instant pot. 5. Put the fish on the rack. 6. Close and seal the lid. 7. Cook the meal on Manual mode at High Pressure for 15 minutes. Make a quick pressure release.

Per Serving:

calories: 447 | fat: 25g | protein: 46g | carbs: 15g | net carbs: 12g | fiber: 3g

Bacon Halibut Steak

Prep time: 15 minutes | Cook time: 10 minutes | Serves 4

24 ounces (680 g) halibut steaks (6 ounces / 170 g each fillet)	1 teaspoon ground black pepper
	4 ounces bacon, sliced
1 teaspoon avocado oil	

1. Sprinkle the halibut steaks with avocado oil and ground black pepper. 2. Then wrap the fish in the bacon slices and put in the air fryer. 3. Cook the fish at 390ºF (199ºC) for 5 minutes per side.

Per Serving:

calories: 430 | fat: 24g | protein: 48g | carbs: 1g | net carbs: 1g | fiber: 0g

Bacon-Wrapped Scallops

Prep time: 5 minutes | Cook time: 10 minutes | Serves 4

8 (1-ounce / 28-g) sea scallops, cleaned and patted dry
8 slices sugar-free bacon
¼ teaspoon salt
¼ teaspoon ground black pepper

1. Wrap each scallop in 1 slice bacon and secure with a toothpick. Sprinkle with salt and pepper. 2. Place scallops into ungreased air fryer basket. Adjust the temperature to 360ºF (182ºC) and air fry for 10 minutes. Scallops will be opaque and firm, and have an internal temperature of 135ºF (57ºC) when done. Serve warm.

Per Serving:

calories: 267 | fat: 18g | protein: 22g | carbs: 1g | net carbs: 1g | fiber: 0g

Tilapia with Pecans

Prep time: 20 minutes | Cook time: 16 minutes | Serves 5

2 tablespoons ground flaxseeds	2 tablespoons extra-virgin olive oil
1 teaspoon paprika	½ cup pecans, ground
Sea salt and white pepper, to taste	5 tilapia fillets, sliced into halves
1 teaspoon garlic paste	

1. Combine the ground flaxseeds, paprika, salt, white pepper, garlic paste, olive oil, and ground pecans in a Ziploc bag. Add the fish fillets and shake to coat well. 2. Spritz the air fryer basket with cooking spray. Cook in the preheated air fryer at 400ºF (204ºC) for 10 minutes; turn them over and cook for 6 minutes more. Work in batches. 3. Serve with lemon wedges, if desired. Enjoy!

Per Serving:

calories: 415 | fat: 28g | protein: 33g | carbs: 8g | net carbs: 5g | fiber: 3g

Coconut Shrimp with Spicy Dipping Sauce

Prep time: 15 minutes | Cook time: 8 minutes | Serves 4

1 (2½ ounces / 71 g) bag pork rinds
¾ cup unsweetened shredded coconut flakes
¾ cup coconut flour
1 teaspoon onion powder
1 teaspoon garlic powder
Spicy Dipping Sauce:
½ cup mayonnaise
2 tablespoons Sriracha

2 eggs
1½ pounds (680 g) large shrimp, peeled and deveined
½ teaspoon salt
¼ teaspoon freshly ground black pepper

Zest and juice of ½ lime
1 clove garlic, minced

1. Preheat the air fryer to 390ºF (199ºC). 2. In a food processor fitted with a metal blade, combine the pork rinds and coconut flakes. Pulse until the mixture resembles coarse crumbs. Transfer to a shallow bowl. 3. In another shallow bowl, combine the coconut flour, onion powder, and garlic powder; mix until thoroughly combined. 4. In a third shallow bowl, whisk the eggs until slightly frothy. 5. In a large bowl, season the shrimp with the salt and pepper, tossing gently to coat. 6. Working a few pieces at a time, dredge the shrimp in the flour mixture, followed by the eggs, and finishing with the pork rind crumb mixture. Arrange the shrimp on a baking sheet until ready to air fry. 7. Working in batches if necessary, arrange the shrimp in a single layer in the air fryer basket. Pausing halfway through the cooking time to turn the shrimp, air fry for 8 minutes until cooked through. 8. To make the sauce: In a small bowl, combine the mayonnaise, Sriracha, lime zest and juice, and garlic. Whisk until thoroughly combined. Serve alongside the shrimp.

Per Serving:

calories: 473 | fat: 33g | protein: 30g | carbs: 13g | net carbs: 7g | fiber: 6g

Tuna Cakes

Prep time: 10 minutes | Cook time: 10 minutes | Serves 4

4 (3 ounces / 85 g) pouches tuna, drained
1 large egg, whisked
2 tablespoons peeled and

chopped white onion
½ teaspoon Old Bay seasoning

1. In a large bowl, mix all ingredients together and form into four patties. 2. Place patties into ungreased air fryer basket. Adjust the temperature to 400ºF (204ºC) and air fry for 10 minutes. Patties will be browned and crispy when done. Let cool 5 minutes before serving.

Per Serving:

calories: 110 | fat: 2g | protein: 20g | carbs: 2g | net carbs: 2g | fiber: 0g

Coconut Milk-Braised Squid

Prep time: 10 minutes | Cook time: 20 minutes | Serves 3

1 pound (454 g) squid, sliced
1 teaspoon sugar-free tomato paste

1 cup coconut milk
1 teaspoon cayenne pepper
½ teaspoon salt

1. Put all ingredients from the list above in the instant pot. 2. Close and seal the lid and cook the squid on Manual (High Pressure) for 20 minutes. 3. When the cooking time is finished, do the quick pressure release. 4. Serve the squid with coconut milk gravy.

Per Serving:

calories: 326 | fat: 21g | protein: 25g | carbs: 10g | net carbs: 8g | fiber: 2g

One-Pot Shrimp Alfredo and Zoodles

Prep time: 10 minutes | Cook time: 25 minutes | Serves 5

Zoodles:
3 medium zucchini (about 21 ounces / 595 g)
Shrimp and Sauce:
2 tablespoons butter or ghee
3 garlic cloves, minced
1 pound (454 g) shrimp, peeled and deveined
4 ounces (113 g) cream cheese, at room temperature
½ cup heavy (whipping) cream

1 teaspoon sea salt

½ teaspoon sea salt
¼ teaspoon freshly ground black pepper
1 cup freshly grated Parmesan cheese
¼ teaspoon cayenne pepper (optional)

Make the Zoodles 1. Trim off the ends of the zucchini. Using a vegetable spiral slicer, swirl the zucchini into noodle shapes (zoodles). 2. Lay the zoodles on a kitchen towel and sprinkle with the salt. Let sit while you prepare the Alfredo sauce. 3. While the sauce is simmering, fold the zoodles up in the towel and squeeze out as much water as you can. Make the Shrimp and Sauce 4. In a large pot, melt the butter over medium heat. Add the garlic and cook for 3 minutes until fragrant. Add the shrimp and cook for 4 to 6 minutes, just until the shrimp start to turn pink. Remove the shrimp to a plate. 5. Add the cream cheese to the pot and whisk until melted. Pour in the cream slowly, whisking constantly. Add the salt and pepper. Let the sauce simmer for 5 to 10 minutes, whisking often, until thickened. 6. Remove the pot from the heat and stir in the Parmesan and cayenne (if using). Taste and adjust the salt and pepper to your liking. 7. Add the zoodles, cover, and cook for 5 minutes. The zoodles will release a bit of water, which will thin out the thick sauce a bit. 8. Add the shrimp and toss before serving.

Per Serving:

calories: 329 | fat: 25g | protein: 20g | carbs: 6g | net carbs: 5g | fiber: 1g

Snapper in Spicy Tomato Sauce

Prep time: 5 minutes | Cook time: 5 minutes | Serves 6

2 teaspoons coconut oil, melted

1 teaspoon celery seeds

½ teaspoon fresh grated ginger

½ teaspoon cumin seeds

1 yellow onion, chopped

2 cloves garlic, minced

1½ pounds (680 g) snapper fillets

¾ cup vegetable broth

1 (14 ounces / 113 g) can fire-roasted diced tomatoes

1 bell pepper, sliced

1 jalapeño pepper, minced

Sea salt and ground black pepper, to taste

¼ teaspoon chili flakes

½ teaspoon turmeric powder

1. Set the Instant Pot to Sauté. Add and heat the sesame oil until hot. Sauté the celery seeds, fresh ginger, and cumin seeds. 2. Add the onion and continue to sauté until softened and fragrant. 3. Mix in the minced garlic and continue to cook for 30 seconds. Add the remaining ingredients and stir well. 4. Lock the lid. Select the Manual mode and set the cooking time for 3 minutes at Low Pressure. 5. When the timer beeps, perform a quick pressure release. Carefully remove the lid. 6. Serve warm

Per Serving:

calories: 177 | fat: 6g | protein: 26g | carbs: 5g | net carbs: 4g | fiber: 1g

Spicy Shrimp Fried Rice

Prep time: 15 minutes | Cook time: 15 minutes | Serves 4

¼ teaspoon cayenne pepper

¼ teaspoon chili powder

¼ teaspoon paprika

¼ teaspoon pink Himalayan salt

¼ teaspoon ground black pepper

1 pound medium-sized shrimp, peeled and deveined

2 tablespoons ghee, divided

4 cups riced cauliflower (see Tip)

For Garnish (optional):

Sliced scallions

½ medium-sized white onion, finely chopped

2 teaspoons minced fresh ginger

1 cup fresh broccoli florets, chopped

3 tablespoons soy sauce

1 tablespoon Sriracha sauce

1½ teaspoons unseasoned rice wine vinegar

2 large eggs

2 teaspoons toasted sesame oil

Black and white sesame seeds

1. Put the cayenne, chili powder, paprika, salt, and pepper in a medium-sized bowl. Mix to blend, then add the shrimp. Toss the shrimp in the seasoning blend until evenly coated. 2. Heat 1 tablespoon of the ghee in a large skillet over medium-high heat. Place the seasoned shrimp in the hot skillet and cook until pink, about 2 minutes on each side. Remove to a small bowl and set aside. 3. Add the remaining tablespoon of ghee to the hot skillet and pour in the riced cauliflower. Spread it out with a spatula so it

lies flat on the surface of the skillet and cook until it crisps up, 3 to 5 minutes. 4. Stir the rice, then add the onion and ginger. Cook for 2 minutes, until the onion is slightly tender. Add the broccoli and cook for 1 to 2 minutes, until bright green in color. Add the soy sauce, Sriracha, and vinegar. Combine using the spatula. 5. Make a well in the center of the skillet and crack in the eggs. Scramble using the spatula, then combine with the rest of the contents of the skillet. 6. Add the shrimp and toss to combine. Drizzle with the sesame oil and garnish with sliced scallions and sesame seeds, if desired. Serve immediately. 7. Store leftovers in a sealed container in the refrigerator for up to 4 days. Reheat in the microwave for 60 to 90 seconds.

Per Serving:

calories: 283 | fat: 13g | protein: 32g | carbs: 13g | net carbs: 9g | fiber: 4g

Sweet Tilapia Fillets

Prep time: 5 minutes | Cook time: 14 minutes | Serves 4

2 tablespoons erythritol

1 tablespoon apple cider vinegar

4 tilapia fillets, boneless

1 teaspoon olive oil

1. Mix apple cider vinegar with olive oil and erythritol. 2. Then rub the tilapia fillets with the sweet mixture and put in the air fryer basket in one layer. 3. Cook the fish at 360ºF (182ºC) for 7 minutes per side.

Per Serving:

calories: 110 | fat: 2g | protein: 23g | carbs: 1g | net carbs: 1g | fiber: 0g

Crab-Stuffed Avocado Boats

Prep time: 5 minutes | Cook time: 7 minutes | Serves 4

2 medium avocados, halved and pitted

8 ounces (227 g) cooked crab meat

¼ teaspoon Old Bay

seasoning

2 tablespoons peeled and diced yellow onion

2 tablespoons mayonnaise

1. Scoop out avocado flesh in each avocado half, leaving ½ inch around edges to form a shell. Chop scooped-out avocado. 2. In a medium bowl, combine crab meat, Old Bay seasoning, onion, mayonnaise, and chopped avocado. Place ¼ mixture into each avocado shell. 3. Place avocado boats into ungreased air fryer basket. Adjust the temperature to 350ºF (177ºC) and air fry for 7 minutes. Avocado will be browned on the top and mixture will be bubbling when done. Serve warm.

Per Serving:

calories: 272 | fat: 21g | protein: 11g | carbs: 9g | net carbs: 6g | fiber: 3g

Nut-Crusted Baked Fish

Prep time: 10 minutes | Cook time: 20 minutes | Serves 4

½ cup extra-virgin olive oil, divided

1 pound (454 g) flaky white fish (such as cod, haddock, or halibut), skin removed

½ cup shelled finely chopped pistachios

½ cup ground flaxseed

Zest and juice of 1 lemon,

divided

1 teaspoon ground cumin

1 teaspoon ground allspice

½ teaspoon salt (use 1 teaspoon if pistachios are unsalted)

¼ teaspoon freshly ground black pepper

1. Preheat the oven to 400°F(205ºC). 2. Line a baking sheet with parchment paper or aluminum foil and drizzle 2 tablespoons olive oil over the sheet, spreading to evenly coat the bottom. 3. Cut the fish into 4 equal pieces and place on the prepared baking sheet. 4. In a small bowl, combine the pistachios, flaxseed, lemon zest, cumin, allspice, salt, and pepper. Drizzle in ¼ cup olive oil and stir well. 5. Divide the nut mixture evenly atop the fish pieces. Drizzle the lemon juice and remaining 2 tablespoons oil over the fish and bake until cooked through, 15 to 20 minutes, depending on the thickness of the fish.

Per Serving:

calories: 620 | fat: 51g | protein: 27g | carbs: 13g | net carbs: 5g | fiber: 8g

Scallops & Mozza Broccoli Mash

Prep time: 5 minutes | Cook time: 35 minutes | Serves 4

Mozza Broccoli Mash:

¼ cup (55 g) coconut oil or ghee, or ¼ cup (60 ml) avocado oil

6 cups (570 g) broccoli florets

4 cloves garlic, minced

1 (2-in/5-cm) piece fresh

Scallops:

1 pound (455 g) sea scallops

¼ teaspoon finely ground sea salt

¼ teaspoon ground black

ginger root, grated

⅔ cup (160 ml) chicken bone broth

½ cup (70 g) shredded mozzarella cheese (dairy-free or regular)

pepper

2 tablespoons coconut oil, avocado oil, or ghee

Lemon wedges, for serving

1. Prepare the mash: Heat the oil in a large frying pan over low heat. Add the broccoli, garlic, and ginger and cook, uncovered, for 5 minutes, or until the garlic is fragrant. 2. Pour in the broth, then cover and cook on low for 25 minutes, or until the broccoli is easily mashed. 3. About 5 minutes before the broccoli is ready, prepare the scallops: Pat the scallops dry and season them on both sides with the salt and pepper. Heat the oil in a medium-sized frying pan over medium heat. When the oil is hot, add the scallops. Cook for 2 minutes per side, or until lightly golden. 4. When the broccoli is done, add the cheese and mash with a fork. Divide the mash among 4 dinner plates and top with the scallops. Serve with lemon wedges and enjoy!

Per Serving:

calories: 353 | fat: 25g | protein: 19g | carbs: 12g | net carbs: 5g | fiber: 7g

Tuna Casserole

Prep time: 15 minutes | Cook time: 15 minutes | Serves 4

2 tablespoons salted butter

¼ cup diced white onion

¼ cup chopped white mushrooms

2 stalks celery, finely chopped

½ cup heavy cream

½ cup vegetable broth

2 tablespoons full-fat

mayonnaise

¼ teaspoon xanthan gum

½ teaspoon red pepper flakes

2 medium zucchini, spiralized

2 (5 ounces / 142 g) cans albacore tuna

1 ounce (28 g) pork rinds, finely ground

1. In a large saucepan over medium heat, melt butter. Add onion, mushrooms, and celery and sauté until fragrant, about 3 to 5 minutes. 2. Pour in heavy cream, vegetable broth, mayonnaise, and xanthan gum. Reduce heat and continue cooking an additional 3 minutes, until the mixture begins to thicken. 3. Add red pepper flakes, zucchini, and tuna. Turn off heat and stir until zucchini noodles are coated. 4. Pour into a round baking dish. Top with ground pork rinds and cover the top of the dish with foil. Place into the air fryer basket. 5. Adjust the temperature to 370ºF (188ºC) and set the timer for 15 minutes. 6. When 3 minutes remain, remove the foil to brown the top of the casserole. Serve warm.

Per Serving:

calories: 406 | fat: 30g | protein: 29g | carbs: 5g | net carbs: 3g | fiber: 2g

Tuna Avocado Bites

Prep time: 10 minutes | Cook time: 7 minutes | Makes 12 bites

1 (10 ounces / 283 g) can tuna, drained

¼ cup full-fat mayonnaise

1 stalk celery, chopped

1 medium avocado, peeled,

pitted, and mashed

½ cup blanched finely ground almond flour, divided

2 teaspoons coconut oil

1. In a large bowl, mix tuna, mayonnaise, celery, and mashed avocado. Form the mixture into balls. 2. Roll balls in almond flour and spritz with coconut oil. Place balls into the air fryer basket. 3. Adjust the temperature to 400ºF (204ºC) and set the timer for 7 minutes. 4. Gently turn tuna bites after 5 minutes. Serve warm.

Per Serving:

2 bites: calories: 170 | fat: 13g | protein: 12g | carbs: 4g | net carbs: 1g | fiber: 3g

Lime Lobster Tails

Prep time: 10 minutes | Cook time: 6 minutes | Serves 4

4 lobster tails, peeled
2 tablespoons lime juice
½ teaspoon dried basil

½ teaspoon coconut oil,
melted

1. Mix lobster tails with lime juice, dried basil, and coconut oil.
2. Put the lobster tails in the air fryer and cook at 380°F (193°C) for 6 minutes.

Per Serving:
calories: 110 | fat: 2g | protein: 22g | carbs: 1g | net carbs: 1g | fiber: 0g

Salmon with Dill Butter

Prep time: 7 minutes | Cook time: 8 minutes | Serves 2

1 teaspoon salt
2 tablespoons chopped fresh dill
10 ounces (283 g) salmon

fillet
¼ cup butter
½ cup water

1. Put butter and salt in the baking pan. 2. Add salmon fillet and dill. Cover the pan with foil. 3. Pour water in the instant pot and insert the baking pan with fish inside. 4. Set the Steam mode and cook the salmon for 8 minutes. 5. Unwrap the cooked salmon and serve!

Per Serving:
calories: 399 | fat: 32g | protein: 28g | carbs: 2g | net carbs: 2g | fiber: 0g

Simple Nut-Crusted Mahi Mahi

Prep time: 5 minutes | Cook time: 15 minutes | Serves 4

Coconut oil, for greasing
4 (4 ounces / 113 g) mahi mahi fillets, rinsed and patted dry
1 teaspoon sea salt, plus a pinch
½ teaspoon freshly ground black pepper, plus a pinch

½ cup roasted and salted macadamia nuts, coarsely chopped
2 tablespoons almond flour (or crushed pork rinds)
½ teaspoon garlic powder
½ teaspoon onion powder
4 tablespoons mayonnaise

1. Preheat the oven to 400°F (205°C). Grease an 8-inch square baking dish with coconut oil. 2. Place the mahi mahi in the prepared baking dish. 3. Sprinkle each fillet with salt and pepper on both sides. 4. In small bowl, mix together the macadamia nuts, almond flour, garlic powder, onion powder, and a pinch salt and pepper. 5. Spread 1 tablespoon of mayonnaise on each fillet. Divide the nut mixture among the tops of the 4 fillets, gently patting it down so it adheres to the mayonnaise. 6. Bake for about 15 minutes until golden brown and cooked through.

Per Serving:
1 fillet: calories: 364 | fat: 28g | protein: 24g | carbs: 4g | net carbs: 2g | fiber: 2g

Cajun Cod Fillet

Prep time: 10 minutes | Cook time: 4 minutes | Serves 2

10 ounces (283 g) cod fillet
1 tablespoon olive oil

1 teaspoon Cajun seasoning
2 tablespoons coconut aminos

1. Sprinkle the cod fillet with coconut aminos and Cajun seasoning. 2. Then heat up olive oil in the instant pot on Sauté mode. 3. Add the spiced cod fillet and cook it for 4 minutes from each side. 4. Then cut it into halves and sprinkle with the oily liquid from the instant pot.

Per Serving:
calories: 189 | fat: 8g | protein: 25g | carbs: 3g | net carbs: 3g | fiber: 0g

Cod with Jalapeño

Prep time: 5 minutes | Cook time: 14 minutes | Serves 4

4 cod fillets, boneless
1 jalapeño, minced

1 tablespoon avocado oil
½ teaspoon minced garlic

1. In the shallow bowl, mix minced jalapeño, avocado oil, and minced garlic. 2. Put the cod fillets in the air fryer basket in one layer and top with minced jalapeño mixture. 3. Cook the fish at 365°F (185°C) for 7 minutes per side.

Per Serving:
calories: 130 | fat: 3g | protein: 23g | carbs: 0g | net carbs: 0g | fiber: 0g

Parmesan Salmon Loaf

Prep time: 15 minutes | Cook time: 25 minutes | Serves 6

12 ounces (340 g) salmon, boiled and shredded
3 eggs, beaten
½ cup almond flour

1 teaspoon garlic powder
¼ cup grated Parmesan
1 teaspoon butter, softened
1 cup water, for cooking

1. Pour water in the instant pot. 2. Mix up the rest of the ingredients in the mixing bowl and stir until smooth. 3. After this, transfer the salmon mixture in the loaf pan and flatten; insert the pan in the instant pot. Close and seal the lid. 4. Cook the meal on Manual mode (High Pressure) for 25 minutes. 5. When the cooking time is finished, make a quick pressure release and cool the loaf well before serving.

Per Serving:
calories: 172 | fat: 10g | protein: 19g | carbs: 2g | net carbs: 2g | fiber: 0g

Lemon and Dill Salmon Kabobs

Prep time: 10 minutes | Cook time: 15 minutes | Serves 8

1 tablespoon fresh dill

¼ cup olive oil

¼ cup lemon juice

¼ teaspoon salt

¼ teaspoon black pepper

⅛ teaspoon ground cayenne

1 pound salmon, cubed

1 medium zucchini, sliced into ¼ rounds

1 Soak wooden skewers in water for at least 5 minutes in a shallow dish to prevent them from burning on grill. 2 In a medium bowl, combine dill, oil, lemon juice, salt, pepper, and cayenne. 3 Toss salmon cubes with marinade and stir to coat completely. Let marinate 10 minutes while prepping grill. 4 Clean and grease outdoor grill grate. Preheat outdoor grill to medium heat for 5 minutes. 5 Skewer salmon and zucchini on eight skewers using alternating pattern. Brush with remaining marinade. 6 Grill kabobs ½" apart, turning regularly until fully cooked, about 15 minutes total cooking time.

Per Serving:

calories: 137 | fat: 8g | protein: 12g | carbs: 1g | net carbs: 1g | fiber: 0g

Clam Chowder

Prep time: 5 minutes | Cook time: 15 minutes | Serves 4

4 slices bacon, chopped into ½-inch squares

2 tablespoons unsalted butter

½ small yellow onion, chopped

4 ribs celery, cut into ¼-inch-thick half-moons

1 cup chopped cauliflower florets, cut to about ½ inch thick

4 ounces (113 g) chopped mushrooms

4 cloves garlic, minced

1 teaspoon dried tarragon

1 teaspoon salt

¼ teaspoon freshly ground black pepper

8 ounces (227 g) bottled clam juice

1 cup vegetable stock or broth

½ cup heavy cream

8 ounces (227 g) cream cheese, room temperature

3 (6½ ounces / 184 g) cans chopped clams, with juice

¼ cup freshly chopped Italian parsley

1. Place the bacon in a medium saucepan over medium heat. Fry until just browned and most of the fat has been rendered, 3 to 4 minutes. Remove the bacon with a slotted spoon, reserving the rendered fat. 2. Add the butter to the pan with the fat and melt over medium heat. Add the onion, celery, cauliflower, and mushrooms and sauté until vegetables are just tender, 4 to 5 minutes. Add the garlic, tarragon, salt, and pepper and sauté for another 30 seconds or until fragrant. 3. Add the clam juice, stock, cream, and cream

cheese and whisk until the cheese is melted and creamy, 2 to 3 minutes. Add the clams and their juice, bring to a simmer, and cook for 1 to 2 minutes so the flavors meld. Stir in the parsley and serve warm.

Per Serving:

calories: 671 | fat: 54g | protein: 34g | carbs: 15g | net carbs: 13g | fiber: 2g

Rainbow Trout with Mixed Greens

Prep time: 5 minutes | Cook time: 12 minutes | Serves 4

1 cup water

1½ (680 g) pounds rainbow trout fillets

4 tablespoons melted butter, divided

Sea salt and ground black pepper, to taste

1 pound (454 g) mixed greens, trimmed and torn into pieces

1 bunch of scallions

½ cup chicken broth

1 tablespoon apple cider vinegar

1 teaspoon cayenne pepper

1. Pour the water into your Instant Pot and insert a steamer basket. 2. Add the fish to the basket. Drizzle with 1 tablespoon of the melted butter and season with the salt and black pepper. 3. Lock the lid. Select the Manual mode and set the cooking time for 12 minutes at Low pressure. 4. When the timer beeps, perform a quick pressure release. Carefully remove the lid. 5. Wipe down the Instant Pot with a damp cloth. 6. Add and warm the remaining 3 tablespoons of butter. Once hot, add the greens, scallions, broth, vinegar, and cayenne pepper and cook until the greens are wilted, stirring occasionally. 7. Serve the prepared trout fillets with the greens on the side.

Per Serving:

calories: 349 | fat: 18g | protein: 39g | carbs: 8g | net carbs: 3g | fiber: 4g

Ginger Cod

Prep time: 10 minutes | Cook time: 20 minutes | Serves 2

1 teaspoon ginger paste

8 ounces (227 g) cod fillet, chopped

1 tablespoon coconut oil

¼ cup coconut milk

1. Melt the coconut oil in the instant pot on Sauté mode. 2. Then add ginger paste and coconut milk and bring the mixture to boil. 3. Add chopped cod and sauté the meal for 12 minutes. Stir the fish cubes with the help of the spatula from time to time.

Per Serving:

calories: 222 | fat: 15g | protein: 21g | carbs: 2g | net carbs: 1g | fiber: 1g

Golden Shrimp

Prep time: 20 minutes | Cook time: 7 minutes | Serves 4

2 egg whites	1 teaspoon garlic powder
½ cup coconut flour	½ teaspoon dried rosemary
1 cup Parmigiano-Reggiano, grated	½ teaspoon sea salt
½ teaspoon celery seeds	½ teaspoon ground black pepper
½ teaspoon porcini powder	1½ pounds (680 g) shrimp, deveined
½ teaspoon onion powder	

1. Whisk the egg with coconut flour and Parmigiano-Reggiano. Add in seasonings and mix to combine well. 2. Dip your shrimp in the batter. Roll until they are covered on all sides. 3. Cook in the preheated air fryer at 390ºF (199ºC) for 5 to 7 minutes or until golden brown. Work in batches. Serve with lemon wedges if desired.

Per Serving:

calories: 265 | fat: 11g | protein: 33g | carbs: 7g | net carbs: 6g | fiber: 1g

Basil Alfredo Sea Bass

Prep time: 15 minutes | Cook time: 30 minutes | Serves 4

Sea Bass:

4 (6 ounces / 170 g) sea bass pieces	2 tablespoons olive oil

Pesto:

1 cup tightly packed fresh basil leaves	1 tablespoon water
¼ cup grated Parmesan cheese	½ teaspoon salt
3 tablespoons pine nuts, or walnuts	Freshly ground black pepper, to taste
	3 tablespoons olive oil

Alfredo Sauce:

2 tablespoons butter	¾ cup Parmesan cheese
1 tablespoon olive oil	Salt, to taste
1 garlic clove, minced	Freshly ground black pepper, to taste
1 cup heavy (whipping) cream	

Make the Sea Bass 1. Preheat the oven to 375ºF (190ºC). 2. Rub the sea bass with the olive oil and place it in a baking dish or on a rimmed baking sheet. Bake for 20 to 25 minutes or until the fish is completely opaque and the flesh flakes easily with a fork. Make the Pesto 1. In a blender or food processor (I prefer a blender because I like this very finely chopped/blended), combine the basil, Parmesan, pine nuts, water, and salt. Season with pepper. 2. With the blender running, stream the olive oil in. Set aside. Make the Alfredo Sauce 1. In a small saucepan over medium heat, melt the butter and olive oil together. 2. Stir in the garlic and cream. Bring to a low simmer and cook for 5 to 7 minutes until thickened.

3. Slowly add the Parmesan, stirring well to mix as it melts. Continue to stir until smooth. Season with salt and pepper. Set aside. 4. In a small bowl, stir together ½ cup of pesto and ½ cup of Alfredo sauce. Spoon over the fish before serving. Refrigerate leftovers in an airtight container for up to 4 days.

Per Serving:

calories: 768 | fat: 64g | protein: 45g | carbs: 4g | net carbs: 4g | fiber: 0g

Shrimp Ceviche Salad

Prep time: 15 minutes | Cook time: 0 minutes | Serves 4

1 pound (454 g) fresh shrimp, peeled and deveined
1 small red or yellow bell pepper, cut into ½-inch chunks
½ English cucumber, peeled and cut into ½-inch chunks
½ small red onion, cut into thin slivers
¼ cup chopped fresh cilantro or flat-leaf Italian parsley
⅓ cup freshly squeezed lime juice
2 tablespoons freshly squeezed lemon juice
2 tablespoons freshly squeezed clementine juice or orange juice
½ cup extra-virgin olive oil
1 teaspoon salt
½ teaspoon freshly ground black pepper
2 ripe avocados, peeled, pitted, and cut into ½-inch chunks

1. Cut the shrimp in half lengthwise. In a large glass bowl, combine the shrimp, bell pepper, cucumber, onion, and cilantro. 2. In a small bowl, whisk together the lime, lemon, and clementine juices, olive oil, salt, and pepper. Pour the mixture over the shrimp and veggies and toss to coat. Cover and refrigerate for at least 2 hours, or up to 8 hours. Give the mixture a toss every 30 minutes for the first 2 hours to make sure all the shrimp "cook" in the juices. 3. Add the cut avocado just before serving and toss to combine.

Per Serving:

calories: 490 | fat: 36g | protein: 28g | carbs: 17g | net carbs: 11g | fiber: 6g

Apple Cider Mussels

Prep time: 10 minutes | Cook time: 2 minutes | Serves 5

2 pounds (907 g) mussels, cleaned, peeled	1 teaspoon ground cumin
1 teaspoon onion powder	1 tablespoon avocado oil
	¼ cup apple cider vinegar

1. Mix mussels with onion powder, ground cumin, avocado oil, and apple cider vinegar. 2. Put the mussels in the air fryer and cook at 395ºF (202ºC) for 2 minutes.

Per Serving:

calories: 210 | fat: 9g | protein: 23g | carbs: 7g | net carbs: 6g | fiber: 1g

Southern-Style Catfish

Prep time: 10 minutes | Cook time: 12 minutes | Serves 4

4 (7 ounces / 198 g) catfish fillets

⅓ cup heavy whipping cream

1 tablespoon lemon juice

1 cup blanched finely ground almond flour

2 teaspoons Old Bay seasoning

½ teaspoon salt

¼ teaspoon ground black pepper

1. Place catfish fillets into a large bowl with cream and pour in lemon juice. Stir to coat. 2. In a separate large bowl, mix flour and Old Bay seasoning. 3. Remove each fillet and gently shake off excess cream. Sprinkle with salt and pepper. Press each fillet gently into flour mixture on both sides to coat. 4. Place fillets into ungreased air fryer basket. Adjust the temperature to 400°F (204°C) and air fry for 12 minutes, turning fillets halfway through cooking. Catfish will be golden brown and have an internal temperature of at least 145°F (63°C) when done. Serve warm.

Per Serving:

calories: 550 | fat: 41g | protein: 34g | carbs: 9g | net carbs: 5g | fiber: 4g

Spicy Grilled Shrimp with Mojo Verde

Prep time: 20 minutes | Cook time: 8 minutes | Serves 4

½ cup lime or lemon juice

3 teaspoons minced garlic

¼ red onion, thinly sliced

12 jumbo shrimp (peels on),

Dipping Sauce:

3 loosely packed cups fresh cilantro leaves

½ cup MCT oil or extra-virgin olive oil

deveined and butterflied

2 teaspoons cayenne pepper

1 teaspoon ground cumin

1 teaspoon fine sea salt

2 tablespoons minced garlic

2 teaspoons coconut vinegar

1 teaspoon fine sea salt

½ teaspoon ground cumin

1. Preheat a grill to medium-high heat. Place 4 wooden skewers in water to soak while you prepare the ingredients. 2. Place the lime juice in a shallow baking dish. Add the garlic, onion, and shrimp and let marinate for 15 minutes while you prepare the spices and dipping sauce. 3. Place the cayenne pepper, cumin, and salt in a small dish and stir well to combine. Set aside. 4. Make the dipping sauce: Place all the sauce ingredients in a food processor or blender and pulse until smooth. Add more salt to taste, if needed. 5. Remove the shrimp from the marinade and liberally sprinkle them with the spice mixture. Thread 3 shrimp onto each skewer. Grill for 3 to 4 minutes per side, or until the shrimp are pink and cooked through. Remove from the grill and serve each skewer with ¼ cup of the sauce. 6. This dish is best served fresh, but extras can be stored in an airtight container in the fridge for up to 3 days. It can be served cold. To reheat, place the shrimp in a skillet over medium heat and sauté until warmed.

Per Serving:

calories: 365 | fat: 29g | protein: 21g | carbs: 5g | net carbs: 4g | fiber: 1g

Salmon Cakes

Prep time: 10 minutes | Cook time: 15 minutes | Serves 4

1 (16 ounces / 454 g) can pink salmon, drained and bones removed

¼ cup almond flour

¼ cup crushed pork rinds

2 scallions, diced

1 large egg

3 tablespoons mayonnaise

1 teaspoon garlic salt

1 teaspoon freshly ground black pepper

2 tablespoons extra-virgin olive oil

1. Line a plate with paper towels and set aside. 2. In a bowl, combine the salmon, almond flour, pork rinds, scallions, egg, mayonnaise, garlic salt, and pepper, and mix together well, using your hands or a spatula. 3. Form 8 small patties or 4 large patties. If the patties seem too dry, add a little more mayonnaise. If they seem too wet, add a little more almond flour or pork rinds. 4. In a skillet over medium heat, heat the oil. Cook the patties for 4 to 5 minutes on each side, until crispy. Larger patties may need to cook a little longer. 5. Transfer the patties to the lined plate to drain.

Per Serving:

2 small patties: calories: 313 | fat: 21g | protein: 26g | carbs: 5g | net carbs: 5g | fiber: 0g

Tuna with Herbs

Prep time: 20 minutes | Cook time: 17 minutes | Serves 4

1 tablespoon butter, melted

1 medium-sized leek, thinly sliced

1 tablespoon chicken stock

1 tablespoon dry white wine

1 pound (454 g) tuna

½ teaspoon red pepper flakes, crushed

Sea salt and ground black pepper, to taste

½ teaspoon dried rosemary

½ teaspoon dried basil

½ teaspoon dried thyme

2 small ripe tomatoes, puréed

1 cup Parmesan cheese, grated

1. Melt ½ tablespoon of butter in a sauté pan over medium-high heat. Now, cook the leek and garlic until tender and aromatic. Add the stock and wine to deglaze the pan. 2. Preheat the air fryer to 370°F (188°C). 3. Grease a casserole dish with the remaining ½ tablespoon of melted butter. Place the fish in the casserole dish. Add the seasonings. Top with the sautéed leek mixture. Add the tomato purée. Cook for 10 minutes in the preheated air fryer. Top with grated Parmesan cheese; cook an additional 7 minutes until the crumbs are golden. Bon appétit!

Per Serving:

calories: 450 | fat: 22g | protein: 56g | carbs: 8g | net carbs: 6g | fiber: 2g

Shrimp in Curry Sauce

Prep time: 10 minutes | Cook time: 5 minutes | Serves 2

½ ounce grated Parmesan cheese	Sauce
1 egg, beaten	2 tablespoons curry leaves
¼ teaspoon curry powder	2 tablespoons butter
2 teaspoons almond flour	½ onion, diced
12 shrimp, shelled	½ cup heavy cream
3 tablespoons coconut oil	½ ounce cheddar cheese, shredded

1. Combine all dry ingredients for the batter. Melt the coconut oil in a skillet over medium heat. Dip the shrimp in the egg first, and then coat with the dry mixture. Fry until golden and crispy. 2. In another skillet, melt butter. Add onion and cook for 3 minutes. Add curry leaves and cook for 30 seconds. Stir in heavy cream and cheddar and cook until thickened. Add shrimp and coat well. Serve.

Per Serving:

calories: 772 | fat: 73g | protein: 20g | carbs: 11g | net carbs: 8g | fiber: 3g

Sardine Fritter Wraps

Prep time: 5 minutes | Cook time: 8 minutes | Serves 4

⅓ cup (80 ml) refined avocado oil, for frying

Fritters:

2 (4.375 ounces/125 g) cans sardines, drained	2 tablespoons finely diced red bell pepper
½ cup (55 g) blanched almond flour	2 cloves garlic, minced
2 large eggs	½ teaspoon finely ground gray sea salt
2 tablespoons finely chopped fresh parsley	¼ teaspoon ground black pepper

For Serving:

8 romaine lettuce leaves	8 tablespoons (105 g) mayonnaise
1 small English cucumber, sliced thin	Thinly sliced green onions

1. Pour the avocado oil into a large frying pan. Heat on medium for a couple of minutes. 2. Meanwhile, prepare the fritters: Place the fritter ingredients in a medium-sized bowl and stir to combine, being careful not to mash the heck out of the sardines. Spoon about 1 tablespoon of the mixture into the palm of your hand and roll it into a ball, then flatten it like a burger patty. Repeat with the remaining fritter mixture, making a total of 16 small patties. 3. Fry the fritters in the hot oil for 2 minutes per side, then transfer to a cooling rack. You may have to fry the fritters in batches if your pan isn't large enough to fit them all without overcrowding. 4. Meanwhile, divide the lettuce leaves among 4 dinner plates. Top with the sliced cucumber. When the fritters are done, place 2 fritters on each leaf. Top with a dollop of mayonnaise, sprinkle with sliced green onions, and serve!

Per Serving:

calories: 612 | fat: 56g | protein: 23g | carbs: 6g | net carbs: 4g | fiber: 2g

Chili Lime Shrimp

Prep time: 5 minutes | Cook time: 5 minutes | Serves 4

1 pound (454 g) medium shrimp, peeled and deveined	¼ teaspoon salt
	¼ teaspoon ground black pepper
1 tablespoon salted butter, melted	½ small lime, zested and juiced, divided
2 teaspoons chili powder	
¼ teaspoon garlic powder	

1. In a medium bowl, toss shrimp with butter, then sprinkle with chili powder, garlic powder, salt, pepper, and lime zest. 2. Place shrimp into ungreased air fryer basket. Adjust the temperature to 400°F (204°C) and air fry for 5 minutes. Shrimp will be firm and form a "C" shape when done. 3. Transfer shrimp to a large serving dish and drizzle with lime juice. Serve warm.

Per Serving:

calories: 129 | fat: 3g | protein: 23g | carbs: 2g | net carbs: 1g | fiber: 1g

Sole Meunière

Prep time: 5 minutes | Cook time: 10 minutes | Serves 2

½ cup almond flour	Juice of ½ lemon
4 (6 ounces / 170 g) sole fillets	2 tablespoons minced fresh parsley leaves
Salt, to taste	4 lemon wedges (from the other half of the lemon), for serving
Freshly ground black pepper, to taste	
6 tablespoons butter, divided	

1. Put the almond flour into a shallow dish. 2. Pat the fish dry with a paper towel and coat each side with almond flour. Season with salt and pepper. 3. In a large skillet over medium heat, melt 3 tablespoons of butter. 4. Add the fish to the skillet and cook for 2 to 3 minutes per side or until the fish is completely opaque. Transfer the fish to a serving platter. 5. Return the skillet to the heat and add the remaining 3 tablespoons of butter and the lemon juice. When melted, pour it over the fish, garnish with the parsley, and serve with the lemon wedges. Refrigerate leftovers in an airtight container for up to 4 days.

Per Serving:

calories: 624 | fat: 40g | protein: 65g | carbs: 2g | net carbs: 2g | fiber: 0g

Chapter 8

Poultry

Pesto Chicken with Stewed Vegetables

Prep time: 15 minutes | Cook time: 6 to 8 hours | Serves 2

1 zucchini, cut into 1-inch pieces	1 teaspoon extra-virgin olive oil
1 cup grape tomatoes	⅛ teaspoon sea salt
1 red bell pepper, cored and sliced thin	Freshly ground black pepper
½ red onion, halved and sliced thin	2 bone-in, skinless chicken thighs, about 8 ounces (227 g) each
1 tablespoon assorted fresh herbs	¼ cup pesto

1. Put the zucchini, grape tomatoes, red bell pepper, onion, and herbs in the slow cooker and gently stir until mixed together. Drizzle the vegetables with the olive oil. Season with the salt and a few grinds of the black pepper. 2. In a medium bowl, coat the chicken on all sides with the pesto, then place the chicken on top of the vegetables. 3. Cover and cook on low for 6 to 8 hours until the vegetables are very tender and the chicken is cooked through.
Per Serving:
calories: 663 | fat: 51g | protein: 37g | carbs: 14g | net carbs: 10g | fiber: 4g

Chicken Kiev

Prep time: 15 minutes | Cook time: 25 minutes | Serves 4

1 cup (2 sticks) unsalted butter, softened (or butter-flavored coconut oil for dairy-free)
2 tablespoons lemon juice
2 tablespoons plus 1 teaspoon chopped fresh parsley leaves, divided, plus more for garnish
2 tablespoons chopped fresh tarragon leaves
3 cloves garlic, minced
1 teaspoon fine sea salt, divided
4 (4 ounces / 113 g) boneless, skinless chicken breasts
2 large eggs
2 cups pork dust
1 teaspoon ground black pepper
Sprig of fresh parsley, for garnish
Lemon slices, for serving

1. Spray the air fryer basket with avocado oil. Preheat the air fryer to 350ºF (177ºC). 2. In a medium-sized bowl, combine the butter, lemon juice, 2 tablespoons of the parsley, the tarragon, garlic, and ¼ teaspoon of the salt. Cover and place in the fridge to harden for 7 minutes. 3. While the butter mixture chills, place one of the chicken breasts on a cutting board. With a sharp knife held parallel to the cutting board, make a 1-inch-wide incision at the top of the breast. Carefully cut into the breast to form a large pocket, leaving a ½-inch border along the sides and bottom. Repeat with

the other 3 breasts. 4. Stuff one-quarter of the butter mixture into each chicken breast and secure the openings with toothpicks. 5. Beat the eggs in a small shallow dish. In another shallow dish, combine the pork dust, the remaining 1 teaspoon of parsley, the remaining ¾ teaspoon of salt, and the pepper. 6. One at a time, dip the chicken breasts in the egg, shake off the excess egg, and dredge the breasts in the pork dust mixture. Use your hands to press the pork dust onto each breast to form a nice crust. If you desire a thicker coating, dip it again in the egg and pork dust. As you finish, spray each coated chicken breast with avocado oil and place it in the air fryer basket. 7. Roast the chicken in the air fryer for 15 minutes, flip the breasts, and cook for another 10 minutes, or until the internal temperature of the chicken is 165ºF (74ºC) and the crust is golden brown. 8. Serve garnished with chopped fresh parsley and a parsley sprig, with lemon slices on the side. 9. Store leftovers in an airtight container in the refrigerator for up to 4 days or in the freezer for up to a month. Reheat in a preheated 350ºF (177ºC) air fryer for 5 minutes, or until heated through.
Per Serving:
calories: 569 | fat: 40g | protein: 48g | carbs: 3g | net carbs: 3g | fiber: 0g

Chicken Meatballs with Green Cabbage

Prep time: 15 minutes | Cook time: 4 minutes | Serves 4

1 pound (454 g) ground chicken	1½ teaspoons freshly ground black pepper, divided
¼ cup heavy (whipping) cream	¼ teaspoon ground allspice
2 teaspoons salt, divided	4 to 6 cups thickly chopped green cabbage
½ teaspoon ground caraway seeds	½ cup coconut milk
	2 tablespoons unsalted butter

1. To make the meatballs, put the chicken in a bowl. Add the cream, 1 teaspoon of salt, the caraway, ½ teaspoon of pepper, and the allspice. Mix thoroughly. Refrigerate the mixture for 30 minutes. Once the mixture has cooled, it is easier to form the meatballs. 2. Using a small scoop, form the chicken mixture into small-to medium-size meatballs. Place half the meatballs in the inner cooking pot of your Instant Pot and cover them with half the cabbage. Place the remaining meatballs on top of the cabbage, then cover them with the rest of the cabbage. 3. Pour in the milk, place pats of the butter here and there, and sprinkle with the remaining 1 teaspoon of salt and 1 teaspoon of pepper. 4. Lock the lid into place. Select Manual and adjust the pressure to High. Cook for 4 minutes. When the cooking is complete, quick-release the pressure. Unlock the lid. Serve the meatballs on top of the cabbage.
Per Serving:
calories: 338 | fat: 23g | protein: 23g | carbs: 7g | net carbs: 4g | fiber: 3g

Rotisserie Chicken

Prep time: 5 minutes | Cook time: 8 hours | Serves 2

Nonstick cooking spray	¼ teaspoon freshly ground
3 garlic cloves, crushed	black pepper
1 teaspoon salt	1 (2½ to 3 pounds / 1.1 to 1.4
1½ teaspoons ground smoked	kg) roasting or broiler chicken
paprika	1 lemon
1 teaspoon dried thyme leaves	

1. Spray the slow cooker with nonstick cooking spray. Tear off 4 (18-inch-long) pieces of foil. Scrunch the foil into balls and place in the slow cooker. 2. In a small bowl, mix the crushed garlic, salt, paprika, thyme, and pepper until well combined. Sprinkle one-quarter of this mixture inside the chicken; rub the rest onto the chicken skin. 3. Roll the lemon on the counter beneath your palm to soften it. Quarter the lemon. Put 2 quarters inside the chicken. Squeeze the remaining 2 quarters over the chicken, and put those pieces in the slow cooker between the foil balls. 4. Place the chicken, breast-side down, on top of the foil balls. 5. Cover and cook on low for 8 hours, or until the chicken registers 165ºF (74ºC) on a meat thermometer and is very tender. 6. Carve and serve.
Per Serving:
calories: 547 | fat: 13g | protein: 98g | carbs: 4g | net carbs: 3g | fiber: 1g
g | net carbs: 9g | fiber: 3g

Chicken Tacos with Fried Cheese Shells

Prep time: 5 minutes | Cook time: 25 minutes | Serves 6

Chicken:

4 (6 ounces / 170 g) boneless,	¼ teaspoon pepper
skinless chicken breasts	1 tablespoon chili powder
1 cup chicken broth	2 teaspoons garlic powder
1 teaspoon salt	2 teaspoons cumin

Cheese Shells:

1½ cups shredded whole-milk	Mozzarella cheese

1. Combine all ingredients for the chicken in the Instant Pot. 2. Secure the lid. Select the Manual mode and set the cooking time for 20 minutes at High Pressure. 3. Once cooking is complete, do a quick pressure release. Carefully open the lid. 4. Shred the chicken and serve in bowls or cheese shells. 5. Make the cheese shells: Heat a nonstick skillet over medium heat. 6. Sprinkle ¼ cup of Mozzarella cheese in the skillet and fry until golden. Flip and turn off the heat. Allow the cheese to get brown. Fill with chicken and fold. The cheese will harden as it cools. Repeat with the remaining cheese and filling. 7. Serve warm.
Per Serving:
calories: 233 | fat: 8g | protein: 32g | carbs: 2g | net carbs: 2g | fiber: 2g

Duck & Vegetable Casserole

Prep time: 15 minutes | Cook time: 20 minutes | Serves 2

2 duck breasts, skin on and	1 carrot, chopped
sliced	2 green bell peppers, seeded
2 zucchinis, sliced	and chopped
1 tablespoon coconut oil	Salt and ground black pepper,
1 green onion bunch, chopped	to taste

1. Set a pan over medium heat and warm oil, stir in the green onions, and cook for 2 minutes. Place in the zucchini, bell peppers, black pepper, salt, and carrot, and cook for 10 minutes. 2. Set another pan over medium heat, add in duck slices and cook each side for 3 minutes. 3. Pour the mixture into the vegetable pan. Cook for 3 minutes. Set in bowls and enjoy.
Per Serving:
calories: 630 | fat: 44g | protein: 44g | carbs: 11

Poblano Chicken

Prep time: 10 minutes | Cook time: 29 minutes | Serves 4

2 Poblano peppers, sliced	½ cup coconut cream
16 ounces (454 g) chicken	1 tablespoon butter
fillet	½ teaspoon chili powder
½ teaspoon salt	

1. Heat up the butter on Sauté mode for 3 minutes. 2. Add Poblano and cook them for 3 minutes. 3. Meanwhile, cut the chicken fillet into the strips and sprinkle with salt and chili powder. 4. Add the chicken strips to the instant pot. 5. Then add coconut cream and close the lid. Cook the meal on Sauté mode for 20 minutes.
Per Serving:
calories: 320 | fat: 18g | protein: 34g | carbs: 4g | net carbs: 3g | fiber: 1g

Lemon & Rosemary Chicken in a Skillet

Prep time: 5 minutes | Cook time: 14 minutes | Serves 4

8 chicken thighs	1 tablespoon chopped
1 teaspoon salt	rosemary
2 tablespoons lemon juice	¼ teaspoon black pepper
1 teaspoon lemon zest	1 garlic clove, minced
2 tablespoons olive oil	

1. Combine all ingredients in a bowl. Place in the fridge for one hour. Heat a skillet over medium heat. Add the chicken along with the juices and cook until crispy, about 7 minutes per side.
Per Serving:
calories: 457 | fat: 33g | protein: 37g | carbs: 3g | net carbs: 2g | fiber: 1g

Chicken Pesto Parmigiana

Prep time: 10 minutes | Cook time: 23 minutes | Serves 4

2 large eggs

1 tablespoon water

Fine sea salt and ground black pepper, to taste

1 cup powdered Parmesan cheese (about 3 ounces / 85 g)

2 teaspoons Italian seasoning

4 (5 ounces / 142 g) boneless, skinless chicken breasts or thighs, pounded to ¼ inch thick

1 cup pesto

1 cup shredded Mozzarella cheese (about 4 ounces / 113 g)

Finely chopped fresh basil, for garnish (optional)

Grape tomatoes, halved, for serving (optional)

1. Spray the air fryer basket with avocado oil. Preheat the air fryer to 400ºF (204ºC). 2. Crack the eggs into a shallow baking dish, add the water and a pinch each of salt and pepper, and whisk to combine. In another shallow baking dish, stir together the Parmesan and Italian seasoning until well combined. 3. Season the chicken breasts well on both sides with salt and pepper. Dip one chicken breast in the eggs and let any excess drip off, then dredge both sides of the breast in the Parmesan mixture. Spray the breast with avocado oil and place it in the air fryer basket. Repeat with the remaining 3 chicken breasts. 4. Air fry the chicken in the air fryer for 20 minutes, or until the internal temperature reaches 165ºF (74ºC) and the breading is golden brown, flipping halfway through. 5. Dollop each chicken breast with ¼ cup of the pesto and top with the Mozzarella. Return the breasts to the air fryer and cook for 3 minutes, or until the cheese is melted. Garnish with basil and serve with halved grape tomatoes on the side, if desired. 6. Store leftovers in an airtight container in the refrigerator for up to 4 days. Reheat in a preheated 400ºF (204ºC) air fryer for 5 minutes, or until warmed through.

Per Serving:

calories: 725 | fat: 54g | protein: 62g | carbs: 8g | net carbs: 7g | fiber: 1g

Kung Pao Chicken

Prep time: 5 minutes | Cook time: 17 minutes | Serves 5

2 tablespoons coconut oil	½ teaspoon chili powder
1 pound (454 g) boneless, skinless chicken breasts, cubed	½ teaspoon finely grated ginger
1 cup cashews, chopped	½ teaspoon kosher salt
6 tablespoons hot sauce	½ teaspoon freshly ground black pepper

1. Set the Instant Pot to Sauté and melt the coconut oil. 2. Add the remaining ingredients to the Instant Pot and mix well. 3. Secure the lid. Select the Manual mode and set the cooking time for 17 minutes at High Pressure. 4. Once cooking is complete, do a quick pressure release. Carefully open the lid. 5. Serve warm.

Per Serving:

calories: 381 | fat: 25g | protein: 31g | carbs: 10g | net carbs: 9g | fiber: 1g

Paprika Chicken

Prep time: 10 minutes | Cook time: 25 minutes | Serves 4

4 (4 ounces) chicken breasts, skin-on	½ cup heavy (whipping) cream
Sea salt	2 teaspoons smoked paprika
Freshly ground black pepper	½ cup sour cream
1 tablespoon olive oil	2 tablespoons chopped fresh parsley
½ cup chopped sweet onion	

1. Lightly season the chicken with salt and pepper. 2. Place a large skillet over medium-high heat and add the olive oil. 3. Sear the chicken on both sides until almost cooked through, about 15 minutes in total. Remove the chicken to a plate. 4. Add the onion to the skillet and sauté until tender, about 4 minutes. 5. Stir in the cream and paprika and bring the liquid to a simmer. 6. Return the chicken and any accumulated juices to the skillet and simmer the chicken for 5 minutes until completely cooked. 7. Stir in the sour cream and remove the skillet from the heat. 8. Serve topped with the parsley.

Per Serving:

calories: 389 | fat: 30g | protein: 25g | carbs: 4g | net carbs: 4g | fiber: 0g

Classic Whole Chicken

Prep time: 5 minutes | Cook time: 50 minutes | Serves 4

Oil, for spraying	½ teaspoon salt
1 (4 pounds / 1.8 kg) whole chicken, giblets removed	½ teaspoon freshly ground black pepper
1 tablespoon olive oil	¼ teaspoon finely chopped fresh parsley, for garnish
1 teaspoon paprika	
½ teaspoon granulated garlic	

1. Line the air fryer basket with parchment and spray lightly with oil. 2. Pat the chicken dry with paper towels. Rub it with the olive oil until evenly coated. 3. In a small bowl, mix together the paprika, garlic, salt, and black pepper and sprinkle it evenly over the chicken. 4. Place the chicken in the prepared basket, breast-side down. 5. Air fry at 360ºF (182ºC) for 30 minutes, flip, and cook for another 20 minutes, or until the internal temperature reaches 165ºF (74ºC) and the juices run clear. 6. Sprinkle with the parsley before serving.

Per Serving:

calories: 372 | fat: 23g | protein: 38g | carbs: 0g | net carbs: 0g | fiber: 0g

Chicken Laksa

Prep time: 5 minutes | Cook time: 25 minutes | Serves 4

⅓ cup (70 g) coconut oil or ghee, or ⅓ cup (80 ml) avocado oil

¼ cup (40 g) diced white onions

4 stalks lemongrass, cut lengthwise to fit in the pan

1 fresh green chili pepper, diced

1 (2-in/5-cm) piece fresh ginger root, minced

4 cloves garlic, minced

2 teaspoons ground coriander

2 teaspoons curry powder

1 teaspoon ground cumin

½ teaspoon finely ground sea salt

1 pound (455 g) boneless, skinless chicken thighs, sliced

1 (13½ ounces/400 ml) can lite coconut milk

2 cups (475 ml) chicken bone broth

For Serving:

8 ounces (240 g) bean sprouts

4 lime wedges

8 fresh mint leaves

1. Heat the oil in a large saucepan over medium heat. Add the onions, lemongrass, chili pepper, ginger, garlic, coriander, curry powder, cumin, and salt and sauté for 10 minutes, or until fragrant. 2. Add the sliced chicken thighs, coconut milk, and broth. Cover and bring to a boil over high heat. Reduce the heat to low and simmer for 15 minutes, or until the chicken is cooked through. 3. Before serving, remove and discard the pieces of lemongrass. Divide the laksa among 4 large soup bowls. Top each bowl with 2 ounces (60 g) of bean sprouts, then squeeze a lime wedge over each bowl and drop the wedges into the bowls. Garnish each bowl with 2 mint leaves and serve!

Per Serving:

calories: 480 | fat: 33g | protein: 37g | carbs: 9g | net carbs: 8g | fiber: 2g

Chicken Broth

Prep time: 5 minutes | Cook time: 8 to 24 hours | Makes 2 to 3 quarts

4 quarts filtered water

1½ to 2 pounds (680 to 907 g) chicken bones with cartilage

Cloves from 1 head of garlic, peeled and smashed with the side of a knife

2 tablespoons apple cider vinegar

2 teaspoons sea salt (optional)

Make This in a Slow Cooker: 1. Place all of the ingredients in a slow cooker. Set the heat to high and bring to a boil, then turn the heat down to low. Cook for at least 8 hours and up to 24 hours—the longer it cooks, the better. 2. Turn off the slow cooker and allow the broth to cool. Make This in an Instant Pot: 1. Place all of the ingredients in the multicooker. Cook on high pressure for 2 hours. When cooking is finished, allow the cooker to depressurize on its own; don't flip the valve to release it. 2. Strain the broth through a fine-mesh strainer or cheesecloth. Pour the cooled broth into glass jars and store in the refrigerator for up to a few days. You can also store it in plastic containers in the freezer until you're ready to use it. Make sure the broth has cooled completely before freezing. 3. Before using the broth, chip away at the top and discard any fat that has solidified.

Per Serving:

calories: 233 | fat: 0g | protein: 20g | carbs: 2g | net carbs: 2g | fiber: 0g

Chicken Fajitas

Prep time: 10 minutes | Cook time: 15 to 20 minutes | Serves 4

1 pound (454 g) boneless, skinless chicken breasts and/or thighs, sliced into thin strips

1 teaspoon salt

1 teaspoon dried oregano

1 teaspoon garlic powder

½ teaspoon freshly ground black pepper

1 teaspoon ground cumin

½ teaspoon red pepper flakes

½ teaspoon paprika

¼ teaspoon ground cinnamon

2 tablespoons avocado oil or butter, divided

½ white onion, sliced

½ red bell pepper, sliced into strips

½ green bell pepper, sliced into strips

2 tablespoons chicken broth (optional)

2 to 4 coconut or almond flour wraps, or grain-free chips

1 cup shredded romaine lettuce

Sugar-free salsa, guacamole, sour cream, and shredded cheese, for serving (optional)

1. In a large bowl, combine the chicken with the salt, oregano, garlic powder, pepper, cumin, red pepper flakes, paprika, cinnamon, and 1 tablespoon of oil or butter. 2. Heat the remaining tablespoon of oil or butter in a large, shallow skillet over medium-high heat. Add the onion and cook for 3 to 5 minutes, stirring occasionally, until translucent. 3. Add the bell peppers and continue to cook, stirring, for another 5 minutes, until tender. 4. Add the chicken mixture and continue to cook and stir for another 2 to 3 minutes, then reduce the heat to medium, cover, and cook for about 5 minutes, or until the chicken is cooked through and no longer pink. If the chicken starts to burn, add the chicken broth. 5. Remove the chicken mixture from the heat and let cool a bit. 6. Divide the wraps or chips among plates, sprinkle the shredded romaine on top, and spoon the chicken fajita mixture on top of the lettuce. Serve the fajitas with salsa, guacamole, sour cream, and cheese, if you'd like.

Per Serving:

calories: 235 | fat: 13g | protein: 25g | carbs: 5g | net carbs: 3g | fiber: 2g

Chicken with Lettuce

Prep time: 15 minutes | Cook time: 14 minutes | Serves 4

1 pound (454 g) chicken breast tenders, chopped into bite-size pieces	and thinly sliced
	1 tablespoon olive oil
½ onion, thinly sliced	1 tablespoon fajita seasoning
½ red bell pepper, seeded and thinly sliced	1 teaspoon kosher salt
	Juice of ½ lime
½ green bell pepper, seeded	8 large lettuce leaves
	1 cup prepared guacamole

1. Preheat the air fryer to 400ºF (204ºC). 2. In a large bowl, combine the chicken, onion, and peppers. Drizzle with the olive oil and toss until thoroughly coated. Add the fajita seasoning and salt and toss again. 3. Working in batches if necessary, arrange the chicken and vegetables in a single layer in the air fryer basket. Pausing halfway through the cooking time to shake the basket, air fry for 14 minutes, or until the vegetables are tender and a thermometer inserted into the thickest piece of chicken registers 165ºF (74ºC). 4. Transfer the mixture to a serving platter and drizzle with the fresh lime juice. Serve with the lettuce leaves and top with the guacamole.

Per Serving:

calories: 315 | fat: 19g | protein: 27g | carbs: 11g | net carbs: 7g | fiber: 4g

Chicken Piccata with Mushrooms

Prep time: 25 minutes | Cook time: 25 minutes | Serves 4

1 pound (454 g) thinly sliced chicken breasts	2 cups sliced mushrooms
1½ teaspoons salt, divided	½ cup dry white wine or chicken stock
½ teaspoon freshly ground black pepper	¼ cup freshly squeezed lemon juice
¼ cup ground flaxseed	¼ cup roughly chopped capers
2 tablespoons almond flour	Zucchini noodles, for serving
8 tablespoons extra-virgin olive oil, divided	¼ cup chopped fresh flat-leaf Italian parsley, for garnish
4 tablespoons butter, divided	

1. Season the chicken with 1 teaspoon salt and the pepper. On a plate, combine the ground flaxseed and almond flour and dredge each chicken breast in the mixture. Set aside. 2. In a large skillet, heat 4 tablespoons olive oil and 1 tablespoon butter over medium-high heat. Working in batches if necessary, brown the chicken, 3 to 4 minutes per side. Remove from the skillet and keep warm. 3. Add the remaining 4 tablespoons olive oil and 1 tablespoon butter to the skillet along with mushrooms and sauté over medium heat until just tender, 6 to 8 minutes. 4. Add the white wine, lemon juice, capers, and remaining ½ teaspoon salt to the skillet and bring to a boil, whisking to incorporate any little browned bits

that have stuck to the bottom of the skillet. Reduce the heat to low and whisk in the final 2 tablespoons butter. 5. Return the browned chicken to skillet, cover, and simmer over low heat until the chicken is cooked through and the sauce has thickened, 5 to 6 more minutes. 6. Serve chicken and mushrooms warm over zucchini noodles, spooning the mushroom sauce over top and garnishing with chopped parsley.

Per Serving:

calories: 617 | fat: 49g | protein: 30g | carbs: 10g | net carbs: 6g | fiber: 4g

Eggplant & Tomato Braised Chicken Thighs

Prep time: 10 minutes | Cook time: 25 minutes | Serves 4

2 tablespoons ghee	tomatoes
1 pound chicken thighs	1 eggplant, diced
Salt and black pepper to taste	10 fresh basil leaves, chopped + extra to garnish
2 cloves garlic, minced	
1 (14 ounces) can whole	

Melt ghee in a saucepan over medium heat, season the chicken with salt and black pepper and fry for 4 minutes on each side until golden brown. Remove to a plate. 2. Sauté the garlic in the ghee for 2 minutes, pour in the tomatoes, and cook covered for 8 minutes. Add in the eggplant and basil. Cook for 4 minutes. Season the sauce with salt and black pepper, stir and add the chicken. Coat with sauce and simmer for 3 minutes. 3. Serve chicken with sauce on a bed of squash pasta. Garnish with extra basil.

Per Serving:

calories: 293 | fat: 18g | protein: 23g | carbs: 14g | net carbs: 11g | fiber: 5g

Roasted Stuffed Chicken with Tomato Basil Sauce

Prep time: 5 minutes | Cook time: 30 minutes | Serves 6

4 ounces cream cheese	cheese
3 ounces mozzarella slices	1 tablespoon olive oil
10 ounces spinach	1 cup tomato basil sauce
⅓ cup shredded mozzarella	3 whole chicken breasts

Preheat your oven to 400ºF. Combine the cream cheese, shredded mozzarella cheese, and spinach in the microwave. Cut the chicken a couple of times horizontally and stuff with the spinach mixture. Brush with olive oil. place on a lined baking dish and bake in the oven for 25 minutes. 2. Pour the tomato basil sauce over and top with mozzarella slices. Return to the oven and cook for an additional 5 minutes.

Per Serving:

calories: 436 | fat: 31g | protein: 23g | carbs: 20g | net carbs: 14g | fiber: 6g

Chicken Tenders

Prep time: 10 minutes | Cook time: 25 to 30 minutes | Serves 4

2 cups crushed pork rinds
¼ cup grated Parmesan cheese
1 teaspoon garlic powder
1 teaspoon freshly ground black pepper
1 large egg
½ cup heavy cream
1 pound (454 g) boneless skinless chicken tenderloins (10 to 12 tenderloins), patted dry

1. Preheat the oven to 425ºF (220ºC). Line a baking sheet with parchment paper and set aside. 2. In a shallow bowl, mix the pork rinds, Parmesan cheese, garlic powder, and pepper. 3. In a separate bowl, whisk together the egg and heavy cream. 4. Dip a tenderloin entirely in the egg mixture, then lay the tenderloin in the pork rind mixture, turning to coat both sides. 5. Lay the coated tenderloin on the prepared baking sheet and repeat with the remaining tenderloins. 6. Bake for 25 to 30 minutes.

Per Serving:
calories: 460 | fat: 32g | protein: 41g | carbs: 2g | net carbs: 2g | fiber: 0g

Thai Tacos with Peanut Sauce

Prep time: 10 minutes | Cook time: 6 minutes | Serves 4

1 pound (454 g) ground chicken
¼ cup diced onions (about 1
Sauce:
¼ cup creamy peanut butter, room temperature
2 tablespoons chicken broth, plus more if needed
2 tablespoons lime juice
2 tablespoons grated fresh
For Serving:
2 small heads butter lettuce, leaves separated
Lime slices (optional)
For Garnish (Optional):
small onion)
2 cloves garlic, minced
¼ teaspoon fine sea salt

ginger
2 tablespoons wheat-free tamari or coconut aminos
1½ teaspoons hot sauce
5 drops liquid stevia (optional)

Cilantro leaves
Shredded purple cabbage
Sliced green onions

1. Preheat the air fryer to 350ºF (177ºC). 2. Place the ground chicken, onions, garlic, and salt in a pie pan or a dish that will fit in your air fryer. Break up the chicken with a spatula. Place in the air fryer and bake for 5 minutes, or until the chicken is browned and cooked through. Break up the chicken again into small crumbles. 3. Make the sauce: In a medium-sized bowl, stir together the peanut butter, broth, lime juice, ginger, tamari, hot sauce, and stevia (if using) until well combined. If the sauce is too thick, add another tablespoon or two of broth. Taste and add more hot sauce if desired. 4. Add half of the sauce to the pan with the chicken.

Cook for another minute, until heated through, and stir well to combine. 5. Assemble the tacos: Place several lettuce leaves on a serving plate. Place a few tablespoons of the chicken mixture in each lettuce leaf and garnish with cilantro leaves, purple cabbage, and sliced green onions, if desired. Serve the remaining sauce on the side. Serve with lime slices, if desired. 6. Store leftover meat mixture in an airtight container in the refrigerator for up to 4 days; store leftover sauce, lettuce leaves, and garnishes separately. Reheat the meat mixture in a lightly greased pie pan in a preheated 350ºF (177ºC) air fryer for 3 minutes, or until heated through.
Per Serving:
calories: 276 | fat: 18g | protein: 25g | carbs: 5g | net carbs: 4g | fiber: 1g

Bacon-Wrapped Chicken Tenders

Prep time: 15 minutes | Cook time: 15 minutes | Serves 2

4 ounces (113 g) chicken fillet
2 bacon slices
½ teaspoon ground paprika
¼ teaspoon salt
1 teaspoon olive oil
1 cup water, for cooking

1. Cut the chicken fillet on 2 tenders and sprinkle them with salt, ground paprika, and olive oil. 2. Wrap the chicken tenders in the bacon and transfer in the steamer rack, 3. Pour water and insert the steamer rack with the chicken tenders in the instant pot. 4. Close and seal the lid and cook the meal on Manual mode (High Pressure) for 15 minutes. 5. When the time is finished, allow the natural pressure release for 10 minutes.
Per Serving:
calories: 232 | fat: 14g | protein: 23g | carbs: 1g | net carbs: 1g | fiber: 0g

Chicken with Bacon and Tomato

Prep time: 25 minutes | Cook time: 10 minutes | Serves 4

4 medium-sized skin-on chicken drumsticks
1½ teaspoons herbs de Provence
Salt and pepper, to taste
1 tablespoon rice vinegar
2 tablespoons olive oil
2 garlic cloves, crushed
12 ounces (340 g) crushed canned tomatoes
1 small-size leek, thinly sliced
2 slices smoked bacon, chopped

1. Sprinkle the chicken drumsticks with herbs de Provence, salt and pepper; then, drizzle them with rice vinegar and olive oil. 2. Cook in the baking pan at 360ºF (182ºC) for 8 to 10 minutes. Pause the air fryer; stir in the remaining ingredients and continue to cook for 15 minutes longer; make sure to check them periodically. Bon appétit!
Per Serving:
calories: 325 | fat: 22g | protein: 22g | carbs: 9g | net carbs: 7g | fiber: 2g

Spicy Chicken with Bacon and Peppers

Prep time: 5 minutes | Cook time: 13 minutes | Serves 6

2 slices bacon, chopped	1 tomato, chopped
1½ pounds (680 g) ground chicken	1 cup water
2 garlic cloves, minced	⅓ cup chicken broth
½ cup green onions, chopped	1 teaspoon paprika
1 green bell pepper, seeded and chopped	1 teaspoon onion powder
1 red bell pepper, seeded and chopped	¼ teaspoon ground allspice
1 serrano pepper, chopped	2 bay leaves
	Sea salt and ground black pepper, to taste

1. Press the Sauté button to heat your Instant Pot. 2. Add the bacon and cook for about 3 minutes until crisp. Reserve the bacon in a bowl. 3. Add the ground chicken to the bacon grease of the pot and brown for 2 to 3 minutes, crumbling it with a spatula. Reserve it in the bowl of bacon. 4. Add the garlic, green onions, and peppers and sauté for 3 minutes until tender. Add the remaining ingredients to the Instant Pot, along with the cooked bacon and chicken. Stir to mix well. 5. Lock the lid. Select the Poultry mode and set the cooking time for 5 minutes at High Pressure. 6. When the timer beeps, perform a natural pressure release for 10 minutes, then release any remaining pressure. Carefully remove the lid. Serve warm.

Per Serving:

calories: 236 | fat: 14g | protein: 25g | carbs: 3g | net carbs: 2g | fiber: 1g

Chicken and Bacon Ranch Casserole

Prep time: 5 minutes | Cook time: 30 minutes | Serves 4

4 slices bacon	1 tablespoon coconut oil
4 (6 ounces / 170 g) boneless, skinless chicken breasts, cut into 1-inch cubes	½ cup chicken broth
	½ cup ranch dressing
	½ cup shredded Cheddar cheese
½ teaspoon salt	2 ounces (57 g) cream cheese
¼ teaspoon pepper	

1. Press the Sauté button to heat your Instant Pot. 2. Add the bacon slices and cook for about 7 minutes until crisp, flipping occasionally. 3. Remove from the pot and place on a paper towel to drain. Set aside. 4. Season the chicken cubes with salt and pepper. 5. Set your Instant Pot to Sauté and melt the coconut oil. 6. Add the chicken cubes and brown for 3 to 4 minutes until golden brown. 7. Stir in the broth and ranch dressing. 8. Secure the lid. Select the Manual mode and set the cooking time for 20 minutes at High Pressure. 9. Once cooking is complete, do a quick pressure release. Carefully open the lid. 10. Stir in the Cheddar and cream cheese. Crumble the cooked bacon and scatter on top.

Serve immediately.

Per Serving:

calories: 467 | fat: 26g | protein: 46g | carbs: 1g | net carbs: 1g | fiber: 0g

Coconut Chicken

Prep time: 10 minutes | Cook time: 25 minutes | Serves 4

2 tablespoons olive oil	1 tablespoon curry powder
4 (4 ounces) chicken breasts, cut into 2-inch chunks	1 teaspoon ground cumin
	1 teaspoon ground coriander
½ cup chopped sweet onion	¼ cup chopped fresh cilantro
1 cup coconut milk	

1. In a small bowl, whisk together the olive oil, rosemary, garlic, and salt. 2. Place the racks in a sealable freezer bag and pour the olive oil mixture into the bag. Massage the meat through the bag so it is coated with the marinade. Press the air out of the bag and seal it. 3. Marinate the lamb racks in the refrigerator for 1 to 2 hours. 4. Preheat the oven to 450°F. 5. Place a large ovenproof skillet over medium-high heat. Take the lamb racks out of the bag and sear them in the skillet on all sides, about 5 minutes in total. 6. Arrange the racks upright in the skillet, with the bones interlaced, and roast them in the oven until they reach your desired doneness, about 20 minutes for medium-rare or until the internal temperature reaches 125°F. 7. Let the lamb rest for 10 minutes and then cut the racks into chops. 8. Serve 4 chops per person.

Per Serving:

calories: 354 | fat: 30g | protein: 21g | carbs: 0g | net carbs: 0g | fiber: 0g

Blackened Cajun Chicken Tenders

Prep time: 10 minutes | Cook time: 17 minutes | Serves 4

2 teaspoons paprika	pepper
1 teaspoon chili powder	2 tablespoons coconut oil
½ teaspoon garlic powder	1 pound (454 g) boneless, skinless chicken tenders
½ teaspoon dried thyme	
¼ teaspoon onion powder	¼ cup full-fat ranch dressing
⅛ teaspoon ground cayenne	

1. In a small bowl, combine all seasonings. 2. Drizzle oil over chicken tenders and then generously coat each tender in the spice mixture. Place tenders into the air fryer basket. 3. Adjust the temperature to 375°F (191ºC) and air fry for 17 minutes. 4. Tenders will be 165ºF (74ºC) internally when fully cooked. Serve with ranch dressing for dipping.

Per Serving:

calories: 287 | fat: 18g | protein: 27g | carbs: 3g | net carbs: 2g | fiber: 1g

Italian Chicken with Sauce

Prep time: 15 minutes | Cook time: 20 minutes | Serves 4

2 large skinless chicken breasts (about 1¼ pounds / 567 g)	2 teaspoons Italian seasoning
	1 egg, lightly beaten
Salt and freshly ground black pepper	1 tablespoon olive oil
	1 cup no-sugar-added marinara sauce
½ cup almond meal	4 slices Mozzarella cheese or
½ cup grated Parmesan cheese	½ cup shredded Mozzarella

1. Preheat the air fryer to 360ºF (182ºC). 2. Slice the chicken breasts in half horizontally to create 4 thinner chicken breasts. Working with one piece at a time, place the chicken between two pieces of parchment paper and pound with a meat mallet or rolling pin to flatten to an even thickness. Season both sides with salt and freshly ground black pepper. 3. In a large shallow bowl, combine the almond meal, Parmesan, and Italian seasoning; stir until thoroughly combined. Place the egg in another large shallow bowl. 4. Dip the chicken in the egg, followed by the almond meal mixture, pressing the mixture firmly into the chicken to create an even coating. 5. Working in batches if necessary, arrange the chicken breasts in a single layer in the air fryer basket and coat both sides lightly with olive oil. Pausing halfway through the cooking time to flip the chicken, air fry for 15 minutes, or until a thermometer inserted into the thickest part registers 165ºF (74ºC). 6. Spoon the marinara sauce over each piece of chicken and top with the Mozzarella cheese. Air fry for an additional 3 to 5 minutes until the cheese is melted.

Per Serving:

calories: 462 | fat: 27g | protein: 46g | carbs: 9g | net carbs: 7g | fiber: 2g

Caprese Chicken Skillet

Prep time: 10 minutes | Cook time: 15 minutes | Serves 4

1 tablespoon extra-virgin olive oil
1 pound boneless, skinless chicken thighs
1½ teaspoons pink Himalayan salt, divided
½ teaspoon ground black pepper
1 teaspoon minced garlic
12 cherry tomatoes, halved (about 3 ounces)
¼ teaspoon red pepper flakes
1 medium-sized zucchini, spiral-sliced into noodles
3 or 4 large fresh basil leaves, minced
3 ounces mini mozzarella balls, halved

1. Heat the olive oil in a large skillet over medium-high heat. 2. Chop the chicken into 1-inch pieces and season with 1 teaspoon of the salt and the black pepper. 3. Put the chicken in the hot skillet and cook through, 5 to 7 minutes. (When fully cooked, the chicken will no longer be pink in the middle.) Remove from the skillet and set aside. 4. Turn the heat down to low and use a spatula to scrape up the drippings from the bottom of the skillet. Add the garlic and cook for 20 seconds. Add the tomatoes, remaining ½ teaspoon of salt, and red pepper flakes. Stir to combine and cover with a lid. Cook for 5 to 7 minutes, until the tomatoes have burst and softened. 5. Turn the heat back up to high, add the zucchini noodles and basil, and cook for 1 minute, until the noodles are slightly tender but not mushy. Remove from the heat, add the chicken and mozzarella, and toss to combine. Serve immediately.

Per Serving:

calories: 226 | fat: 12g | protein: 26g | carbs: 4g | net carbs: 3g | fiber: 1g

Chicken Bacon Ranch Casserole

Prep time: 15 minutes | Cook time: 35 minutes | Serves 4

4 bacon slices, chopped	cream
¼ white onion, diced	2 eggs
1 garlic clove, minced	1 cup shredded Cheddar
1 pound (454 g) shredded cooked chicken (boneless skinless breasts or thighs)	cheese, divided
	Salt, to taste
3 tablespoons ranch seasoning	Freshly ground black pepper, to taste
½ cup heavy (whipping)	

1. Preheat the oven to 350ºF (180ºC). 2. In a medium nonstick skillet over medium heat, cook the bacon for about 5 minutes. 3. Add the onion and garlic. Cook for 5 to 7 minutes until the onion is softened and translucent. Remove the skillet from the heat and transfer the bacon-onion mixture to a large bowl, leaving behind most of the bacon fat in the skillet. 4. To the bowl, add the chicken and ranch seasoning. Stir well to combine, making sure everything is coated in the spices. Transfer to a 9-by-13-inch baking dish. 5. In the same bowl, whisk the cream and eggs. Add ½ cup of Cheddar, season with salt and pepper, and whisk to combine. Pour the cheese sauce over the chicken mixture and tap the baking dish on the counter to make sure the cheese sauce covers everything and makes it all the way to the bottom and sides of the dish. Top with the remaining ½ cup of Cheddar. 6. Cover the dish with aluminum foil (or a lid if the baking dish has one) and bake for about 20 minutes or until the cheese melts and the casserole is heated all the way through. Serve immediately. Refrigerate leftovers in an airtight container for up to 1 week. Reheat individual servings for 1 to 2 minutes in the microwave or all at once in a 350ºF (180ºC) oven for 15 to 20 minutes.

Per Serving:

calories: 469 | fat: 29g | protein: 50g | carbs: 2g | net carbs: 2g | fiber: 0g

Cheesy Chicken Bake with Zucchini

Prep time: 20 minutes | Cook time: 40 minutes | Serves 6

2 pounds (907 g) chicken breasts, cubed	½ teaspoon salt
1 tablespoon butter	½ teaspoon black pepper
1 cup green bell peppers, sliced	8 oz cream cheese, softened
1 cup yellow onions, sliced	½ cup mayonnaise
1 zucchini, cubed	2 tablespoons Worcestershire sauce (sugar-free)
2 garlic cloves, divided	2 cups cheddar cheese, shredded
2 teaspoons Italian seasoning	

1. Set oven to 370°F and grease and line a baking dish. 2. Set a pan over medium heat. Place in the butter and let melt, then add in the chicken. Cook until lightly browned, about 5 minutes. Place in onions, zucchini, black pepper, garlic, bell peppers, salt, and 1 teaspoon of Italian seasoning. Cook until tender and set aside. 3. In a bowl, mix cream cheese, garlic, remaining seasoning, mayonnaise, and Worcestershire sauce. Stir in meat and sauteed vegetables. Place the mixture into the prepared baking dish, sprinkle with the shredded cheddar cheese and insert into the oven. Cook until browned for 30 minutes.

Per Serving:

calories: 465 | fat: 37g | protein: 25g | carbs: 8g | net carbs: 4g | fiber: 4g

Turkey Meatloaf Florentine Muffins

Prep time: 10 minutes | Cook time: 25 minutes | Serves 6

½ pound (227 g) frozen spinach, thawed

2 pounds (907 g) ground turkey

½ cup (2 ounces / 57 g) blanched almond flour

2 large eggs

4 cloves garlic, minced

2 teaspoons sea salt

½ teaspoon black pepper

2¼ cups (9 ounces / 255 g) shredded Mozzarella cheese, divided into 1½ cups (6 ounces / 170 g) and ¾ cup (3 ounces / 85 g)

⅓ cup no-sugar-added marinara sauce

1. Preheat the oven to 375°F (190°C). Lightly grease 12 cups of a muffin tin and place on top of a sheet pan for easier cleanup. 2. Drain the spinach and squeeze it tightly in a kitchen towel to remove as much water as possible. 3. In a large bowl, mix together the spinach, turkey, almond flour, eggs, garlic, sea salt, and black pepper. Mix until just combined, but do not overwork the meat. 4. Fill each muffin cup with 2 tablespoons of the turkey mixture. Create a well with the back of a measuring spoon or your hands. Pack each well with 2 tablespoons Mozzarella (1½ cups or 6 ounces / 170 g total). Top with 2 more tablespoons turkey mixture, lightly pressing down along the sides to seal the filling inside. 5. Spread 1 teaspoon marinara sauce over each meatloaf muffin. Sprinkle each with another 1 tablespoon Mozzarella (¾ cup or 3 ounces / 85 g total). 6. Bake for 20 to 25 minutes, until the internal temperature reaches at least 160°F (71°C). Let rest for 5 minutes before serving (temperature will rise another 5 degrees while resting).

Per Serving:

calories: 380 | fat: 16g | protein: 52g | carbs: 6g | net carbs: 4g | fiber: 2g

Slow Cooker Chicken Thighs with Sun-Dried Tomatoes

Prep time: 10 minutes | Cook time: 10 minutes | Serves 4

¼ cup olive oil, divided	½ cup chicken stock
4 (4 ounces) boneless chicken thighs	4 ounces julienned oil-packed sun-dried tomatoes
Sea salt, for seasoning	2 tablespoons minced garlic
Freshly ground black pepper, for seasoning	2 tablespoons dried oregano
1 (28 ounces) can sodium-free diced tomatoes	Pinch red pepper flakes
	2 tablespoons chopped fresh parsley

1. Grease the slow cooker. Coat the bowl of the slow cooker with 1 tablespoon of the olive oil. 2. Brown the chicken. Pat the chicken thighs dry with paper towels and season them lightly with salt and pepper. In a large skillet over medium-high heat, warm the remaining 3 tablespoons of olive oil. Add the chicken thighs and brown them, turning them once, about 10 minutes in total. 3. Cook in the slow cooker. Put the tomatoes, chicken stock, sun-dried tomatoes, garlic, oregano, and red pepper flakes into the slow cooker and stir to combine the ingredients. Add the chicken, making sure it is covered by the sauce, place the lid on the slow cooker, and cook it on high heat for 4 to 6 hours or on low heat for 6 to 8 hours. 4. Serve. Divide the chicken thighs and sauce between four bowls and top with the parsley.

Per Serving:

calories: 468 | fat: 36g | protein: 24g | carbs: 12g | net carbs: 6g | fiber: 6g

Herb and Lemon Whole Chicken

Prep time: 5 minutes | Cook time: 30 to 32 minutes | Serves 4

3 teaspoons garlic powder

3 teaspoons salt

2 teaspoons dried parsley

2 teaspoons dried rosemary

1 teaspoon pepper

1 (4 pounds / 1.8 kg) whole chicken

2 tablespoons coconut oil

1 cup chicken broth

1 lemon, zested and quartered

1. Combine the garlic powder, salt, parsley, rosemary, and pepper in a small bowl. Rub this herb mix over the whole chicken. 2. Set your Instant Pot to Sauté and heat the coconut oil. 3. Add the chicken and brown for 5 to 7 minutes. Using tongs, transfer the chicken to a plate. 4. Pour the broth into the Instant Pot and scrape the bottom with a rubber spatula or wooden spoon until no seasoning is stuck to pot, then insert the trivet. 5. Scatter the lemon zest over chicken. Put the lemon quarters inside the chicken. Place the chicken on the trivet. 6. Secure the lid. Select the Meat/Stew mode and set the cooking time for 25 minutes at High Pressure. 7. Once cooking is complete, do a natural pressure release for 10 minutes, then release any remaining pressure. Carefully open the lid. 8. Shred the chicken and serve warm.

Per Serving:

calories: 860 | fat: 63g | protein: 55g | carbs: 3g | net carbs: 2g | fiber: 1g

Lemon Threaded Chicken Skewers

Prep time: 10 minutes | Cook time: 12 minutes | Serves 4

3 chicken breasts, cut into cubes

2 tablespoons olive oil, divided

2/3 jar preserved lemon, flesh removed, drained

2 cloves garlic, minced

½ cup lemon juice

Salt and black pepper to taste

1 teaspoon rosemary leaves to garnish

2 to 4 lemon wedges to garnish

1. First, thread the chicken onto skewers and set aside. 2. In a wide bowl, mix half of the oil, garlic, salt, pepper, and lemon juice, and add the chicken skewers, and lemon rind. Cover the bowl and let the chicken marinate for at least 2 hours in the refrigerator. 3. When the marinating time is almost over, preheat a grill to 350ºF, and remove the chicken onto the grill. Cook for 6 minutes on each side. 4. Remove and serve warm garnished with rosemary leaves and lemons wedges.

Per Serving:

calories: 277 | fat: 11g | protein: 32g | carbs: 9g | net carbs: 7g | fiber: 2g

Chapter 9

Beef, Pork, and Lamb

Peppercorn-Crusted Beef Tenderloin

Prep time: 10 minutes | Cook time: 25 minutes | Serves 6

2 tablespoons salted butter, melted

2 teaspoons minced roasted garlic

3 tablespoons ground 4-peppercorn blend

1 (2 pounds / 907 g) beef tenderloin, trimmed of visible fat

1. In a small bowl, mix the butter and roasted garlic. Brush it over the beef tenderloin. 2. Place the ground peppercorns onto a plate and roll the tenderloin through them, creating a crust. Place tenderloin into the air fryer basket. 3. Adjust the temperature to 400°F (204°C) and roast for 25 minutes. 4. Turn the tenderloin halfway through the cooking time. 5. Allow meat to rest 10 minutes before slicing.

Per Serving:

calories: 352 | fat: 19g | protein: 41g | carbs: 2g | net carbs: 2g | fiber: 0g

Rack of Lamb in Red Bell Pepper Butter Sauce

Prep time: 10 minutes | Cook time: 30 minutes | Serves 4

1 pound (454 g) rack of lamb	2 tablespoons olive oil
Salt to cure	1large red bell pepper, seeded, diced
3 cloves garlic, minced	
⅓ cup olive oil	2 cloves garlic, minced
⅓ cup white wine	1 cup chicken broth
6 sprigs fresh rosemary	2 ounces butter
Sauce	Salt and white pepper to taste

1. Fill a large bowl with water and soak in the lamb for 30 minutes. Drain the meat after and season with salt. Let the lamb sit on a rack to drain completely and then rinse it afterward. Put in a bowl. 2. Mix the olive oil with wine and garlic, and brush the mixture all over the lamb. Drop the rosemary sprigs on it, cover the bowl with plastic wrap, and place in the refrigerator to marinate the meat. 3. The next day, preheat the grill to 450°F and cook the lamb for 6 minutes on both sides. Remove after and let rest for 4 minutes. 4. Heat the olive oil in a frying pan and sauté the garlic and bell pepper for 5 minutes. Pour in the chicken broth and continue cooking the ingredients until the liquid reduces by half, about 10 minutes. Add the butter, salt, and white pepper. Stir to melt the butter and turn the heat off. 5. Use the stick blender to puree the ingredients until very smooth and strain the sauce through a fine mesh into a bowl. Slice the lamb, serve with the sauce, and your favorite red wine.

Per Serving:

calories: 432 | fat: 28g | protein: 42g | carbs: 3g | net carbs: 3g | fiber: 0g

Beef and Butternut Squash Stew

Prep time: 10 minutes | Cook time: 40 minutes | Serves 4

3 teaspoons olive oil	1 tablespoon Worcestershire sauce
1 pound ground beef	
1 cup beef stock	2 bay leaves
14 ounces canned tomatoes with juice	Salt and black pepper, to taste
	1 onion, chopped
1 tablespoon stevia	1 teaspoon dried sage
1 pound butternut squash, chopped	1 tablespoon garlic, minced

1. Set a pan over medium heat and heat olive oil, stir in the onion, garlic, and beef, and cook for 10 minutes. Add in butternut squash, Worcestershire sauce, bay leaves, stevia, beef stock, canned tomatoes, and sage, and bring to a boil. Reduce heat, and simmer for 30 minutes. 2. Remove and discard the bay leaves and adjust the seasonings. Split into bowls and enjoy.

Per Serving:

calories: 422 | fat: 21g | protein: 29g | carbs: 30g | net carbs: 23g | fiber: 7g

Breakfast Sausage and Egg Casserole

Prep time: 10 minutes | Cook time: 1 hour 25 minutes | Serves 6

3 tablespoons olive oil, divided	Freshly ground black pepper, to taste
¼ onion, chopped	10 eggs
1 garlic clove, minced	1 cup shredded Cheddar cheese
10 ounces (283 g) breakfast sausage	
	2 tablespoons sliced scallion, green parts only
Salt, to taste	

1. Preheat the oven to 350°F (180°C). 2. In a large skillet over medium heat, heat 1½ tablespoons of olive oil. 3. Add the onion and garlic. Sauté for 5 to 7 minutes until the onion is softened and translucent. 4. Add the remaining 1½ tablespoons of olive oil to the skillet along with the sausage. Cook for 5 to 7 minutes or until no pink remains. Season with salt and pepper. Transfer the sausage mixture to a 7-by-11-inch baking dish and arrange in an even layer. 5. In a large bowl, whisk the eggs well, season with salt and pepper, and pour over the sausage layer in the baking dish. Sprinkle with the Cheddar. 6. Bake for 50 minutes to 1 hour, 10 minutes or until the eggs are no longer runny. Serve hot, garnished with a sprinkle of sliced scallion. Refrigerate leftovers in an airtight container for up to 1 week. Reheat in the microwave for about 1 minute or in a 350°F (180°C) oven for 15 to 20 minutes.

Per Serving:

calories: 406 | fat: 34g | protein: 23g | carbs: 2g | net carbs: 2g | fiber: 0g

Beef with Grilled Vegetables

Prep time: 15 minutes | Cook time: 15 minutes | Serves 4

4 sirloin steaks	1 cup snow peas
Salt and black pepper to taste	1 red bell peppers, seeded, cut
4 tablespoons olive oil	into strips
3 tablespoons balsamic vinegar	1 orange bell peppers, seeded,
Vegetables	cut into strips
½ lb asparagus, trimmed	1 medium red onion,
1 cup green beans	quartered

1Set the grill pan over high heat. 2Grab 2 separate bowls; put the beef in one and the vegetables in another. Mix salt, pepper, olive oil, and balsamic vinegar in a small bowl, and pour half of the mixture over the beef and the other half over the vegetables. Coat the ingredients in both bowls with the sauce and cook the beef first. 3Place the steaks in the grill pan and sear both sides for 2 minutes each, then continue cooking for 6 minutes on each side. When done, remove the beef onto a plate; set aside. 4Pour the vegetables and marinade in the pan; and cook for 5 minutes, turning once. Share the vegetables into plates. Top with each piece of beef, the sauce from the pan, and serve with a rutabaga mash.

Per Serving:

calories: 554 | fat: 39g | protein: 38g | carbs: 15g | net carbs: 10g | fiber: 5g

Taco Cheese Cups

Prep time: 10 minutes | Cook time: 20 minutes | Serves 2

For The Cheese Cups	
2 cups shredded cheese (I use	½ pound ground beef
Mexican blend)	½ (1¼-ounce) package taco
For The Ground Beef	seasoning
1 tablespoon ghee	¼ cup water
For The Taco Cups	
½ avocado, diced	Freshly ground black pepper
Pink Himalayan salt	2 tablespoons sour cream

Make The Cheese Cups: 1. Preheat the oven to 350°F. Line a baking sheet with parchment paper or a silicone baking mat. 2. Place ½-cup mounds of the cheese on the prepared pan. Bake for about 7 minutes, or until the edges are brown and the middle has melted. You want these slightly larger than a typical tortilla chip. 3. Put the pan on a cooling rack for 2 minutes while the cheese chips cool. The chips will be floppy when they first come out of the oven, but they will begin to crisp as they cool. 4. Before they are fully crisp, move the cheese chips to a muffin tin. Form the cheese chips around the shape of the muffin cups to create small bowls. (The chips will fully harden in the muffin tin, which will make them really easy to fill.) Make The Ground Beef: 1. In a medium skillet over medium-high heat, heat the ghee. 2. When the ghee is hot, add the ground beef and sauté for about 8 minutes, until browned. 3. Drain the excess grease. Stir in the taco seasoning and water, and bring to a boil. Turn the heat to medium-low and simmer for 5 minutes. Make The Taco Cups: 1. Using a slotted spoon, spoon the ground beef into the taco cups. 2. Season the diced avocado with pink Himalayan salt and pepper, and divide it among the taco cups. 3. Add a dollop of sour cream to each taco cup and serve.

Per Serving:

calories: 894 | fat: 68g | protein: 57g | carbs: 12g | net carbs: 9g | fiber: 3g

Rosemary Mint Marinated Lamb Chops

Prep time: 5 minutes | Cook time: 10 minutes | Serves 4

3 tablespoons extra-virgin olive oil, plus more for greasing
½ teaspoon sea salt
1 tablespoon fresh rosemary leaves (from about 4 sprigs), plus more sprigs for garnish
1 tablespoon chopped mint leaves
½ teaspoon garlic salt
4 (4 ounces / 113 g) lamb chops (about ½-inch thick)
Freshly ground black pepper, to taste

1. In a blender, combine the olive oil, salt, rosemary, mint, and garlic salt and blend until smooth. Rub the mixture all over the lamb chops and let them marinate in an airtight container in the refrigerator for 30 minutes or up to 4 hours. 2. Oil a large skillet over medium-high heat. Add the lamb chops and cook for about 3 minutes on each side (for medium-rare), or to desired doneness. 3. Plate the chops and let them rest for 3 minutes. Pour the leftover extra juices over the lamb chops and garnish with rosemary sprigs and pepper.

Per Serving:

1 chop: calories: 254 | fat: 18g | protein: 23g | carbs: 0g | net carbs: 0g | fiber: 0g

Baked Crustless Pizza

Prep time: 5 minutes | Cook time: 20 minutes | Serves 2

8 ounces (227 g) chopped	10 large black olives, sliced
Italian sausage	½ cup grated Mozzarella
15 slices pepperoni	cheese

1. Preheat the oven to 350°F (180°C). 2. In a skillet over medium heat, cook the sausage. Drain the grease and spread the sausage on the bottom of an 8-by-8-inch baking dish or pie pan. 3. Layer the pepperoni slices, black olives, and cheese over the sausage. 4. Bake, covered, for 10 to 15 minutes or until the cheese is melted and hot throughout.

Per Serving:

½ skillet: calories: 480 | fat: 40g | protein: 27g | carbs: 3g | net carbs: 2g | fiber: 1g

Shredded Mojo Pork with Avocado Salad

Prep time: 10 minutes | Cook time: 45 minutes | Serves 4

Shredded Pork:

2 pounds (910 g) bone-in pork shoulder	4 cloves garlic, minced
1 cup (240 ml) vegetable broth	2 teaspoons finely ground sea salt
¼ cup (60 ml) lime juice	2 bay leaves
2 teaspoons ground cumin	¼ teaspoon ground black pepper
2 teaspoons dried oregano leaves	¼ teaspoon red pepper flakes

Avocado Salad:

¼ cup (60 ml) avocado oil or olive oil	thinly sliced
2 tablespoons lime juice	2 medium Hass avocados, peeled and pitted (about 8 oz/220 g of flesh)
1½ teaspoons chili powder	4 green onions, sliced
¼ teaspoon finely ground sea salt	½ cup (112 g) hulled pumpkin seeds
2 bunches (400 g) radishes,	

1. Place all the ingredients for the shredded pork in a pressure cooker or slow cooker. If using a pressure cooker, seal the lid and cook on high pressure for 45 minutes. When complete, allow the pressure to release naturally before removing the lid. If using a slow cooker, cook on high for 4 hours or low for 6 hours. 2. When the meat is done, drain it almost completely, leaving ¼ cup (60 ml) of cooking liquid in the cooker. Shred the meat with two forks. 3. Prepare the salad: Place the oil, lime juice, chili powder, and salt in a medium-sized salad bowl. Whisk to combine, then add the remaining ingredients and toss to coat. 4. Divide the salad evenly among 4 plates or bowls, then top with the shredded pork.

Per Serving:

calories: 938 | fat: 70g | protein: 64g | carbs: 14g | net carbs: 7g | fiber: 7g

The Classic Juicy Lucy

Prep time: 10 minutes | Cook time: 10 minutes | Serves 4

1 pound (454 g) ground beef	Salt, to taste
8 ounces (227 g) Cheddar cheese, shredded or cubed	Freshly ground black pepper, to taste

1. Divide the ground beef into 4 equal portions. (This makes 4 quarter-pound burgers—if you want 2 larger ones, just divide the meat in half.) Form each portion into a patty, pressing down on the center to flatten it out a bit. 2. Add ¼ of the Cheddar to the center of each burger and roll the sides of the patty up to cover the cheese, like a big meatball. Smooth the burger out in your hands and gently press down with your palms to re-form it into a patty. Season both sides generously with salt and pepper. 3. In a large skillet, cast-iron pan, or on the grill over medium-high heat, cook the burgers for 7 to 10 minutes per side, depending on how you like them done. This timing will give you medium burgers; cook for a little less time if you prefer yours medium-rare. Remove the burgers from the heat and serve immediately with your favorite keto toppings (lettuce, pickles, sliced onion).

Per Serving:

calories: 602 | fat: 53g | protein: 30g | carbs: 1g | net carbs: 1g | fiber: 0g

Italian Sausage and Cheese Meatballs

Prep time: 10 minutes | Cook time: 20 minutes | Serves 4

½ pound (227 g) bulk Italian sausage	Cheddar cheese
½ pound (227 g) 85% lean ground beef	½ teaspoon onion powder
½ cup shredded sharp	½ teaspoon garlic powder
	½ teaspoon black pepper

1. In a large bowl, gently mix the sausage, ground beef, cheese, onion powder, garlic powder, and pepper until well combined. 2. Form the mixture into 16 meatballs. Place the meatballs in a single layer in the air fryer basket. Set the air fryer to 350°F (177°C) for 20 minutes, turning the meatballs halfway through the cooking time. Use a meat thermometer to ensure the meatballs have reached an internal temperature of 160°F / 71°C (medium).

Per Serving:

calories: 379 | fat: 31g | protein: 22g | carbs: 1g | net carbs: 1g | fiber: 0g

Pork Burgers with Sriracha Mayo

Prep time: 10 minutes | Cook time: 10 minutes | Serves 2

12 ounces ground pork	Pink Himalayan salt
2 scallions, white and green parts, thinly sliced	Freshly ground black pepper
1 tablespoon toasted sesame oil	1 tablespoon ghee
	1 tablespoon Sriracha sauce
	2 tablespoons mayonnaise

1. In a large bowl, mix to combine the ground pork with the scallions and sesame oil, and season with pink Himalayan salt and pepper. Form the pork mixture into 2 patties. Create an imprint with your thumb in the middle of each burger so the pork will heat evenly. 2. In a large skillet over medium-high heat, heat the ghee. When the ghee has melted and is very hot, add the burger patties and cook for 4 minutes on each side. 3. Meanwhile, in a small bowl, mix the Sriracha sauce and mayonnaise. 4. Transfer the burgers to a plate and let rest for at least 5 minutes. 5. Top the burgers with the Sriracha mayonnaise and serve.

Per Serving:

calories: 575 | fat: 49g | protein: 31g | carbs: 2g | net carbs: 1g | fiber: 1g

Zucchini Rolls

Prep time: 10 minutes | Cook time: 0 minutes | Serves 4

Rolls:

1 medium zucchini (about 7 ounces/200 g)	strips
	5 medium radishes, sliced thin
1 cup (120 g) cooked beef	

Dipping Sauce:

¼ cup (60 ml) extra-virgin olive oil or refined avocado oil	2 tablespoons hot sauce
	2 teaspoons fresh lime juice

1. Place the zucchini on a cutting board and, using a vegetable peeler, peel long strips from the zucchini until it is next to impossible to create a full, long strip. 2. Place a zucchini strip on a cutting board, with a short end facing you. Place a couple of pieces of beef and 3 or 4 radish slices at the short end closest to you. Roll it up, then stab with a toothpick to secure. Repeat with the remaining zucchini strips, placing the completed rolls on a serving plate. 3. In a small serving dish, whisk together the dipping sauce ingredients. Serve the dipping sauce alongside the rolls.

Per Serving:

calories: 370 | fat: 33g | protein: 14g | carbs: 4g | net carbs: 3g | fiber: 1g

Braised Short Ribs

Prep time: 15 minutes | Cook time: 2 hours 30 minutes | Serves 2

2 tablespoons butter	1 garlic clove
4 bone-in beef chuck short ribs (about 2 pounds / 907 g)	2 sprigs fresh thyme
	1 sprig fresh rosemary
Pink Himalayan sea salt	1½ cups beef broth
Freshly ground black pepper	1½ cups red wine

1. Preheat the oven to 350ºF (180ºC). 2. In a large sauté pan or skillet, melt the butter over medium heat. 3. Season the ribs on all sides with salt and pepper. 4. Add the ribs to the skillet, sear on both sides for 4 to 6 minutes, until uniformly browned. 5. Transfer the ribs to an 8-inch baking pan; leave the drippings in the skillet. 6. Add the garlic, thyme, and rosemary to the skillet and stir for 2 to 3 minutes, until the garlic is browned. 7. Add the broth and wine, and stir to combine. Simmer over low heat until the liquid is reduced by about one-fourth. 8. Pour the sauce over the short ribs and cover the baking pan with aluminum foil. Bake for 2½ hours, until the ribs are very tender. 9. Using a slotted spoon or a fork, transfer the ribs to a serving dish. Pour the cooking liquid through a mesh strainer into a medium bowl. Discard the solids. Drizzle a small amount of the strained liquid over the ribs before serving.

Per Serving:

calories: 696 | fat: 55g | protein: 39g | carbs: 2g | net carbs: 2g | fiber: 0g

Stuffed Cabbage Rolls

Prep time: 10 minutes | Cook time: 1 hour 30 minutes | Serves 8

1 large head cabbage, separated into 16 leaves	Freshly ground black pepper, to taste
1 pound (454 g) ground beef	1 cup chicken broth
1 pound (454 g) sausage	½ cup canned no-sugar-added tomato sauce, warmed
1 small onion, chopped	
2 garlic cloves, minced	Grated Parmesan cheese, for topping
Salt, to taste	

1. Bring a large saucepan of water to a boil over high heat. Add the cabbage leaves and boil for 2 to 3 minutes or until soft. Remove from the water and set aside to drain. Discard the water. 2. In a large bowl, mix together the beef, sausage, onion, and garlic. Season well with salt and pepper. Spoon the meat mixture into each leaf and fold the sides over, rolling each leaf up to hold the meat mixture. Secure with a toothpick and transfer to the pan. 3. Add the chicken broth. Cover the pan and simmer over low heat for about 1 hour, 30 minutes or until the meat is cooked through. Remove the rolls from the broth and top with the warmed tomato sauce and a sprinkle of Parmesan. Refrigerate leftovers in an airtight container for up to 3 days.

Per Serving:

2 rolls: calories: 331 | fat: 23g | protein: 22g | carbs: 11g | net carbs: 7g | fiber: 4g

Bo Ssäm

Prep time: 10 minutes | Cook time: 8 minutes | Serves 6

1 tablespoon vegetable oil	1 tablespoon minced garlic
1 pound (454 g) ground pork	1 tablespoon coconut aminos
2 tablespoons gochujang	1 teaspoon hot sesame oil
1 tablespoon Doubanjiang	1 teaspoon salt
½ teaspoon ground Sichuan peppercorns	¼ cup water
	1 bunch bok choy, chopped (about 4 to 6 cups)
1 tablespoon minced fresh ginger	

1. Preheat the Instant Pot on Sauté mode. Add the oil and heat until it is shimmering. 2. Add the ground pork, breaking up all lumps, and cook for 4 minutes or until the pork is no longer pink. 3. Add the gochujang, doubanjiang, peppercorns, ginger, garlic, coconut aminos, sesame oil, and salt. Stir to combine. 4. Add the water and bok choy. 5. Lock the lid. Select Manual mode. Set cooking time for 4 minutes on High Pressure. 6. When cooking is complete, quick-release the pressure. Unlock the lid. 7. Serve immediately.

Per Serving:

calories: 239 | fat: 19g | protein: 14g | carbs: 2g | net carbs: 1g | fiber: 1g

Bacon and Cheese Stuffed Pork Chops

Prep time: 10 minutes | Cook time: 12 minutes | Serves 4

½ ounce (14 g) plain pork rinds, finely crushed
½ cup shredded sharp Cheddar cheese
4 slices cooked sugar-free bacon, crumbled

4 (4 ounces / 113 g) boneless pork chops
½ teaspoon salt
¼ teaspoon ground black pepper

1. In a small bowl, mix pork rinds, Cheddar, and bacon. 2. Make a 3-inch slit in the side of each pork chop and stuff with ¼ pork rind mixture. Sprinkle each side of pork chops with salt and pepper. 3. Place pork chops into ungreased air fryer basket, stuffed side up. Adjust the temperature to 400ºF (204ºC) and air fry for 12 minutes. Pork chops will be browned and have an internal temperature of at least 145ºF (63ºC) when done. Serve warm.

Per Serving:

calories: 357 | fat: 17g | protein: 39g | carbs: 1g | net carbs: 1g | fiber: 0g

Beef Barbacoa

Prep time: 20 minutes | Cook time: 3 hours | Serves 4

1 cup beef broth
½ cup tomato purée
¼ cup granulated erythritol
¼ cup chili powder
2 tablespoons freshly squeezed lime juice
2 dried chipotle chiles, crushed
2 tablespoons apple cider vinegar
4 garlic cloves, minced
1 teaspoon dried oregano
1 teaspoon ground cumin

½ teaspoon pink Himalayan sea salt
¼ teaspoon freshly ground black pepper
⅛ teaspoon ground cinnamon
⅛ teaspoon ground allspice
⅛ teaspoon ground cloves
1½ pounds (680 g) boneless chuck roast
2 bay leaves
4 low-carb tortillas
Taco toppings of choice

1. In a large bowl, combine the broth, tomato purée, erythritol, chili powder, lime juice, chipotles, vinegar, garlic, oregano, cumin, salt, pepper, cinnamon, allspice, and cloves. 2. If you wish to have a super-smooth sauce and don't mind the added dishes, transfer the mixture to a food processor and run on high speed until the sauce is smooth. 3. Place the chuck roast into a slow cooker. Add the bay leaves and pour in the sauce. 4. Cover and cook on high power for 3 to 4 hours. 5. Remove the inner pot from the slow cooker and discard the bay leaves. Using 2 forks, shred the beef. 6. Pile the barbecued beef into the tortillas, and serve along with your favorite taco toppings.

Per Serving:

calories: 528 | fat: 34g | protein: 40g | carbs: 30g | net carbs: 11g | fiber: 19g

Pork Milanese

Prep time: 10 minutes | Cook time: 12 minutes | Serves 4

4 (1-inch) boneless pork chops
Fine sea salt and ground black pepper, to taste
2 large eggs

¾ cup powdered Parmesan cheese
Chopped fresh parsley, for garnish
Lemon slices, for serving

1. Spray the air fryer basket with avocado oil. Preheat the air fryer to 400ºF (204ºC). 2. Place the pork chops between 2 sheets of plastic wrap and pound them with the flat side of a meat tenderizer until they're ¼ inch thick. Lightly season both sides of the chops with salt and pepper. 3. Lightly beat the eggs in a shallow bowl. Divide the Parmesan cheese evenly between 2 bowls and set the bowls in this order: Parmesan, eggs, Parmesan. Dredge a chop in the first bowl of Parmesan, then dip it in the eggs, and then dredge it again in the second bowl of Parmesan, making sure both sides and all edges are well coated. Repeat with the remaining chops. 4. Place the chops in the air fryer basket and air fry for 12 minutes, or until the internal temperature reaches 145ºF (63ºC), flipping halfway through. 5. Garnish with fresh parsley and serve immediately with lemon slices. Store leftovers in an airtight container in the refrigerator for up to 3 days. Reheat in a preheated 390ºF (199ºC) air fryer for 5 minutes, or until warmed through.

Per Serving:

calories: 343 | fat: 20g | protein: 36g | carbs: 4g | net carbs: 4g | fiber: 0g

Garlic Balsamic London Broil

Prep time: 30 minutes | Cook time: 8 to 10 minutes | Serves 8

2 pounds (907 g) London broil
3 large garlic cloves, minced
3 tablespoons balsamic vinegar
3 tablespoons whole-grain mustard

2 tablespoons olive oil
Sea salt and ground black pepper, to taste
½ teaspoon dried hot red pepper flakes

1. Score both sides of the cleaned London broil. 2. Thoroughly combine the remaining ingredients; massage this mixture into the meat to coat it on all sides. Let it marinate for at least 3 hours. 3. Set the air fryer to 400ºF (204ºC); Then cook the London broil for 15 minutes. Flip it over and cook another 10 to 12 minutes. Bon appétit!

Per Serving:

calories: 285 | fat: 13g | protein: 37g | carbs: 2g | net carbs: 2g | fiber: 0g

Low Carb Pork Tenderloin

Prep time: 15 minutes | Cook time: 30 minutes | Serves 2

9 ounces (255 g) pork tenderloin	½ teaspoon white pepper
1 teaspoon erythritol	1 garlic clove, minced
½ teaspoon dried dill	3 tablespoons butter
	¼ cup water

1. Rub the pork tenderloin with erythritol, dried dill, white pepper, and minced garlic. 2. Then melt the butter in the instant pot on Sauté mode. 3. Add pork tenderloin and cook it for 8 minutes from each side (use Sauté mode). 4. Then add water and close the lid. 5. Cook the meat on Sauté mode for 10 minutes. 6. Cool the cooked tenderloin for 10 to 15 minutes and slice.

Per Serving:

calories: 339 | fat: 22g | protein: 34g | carbs: 4g | net carbs: 4g | fiber: 0g

Greek Stuffed Tenderloin

Prep time: 10 minutes | Cook time: 10 minutes | Serves 4

1½ pounds (680 g) venison or beef tenderloin, pounded to ¼ inch thick	¼ cup finely chopped onions
	2 cloves garlic, minced
3 teaspoons fine sea salt	For Garnish/Serving (Optional):
1 teaspoon ground black pepper	Prepared yellow mustard
2 ounces (57 g) creamy goat cheese	Halved cherry tomatoes
	Extra-virgin olive oil
½ cup crumbled feta cheese (about 2 ounces / 57 g)	Sprigs of fresh rosemary
	Lavender flowers

1. Spray the air fryer basket with avocado oil. Preheat the air fryer to 400ºF (204ºC). 2. Season the tenderloin on all sides with the salt and pepper. 3. In a medium-sized mixing bowl, combine the goat cheese, feta, onions, and garlic. Place the mixture in the center of the tenderloin. Starting at the end closest to you, tightly roll the tenderloin like a jelly roll. Tie the rolled tenderloin tightly with kitchen twine. 4. Place the meat in the air fryer basket and air fry for 5 minutes. Flip the meat over and cook for another 5 minutes, or until the internal temperature reaches 135ºF (57ºC) for medium-rare. 5. To serve, smear a line of prepared yellow mustard on a platter, then place the meat next to it and add halved cherry tomatoes on the side, if desired. Drizzle with olive oil and garnish with rosemary sprigs and lavender flowers, if desired. 6. Best served fresh. Store leftovers in an airtight container in the fridge for 3 days. Reheat in a preheated 350ºF (177ºC) air fryer for 4 minutes, or until heated through.

Per Serving:

calories: 433 | fat: 22g | protein: 53g | carbs: 3g | net carbs: 3g | fiber: 0g

Cheese Wine Pork Cutlets

Prep time: 30 minutes | Cook time: 15 minutes | Serves 2

1 cup water	½ teaspoon porcini powder
1 cup red wine	Sea salt and ground black pepper, to taste
1 tablespoon sea salt	
2 pork cutlets	1 egg
¼ cup almond meal	¼ cup yogurt
¼ cup flaxseed meal	1 teaspoon brown mustard
½ teaspoon baking powder	⅓ cup Parmesan cheese, grated
1 teaspoon shallot powder	

1. In a large ceramic dish, combine the water, wine and salt. Add the pork cutlets and put for 1 hour in the refrigerator. 2. In a shallow bowl, mix the almond meal, flaxseed meal, baking powder, shallot powder, porcini powder, salt, and ground pepper. In another bowl, whisk the eggs with yogurt and mustard. 3. In a third bowl, place the grated Parmesan cheese. 4. Dip the pork cutlets in the seasoned flour mixture and toss evenly; then, in the egg mixture. Finally, roll them over the grated Parmesan cheese. 5. Spritz the bottom of the air fryer basket with cooking oil. Add the breaded pork cutlets and cook at 395ºF (202ºC) and for 10 minutes. 6. Flip and cook for 5 minutes more on the other side. Serve warm.

Per Serving:

calories: 541 | fat: 32g | protein: 53g | carbs: 9g | net carbs: 6g | fiber: 3g

Italian Sausage Stew

Prep time: 15 minutes | Cook time: 22 minutes | Serves 6

1 pound Italian sausage, sliced	4 garlic cloves
1 red bell pepper, seeded and chopped	24 ounces canned diced tomatoes
2 onions, chopped	16 ounces okra, trimmed and sliced
Salt and black pepper, to taste	
1 cup fresh parsley, chopped	6 ounces tomato sauce
6 green onions, chopped	2 tablespoons coconut aminos
¼ cup avocado oil	1 tablespoon hot sauce
1 cup beef stock	

1. Set a pot over medium heat and warm oil, place in the sausages, and cook for 2 minutes. Stir in the onions, green onions, garlic, black pepper, bell pepper, and salt, and cook for 5 minutes. 2. Add in the hot sauce, stock, tomatoes, coconut aminos, okra, and tomato sauce, bring to a simmer and cook for 15 minutes. Adjust the seasoning with salt and black pepper. Share into serving bowls and sprinkle with fresh parsley to serve.

Per Serving:

calories: 435 | fat: 28g | protein: 23g | carbs: 20g | net carbs: 16g | fiber: 4g

Coconut Milk Ginger Marinated Pork Tenderloin

Prep time: 5 minutes | Cook time: 25 minutes | Serves 4

¼ cup coconut oil, divided

1½ pounds boneless pork chops, about ¾ inch thick

1 tablespoon grated fresh ginger

2 teaspoons minced garlic

1 cup coconut milk

1 teaspoon chopped fresh basil

Juice of 1 lime

½ cup shredded unsweetened coconut

1. Brown the pork. In a large skillet over medium heat, warm 2 tablespoons of the coconut oil. Add the pork chops to the skillet and brown them all over, turning them several times, about 10 minutes in total. 2. Braise the pork. Move the pork to the side of the skillet and add the remaining 2 tablespoons of coconut oil. Add the ginger and garlic and sauté until they've softened, about 2 minutes. Stir in the coconut milk, basil, and lime juice and move the pork back to the center of the skillet. Cover the skillet and simmer until the pork is just cooked through and very tender, 12 to 15 minutes. 3. Serve. Divide the pork chops between four plates and top them with the shredded coconut.

Per Serving:

calories: 479 | fat: 38g | protein: 32g | carbs: 6g | net carbs: 3g | fiber: 3g

Thai Beef Lettuce Wraps

Prep time: 10 minutes | Cook time: 15 minutes | Serves 4

1 tablespoon avocado oil

2 cloves garlic, minced

1 pound (454 g) ground beef

½ teaspoon sea salt

¼ teaspoon black pepper

3 tablespoons coconut aminos

1 tablespoon fish sauce

1½ tablespoons lime juice

1½ tablespoons red curry paste, or to taste

16 leaves butter lettuce, or any variety of large lettuce leaves

½ cup finely chopped red bell peppers

1 medium (6-ounce/ 170-g) avocado, diced

1. In a sauté pan, heat the oil over medium heat. Add the garlic and sauté for about 1 minute, until fragrant. Add the ground beef and season with the sea salt and black pepper. Increase the heat to medium-high and cook, breaking apart with a spatula, about 10 minutes, until browned. 2. Add the coconut aminos, fish sauce, lime juice, and red curry paste. Adjust the curry paste to taste. Cook for 2 to 5 minutes, stirring occasionally, until most of the liquid is evaporated. Add sea salt and black pepper to taste, if needed. 3. Dividing evenly, fill the lettuce leaves with the cooked Thai beef, bell peppers, and diced avocado.

Per Serving:

calories: 511 | fat: 37g | protein: 34g | carbs: 10g | net carbs: 6g | fiber: 4g

Italian Beef Burgers

Prep time: 10 minutes | Cook time: 12 minutes | Serves 4

1 pound 75% lean ground beef

¼ cup ground almonds

2 tablespoons chopped fresh basil

1 teaspoon minced garlic

¼ teaspoon sea salt

1 tablespoon olive oil

1 tomato, cut into 4 thick slices

¼ sweet onion, sliced thinly

1. In a medium bowl, mix together the ground beef, ground almonds, basil, garlic, and salt until well mixed. 2. Form the beef mixture into four equal patties and flatten them to about ½ inch thick. 3. Place a large skillet on medium-high heat and add the olive oil. 4. Panfry the burgers until cooked through, flipping them once, about 12 minutes in total. 5. Pat away any excess grease with paper towels and serve the burgers with a slice of tomato and onion.

Per Serving:

calories: 441 | fat: 37g | protein: 22g | carbs: 4g | net carbs: 3g | fiber: 1g

Fajita Meatball Lettuce Wraps

Prep time: 10 minutes | Cook time: 10 minutes | Serves 4

1 pound (454 g) ground beef (85% lean)

½ cup salsa, plus more for serving if desired

¼ cup chopped onions

¼ cup diced green or red bell peppers

1 large egg, beaten

1 teaspoon fine sea salt

½ teaspoon chili powder

½ teaspoon ground cumin

1 clove garlic, minced

For Serving (Optional):

8 leaves Boston lettuce

Pico de gallo or salsa

Lime slices

1. Spray the air fryer basket with avocado oil. Preheat the air fryer to 350°F (177°C). 2. In a large bowl, mix together all the ingredients until well combined. 3. Shape the meat mixture into eight 1-inch balls. Place the meatballs in the air fryer basket, leaving a little space between them. Air fry for 10 minutes, or until cooked through and no longer pink inside and the internal temperature reaches 145°F (63°C). 4. Serve each meatball on a lettuce leaf, topped with pico de gallo or salsa, if desired. Serve with lime slices if desired. 5. Store leftovers in an airtight container in the fridge for 3 days or in the freezer for up to a month. Reheat in a preheated 350°F (177°C) air fryer for 4 minutes, or until heated through.

Per Serving:

calories: 277 | fat: 18g | protein: 21g | carbs: 6g | net carbs: 4g | fiber: 2g

Italian Sausage Broccoli Sauté

Prep time: 10 minutes | Cook time: 20 minutes | Serves 4

2 tablespoons good-quality olive oil

1 pound Italian sausage meat, hot or mild

4 cups small broccoli florets

1 tablespoon minced garlic

Freshly ground black pepper, for seasoning

1. Cook the sausage. In a large skillet over medium heat, warm the olive oil. Add the sausage and sauté it until it's cooked through, 8 to 10 minutes. Transfer the sausage to a plate with a slotted spoon and set the plate aside. 2. Sauté the vegetables. Add the broccoli to the skillet and sauté it until it's tender, about 6 minutes. Stir in the garlic and sauté for another 3 minutes. 3. Finish the dish. Return the sausage to the skillet and toss to combine it with the other ingredients. Season the mixture with pepper. 4. Serve. Divide the mixture between four plates and serve it immediately.

Per Serving:

calories: 486 | fat: 43g | protein: 19g | carbs: 7g | net carbs: 5g | fiber: 2g

Bacon Mac 'n' Cheese

Prep time: 10 minutes | Cook time: 50 minutes | Serves 4

1 large head cauliflower (about 1⅔ pounds/750 g), cored and broken into ½-inch (1.25-cm) pieces

⅓ cup (22 g) finely chopped fresh parsley

6 strips bacon (about 6 ounces/170 g), cooked until crisp, then crumbled (reserve the grease)

2 cups (475 ml) unsweetened nondairy milk

2 tablespoons unflavored

gelatin

1 tablespoon fresh lemon juice

1 teaspoon onion powder

1 teaspoon finely ground gray sea salt

¼ teaspoon garlic powder

⅓ cup (22 g) nutritional yeast

2 large eggs, beaten

2 teaspoons prepared yellow mustard

2 ounces (60 g) pork dust or ground pork rinds

1. Preheat the oven to 350°F (177°C) and grease a shallow 1½-quart (1.4-L) casserole dish with coconut oil. Set aside. 2. Place the cauliflower, parsley, and bacon in a large bowl and toss to combine. 3. Place the reserved bacon grease, milk, gelatin, lemon juice, onion powder, salt, and garlic powder in a medium-sized saucepan. Bring to a boil over medium heat, whisking occasionally. Once boiling, continue to boil for 5 minutes. 4. Whisk in the nutritional yeast, eggs, and mustard and gently cook for 3 minutes, whisking constantly. 5. Remove the saucepan from the heat and pour the "cheese" sauce over the cauliflower mixture. (If you've overcooked the sauce or didn't whisk it well enough, you may end up with small pieces of cooked egg; for an ultra-smooth sauce, pour the sauce through a fine-mesh strainer.) Toss with a spatula until all the cauliflower pieces are coated in the cheese

sauce. 6. Transfer the coated cauliflower to the prepared casserole dish and smooth it out with the back of a spatula. Sprinkle the pork dust evenly over the top. Bake for 40 to 45 minutes, until the cauliflower is fork-tender, checking with a sharp knife on the edge of the casserole. 7. Allow to sit for 15 minutes before serving.

Per Serving:

calories: 440 | fat: 27g | protein: 35g | carbs: 15g | net carbs: 8g | fiber: 7g

Braised Pork Belly

Prep time: 15 minutes | Cook time: 37 minutes | Serves 4

1 pound (454 g) pork belly

1 tablespoon olive oil

Salt and ground black pepper to taste

1 clove garlic, minced

1 cup dry white wine

Rosemary sprig

1. Select the Sauté mode on the Instant Pot and heat the oil. 2. Add the pork belly and sauté for 2 minutes per side, until starting to brown. 3. Season the meat with salt and pepper, add the garlic. 4. Pour in the wine and add the rosemary sprig. Bring to a boil. 5. Select the Manual mode and set the cooking time for 35 minutes at High pressure. 6. Once cooking is complete, use a natural pressure release for 10 minutes, then release any remaining pressure. Open the lid. 7. Slice the meat and serve.

Per Serving:

calories: 666 | fat: 64g | protein: 11g | carbs: 2g | net carbs: 1g | fiber: 0g

Mustard Lamb Chops

Prep time: 5 minutes | Cook time: 14 minutes | Serves 4

Oil, for spraying

1 tablespoon Dijon mustard

2 teaspoons lemon juice

½ teaspoon dried tarragon

¼ teaspoon salt

¼ teaspoon freshly ground black pepper

4 (1¼-inch-thick) loin lamb chops

1. Preheat the air fryer to 390°F (199°C). Line the air fryer basket with parchment and spray lightly with oil. 2. In a small bowl, mix together the mustard, lemon juice, tarragon, salt, and black pepper. 3. Pat dry the lamb chops with a paper towel. Brush the chops on both sides with the mustard mixture. 4. Place the chops in the prepared basket. You may need to work in batches, depending on the size of your air fryer. 5. Cook for 8 minutes, flip, and cook for another 6 minutes, or until the internal temperature reaches 125°F (52°C) for rare, 145°F (63°C) for medium-rare, or 155°F (68°C) for medium.

Per Serving:

calories: 244 | fat: 13g | protein: 27g | carbs: 1g | net carbs: 1g | fiber: 0g

Classic Pork and Cauliflower Keema

Prep time: 15 minutes | Cook time: 8 minutes | Serves 6

1 tablespoon sesame oil	minced
½ cup yellow onion, chopped	4 cloves, whole
1 garlic cloves, minced	1 teaspoon garam masala
1 (1-inch) piece fresh ginger, minced	½ teaspoon ground cumin
	¼ teaspoon turmeric powder
1½ pounds (680 g) ground pork	1 teaspoon brown mustard seeds
1 cup cauliflower, chopped into small florets	½ teaspoon hot paprika
1 ripe tomatoes, puréed	Sea salt and ground black pepper, to taste
1 jalapeño pepper, seeded and	1 cup wate

1. Press the Sauté button to heat up the Instant Pot. Heat the sesame oil. Once hot, sauté yellow onion for 3 minutes or until softened. 2. Stir in garlic and ginger; cook for an additional minute. Add the remaining ingredients. 3. Secure the lid. Choose the Manual mode and set cooking time for 5 minutes on High pressure. 4. Once cooking is complete, use a quick pressure release. Carefully remove the lid. 5. Serve immediately.

Per Serving:
calories: 389 | fat: 29g | protein: 30g | carbs: 5g | net carbs: 3g | fiber: 3g

London Broil with Herb Butter

Prep time: 30 minutes | Cook time: 20 to 25 minutes | Serves 4

1½ pounds (680 g) London broil top round steak	6 tablespoons unsalted butter, softened
¼ cup olive oil	1 tablespoon chopped fresh parsley
2 tablespoons balsamic vinegar	¼ teaspoon salt
1 tablespoon Worcestershire sauce	¼ teaspoon dried ground rosemary or thyme
4 cloves garlic, minced	¼ teaspoon garlic powder
Herb Butter:	Pinch of red pepper flakes

1. Place the beef in a gallon-size resealable bag. In a small bowl, whisk together the olive oil, balsamic vinegar, Worcestershire sauce, and garlic. Pour the marinade over the beef, massaging gently to coat, and seal the bag. Let sit at room temperature for an hour or refrigerate overnight. 2. To make the herb butter: In a small bowl, mix the butter with the parsley, salt, rosemary, garlic powder, and red pepper flakes until smooth. Cover and refrigerate until ready to use. 3. Preheat the air fryer to 400ºF (204ºC). 4. Remove the beef from the marinade (discard the marinade) and place the beef in the air fryer basket. Pausing halfway through the cooking time to turn the meat, air fry for 20 to 25 minutes, until a thermometer inserted into the thickest part indicates the desired doneness, 125ºF / 52ºC (rare) to 150ºF / 66ºC (medium). Let the beef rest for 10 minutes before slicing. Serve topped with the herb butter.

Per Serving:
calories: 519 | fat: 38g | protein: 39g | carbs: 3g | net carbs: 3g | fiber: 0g

Pork Kebab with Yogurt Sauce

Prep time: 25 minutes | Cook time: 12 minutes | Serves 4

2 teaspoons olive oil	1 teaspoon paprika
½ pound (227 g) ground pork	2 garlic cloves, minced
½ pound (227 g) ground beef	1 teaspoon dried marjoram
1 egg, whisked	1 teaspoon mustard seeds
Sea salt and ground black pepper, to taste	½ teaspoon celery seeds
Yogurt Sauce:	
2 tablespoons olive oil	¼ teaspoon red pepper flakes, crushed
2 tablespoons fresh lemon juice	½ cup full-fat yogurt
Sea salt, to taste	1 teaspoon dried dill weed

1. Spritz the sides and bottom of the air fryer basket with 2 teaspoons of olive oil. 2. In a mixing dish, thoroughly combine the ground pork, beef, egg, salt, black pepper, paprika, garlic, marjoram, mustard seeds, and celery seeds. 3. Form the mixture into kebabs and transfer them to the greased basket. Cook at 365ºF (185ºC) for 11 to 12 minutes, turning them over once or twice. 4. In the meantime, mix all the sauce ingredients and place in the refrigerator until ready to serve. Serve the pork kebabs with the yogurt sauce on the side. Enjoy!

Per Serving:
calories: 464 | fat: 38g | protein: 22g | carbs: 6g | net carbs: 5g | fiber: 1g

Homemade Classic Beef Burgers

Prep time: 10 minutes | Cook time: 6 minutes | Serves 4

1 pound (454 g) ground beef	4 low carb buns, halved
½ teaspoon onion powder	¼ cup mayonnaise
½ teaspoon garlic powder	1 teaspoon sriracha sauce
2 tablespoons ghee	4 tablespoons cabbage slaw
1 teaspoon Dijon mustard	Salt and black pepper to taste

1. Mix together the beef, onion powder, garlic powder, mustard, salt, and black pepper; create 4 burgers. Melt the ghee in a skillet and cook the burgers for about 3 minutes per side. 2. Serve in buns topped with mayo, sriracha, and cabbage slaw.

Per Serving:
calories: 679 | fat: 55g | protein: 39g | carbs: 7g | net carbs: 6g | fiber: 1g

Herb-Crusted Lamb Chops

Prep time: 10 minutes | Cook time: 5 minutes | Serves 2

1 large egg	½ teaspoon ground black
2 cloves garlic, minced	pepper
¼ cup pork dust	4 (1-inch-thick) lamb chops
¼ cup powdered Parmesan	For Garnish/Serving
cheese	(Optional):
1 tablespoon chopped fresh	Sprigs of fresh oregano
oregano leaves	Sprigs of fresh rosemary
1 tablespoon chopped fresh	Sprigs of fresh thyme
rosemary leaves	Lavender flowers
1 teaspoon chopped fresh	Lemon slices
thyme leaves	

1. Spray the air fryer basket with avocado oil. Preheat the air fryer to 400ºF (204ºC). 2. Beat the egg in a shallow bowl, add the garlic, and stir well to combine. In another shallow bowl, mix together the pork dust, Parmesan, herbs, and pepper. 3. One at a time, dip the lamb chops into the egg mixture, shake off the excess egg, and then dredge them in the Parmesan mixture. Use your hands to coat the chops well in the Parmesan mixture and form a nice crust on all sides; if necessary, dip the chops again in both the egg and the Parmesan mixture. 4. Place the lamb chops in the air fryer basket, leaving space between them, and air fry for 5 minutes, or until the internal temperature reaches 145ºF (63ºC) for medium doneness. Allow to rest for 10 minutes before serving. 5. Garnish with sprigs of oregano, rosemary, and thyme, and lavender flowers, if desired. Serve with lemon slices, if desired. 6. Best served fresh. Store leftovers in an airtight container in the fridge for up to 4 days. Serve chilled over a salad, or reheat in a 350ºF (177ºC) air fryer for 3 minutes, or until heated through.

Per Serving:

calories: 386 | fat: 26g | protein: 31g | carbs: 4g | net carbs: 3g | fiber: 1g

Italian Beef Meatloaf

Prep time: 10 minutes | Cook time: 25 minutes | Serves 6

1 pound (454 g) ground beef	½ cup water
1 cup crushed pork rinds	½ cup sugar-free tomato sauce
1 egg	1 tablespoon chopped fresh
¼ cup grated Parmesan cheese	herbs (such as parsley or
¼ cup Italian dressing	basil)
2 teaspoons Italian seasoning	1 clove garlic, minced

1. In large bowl, combine the beef, pork rinds, egg, cheese, dressing, and Italian seasoning. Use a wooden spoon to incorporate everything into the meat, but do not overwork the meat or it will turn out tough. 2. Turn the meat mixture out onto a piece of aluminum foil. Use your hands to shape into a loaf. Wrap the foil up around the meat like a packet, but do not cover the top. Place the trivet in the pot and add the water. Place the meatloaf on top of the trivet. 3. Close the lid and seal the vent. Cook on High Pressure 20 minutes. Quick release the steam. 4. While the meat is cooking, whisk together the tomato sauce, herbs, and garlic in a small bowl. Heat the broiler. 5. Remove the meat and foil packet from the pot. Place on a baking sheet and spread the tomato sauce mixture on top. Broil until the glaze becomes sticky, about 5 minutes. Slice into six equal pieces.

Per Serving:

calories: 358 | fat: 25g | protein: 29g | carbs: 2g | net carbs: 2g | fiber: 0g

Shoulder Chops with Lemon-Thyme Gravy

Prep time: 30 minutes | Cook time: 40 minutes | Serves 6

¼ cup (60 ml) refined avocado oil or melted coconut oil, for frying
2½ pounds (1.2 kg) bone-in pork shoulder blade chops (aka shoulder chops, blade steaks, or pork shoulder steaks), about ½ inch (1.25 cm) thick
1½ teaspoons finely ground gray sea salt, divided
1 teaspoon ground black pepper
⅓ cup (80 ml) white wine, such as Pinot Grigio, Sauvignon Blanc, or unoaked Chardonnay
2 tablespoons unflavored gelatin
Grated zest of 1 lemon
Juice of 1 lemon
1 teaspoon dried thyme leaves
⅔ cup (160 ml) full-fat coconut milk

1. Place the oil in a large frying pan over high heat. While the oil is heating, sprinkle 1 teaspoon of the salt and the pepper on both sides of the chops. Place the chops in the hot oil and sear for 4 minutes per side. Transfer the seared chops to a clean plate. 2. Remove the pan from the heat. Leaving the fat in the pan, add the wine, gelatin, lemon zest, lemon juice, thyme, and remaining ½ teaspoon of salt. Whisk to combine. 3. Return the chops to the frying pan. Cover and cook over medium-low heat for 30 minutes, flipping them halfway through cooking. 4. Place an oven rack in the top position and turn on the broiler to low, if that is an option (if not, simply "broil" is fine). Place the chops in an oven-safe pan (I like to use cast iron) and set the pan on the top rack of the oven. Broil the chops for 3 minutes per side, or until just browned. Allow to rest for 5 minutes. 5. Meanwhile, add the coconut milk to the liquid in the frying pan. Cook over medium heat for 15 minutes, whisking occasionally, until slightly thickened. 6. If serving individually instead of family style, remove the bones from each chop and divide the steaks into 6 servings. Serve the chops drizzled with the gravy.

Per Serving:

calories: 511 | fat: 40g | protein: 33g | carbs: 2g | net carbs: 2g | fiber: 0g

Chapter 10

Stews and Soups

Chicken Enchilada Soup

Prep time: 10 minutes | Cook time: 40 minutes | Serves 6

2 (6 ounces / 170 g) boneless, skinless chicken breasts
½ tablespoon chili powder
½ teaspoon salt
½ teaspoon garlic powder
¼ teaspoon pepper
½ cup red enchilada sauce
½ medium onion, diced
1 (4 ounces / 113 g) can green chilies
2 cups chicken broth
⅛ cup pickled jalapeños
4 ounces (113 g) cream cheese
1 cup uncooked cauliflower rice
1 avocado, diced
1 cup shredded mild Cheddar cheese
½ cup sour cream

1. Sprinkle seasoning over chicken breasts and set aside. Pour enchilada sauce into Instant Pot and place chicken on top. 2. Add onion, chilies, broth, and jalapeños to the pot, then place cream cheese on top of chicken breasts. Click lid closed. Adjust time for 25 minutes. When timer beeps, quick-release the pressure and shred chicken with forks. 3. Mix soup together and add cauliflower rice, with pot on Keep Warm setting. Replace lid and let pot sit for 15 minutes, still on Keep Warm. This will cook cauliflower rice. Serve with avocado, Cheddar, and sour cream.

Per Serving:
calories: 318 | fat: 19g | protein: 21g | carbs: 10g | net carbs: 7g | fiber: 3g

Chicken and Mushroom Soup

Prep time: 5 minutes | Cook time: 15 minutes | Serves 4

1 onion, cut into thin slices
3 garlic cloves, minced
2 cups chopped mushrooms
1 yellow summer squash, chopped
1 pound (454 g) boneless, skinless chicken breast, cut into large chunks
2½ cups chicken broth
1 teaspoon salt
1 teaspoon freshly ground black pepper
1 teaspoon Italian seasoning or poultry seasoning
1 cup heavy (whipping) cream

1. Put the onion, garlic, mushrooms, squash, chicken, chicken broth, salt, pepper, and Italian seasoning in the inner cooking pot of the Instant Pot. 2. Lock the lid into place. Select Manual and adjust the pressure to High. Cook for 15 minutes. When the cooking is complete, let the pressure release naturally for 10 minutes, then quick-release any remaining pressure. Unlock the lid. 3. Using tongs, transfer the chicken pieces to a bowl and set aside. 4. Tilt the pot slightly. Using an immersion blender, roughly purée the vegetables, leaving a few intact for texture and visual appeal. 5. Shred the chicken and stir it back in to the soup. 6. Add the cream and stir well. Serve.

Per Serving:
calories: 427 | fat: 28g | protein: 31g | carbs: 13g | net carbs: 11g

| fiber: 2g

Beef and Spinach Stew

Prep time: 20 minutes | Cook time: 30 minutes | Serves 4

1 pound (454 g) beef sirloin, chopped
2 cups spinach, chopped
3 cups chicken broth
1 cup coconut milk
1 teaspoon allspices
1 teaspoon coconut aminos

1. Put all ingredients in the Instant Pot. Stir to mix well. 2. Close the lid. Set the Manual mode and set cooking time for 30 minutes on High Pressure. 3. When timer beeps, use a natural pressure release for 10 minutes, then release any remaining pressure. Open the lid. 4. Blend with an immersion blender until smooth. 5. Serve warm.

Per Serving:
calories: 383 | fat: 22g | protein: 40g | carbs: 5g | net carbs: 3g | fiber: 2g

Bacon Soup

Prep time: 10 minutes | Cook time: 1 hour 20 minutes | Serves 6

⅓ cup (69 g) lard
1 pound (455 g) pork stewing pieces
¾ cup (110 g) sliced shallots
10 strips bacon (about 10 ounces/285 g), cut into about ½-inch (1.25-cm) pieces
1¾ cups (415 ml) chicken bone broth
3 medium turnips (about 12½ ounces/355 g), cubed
¼ cup (60 ml) white wine, such as Pinot Grigio,
Sauvignon Blanc, or unoaked Chardonnay
1 tablespoon prepared yellow mustard
4 sprigs fresh thyme
½ cup (120 ml) full-fat coconut milk
2 tablespoons apple cider vinegar
2 tablespoons unflavored gelatin
1 tablespoon dried tarragon leaves

1. Melt the lard in a large saucepan over medium heat. Once the lard has melted, add the pork pieces and cook for 8 minutes, or until lightly browned on the outside. 2. Add the sliced shallots and bacon pieces. Sauté for an additional 5 minutes or until the shallots become fragrant. 3. Add the bone broth, turnips, wine, mustard, and thyme sprigs. Cover and bring to a boil, then reduce the heat to medium-low and cook until the meat and turnips are fork-tender, about 1 hour. 4. Remove the thyme sprigs and add the coconut milk, vinegar, gelatin, and tarragon. Increase the heat to medium and boil, covered, for another 10 minutes. 5. Divide the soup among 6 small bowls and serve.

Per Serving:
calories: 571 | fat: 41g | protein: 40g | carbs: 10g | net carbs: 9g | fiber: 1g

Beef and Eggplant Tagine

Prep time: 15 minutes | Cook time: 25 minutes | Serves 6

1 pound (454 g) beef fillet, chopped	4 cups beef broth
1 eggplant, chopped	1 teaspoon ground allspices
6 ounces (170 g) scallions, chopped	1 teaspoon erythritol
	1 teaspoon coconut oil

1. Put all ingredients in the Instant Pot. Stir to mix well. 2. Close the lid. Select Manual mode and set cooking time for 25 minutes on High Pressure. 3. When timer beeps, use a natural pressure release for 15 minutes, then release any remaining pressure. Open the lid. 4. Serve warm.

Per Serving:

calories: 158 | fat: 5g | protein: 21g | carbs: 8g | net carbs: 5g | fiber: 4g

Coconut Shrimp Saffron Soup

Prep time: 5 minutes | Cook time: 15 minutes | Serves 4

1 tablespoon coconut oil	deveined, and chopped
1 red bell pepper, chopped	1 cup shredded kale
2 teaspoons minced garlic	Juice of 1 lime
2 teaspoons grated fresh ginger	½ cup warm water
4 cups chicken stock	Pinch saffron threads
1 (15 ounces) can coconut milk	Sea salt, for seasoning
1 pound shrimp, peeled,	2 tablespoons chopped fresh cilantro

1. Sauté the vegetables. In a large saucepan over medium heat, warm the coconut oil. Add the red pepper, garlic, and ginger and sauté until they've softened, about 5 minutes. 2. Simmer the soup. Add the chicken stock and coconut milk and bring the soup to a boil, then reduce the heat to low and stir in the shrimp, kale, and lime juice. Simmer the soup until the shrimp is cooked through, about 5 minutes. 3. Mix in the saffron. While the soup is simmering, stir the saffron and the warm water together in a small bowl and let it sit for 5 minutes. Stir the saffron mixture into the soup when the shrimp is cooked, and simmer the soup for 3 minutes more. 4. Season and serve. Season with salt. Ladle the soup into bowls, garnish it with the cilantro, and serve it hot. Tip: As mentioned above, there's a reason that saffron is expensive, so if you come across some that is cheap, take a close look to make sure it's the real deal. Take a look at the threads, and if the saffron is a uniform color on the whole strand (instead of having a lighter tip), it is probably not real saffron.

Per Serving:

calories: 504 | fat: 36g | protein: 32g | carbs: 15g | net carbs: 12g | fiber: 3g

Chili-Infused Lamb Soup

Prep time: 5 minutes | Cook time: 25 minutes | Serves 6

1 tablespoon coconut oil	2 cups coconut milk
¾ pound ground lamb	1½ tablespoons red chili paste
2 cups shredded cabbage	or as much as you want
½ onion, chopped	Zest and juice of 1 lime
2 teaspoons minced garlic	1 cup shredded kale
4 cups chicken broth	

1. Cook the lamb. In a medium stockpot over medium-high heat, warm the coconut oil. Add the lamb and cook it, stirring it often, until it has browned, about 6 minutes. 2. Cook the vegetables. Add the cabbage, onion, and garlic and sauté until they've softened, about 5 minutes. 3. Simmer the soup. Stir in the chicken broth, coconut milk, red chili paste, lime zest, and lime juice. Bring it to a boil, then reduce the heat to low and simmer until the cabbage is tender, about 10 minutes. 4. Add the kale. Stir in the kale and simmer the soup for 3 more minutes. 5. Serve. Spoon the soup into six bowls and serve.

Per Serving:

calories: 380 | fat: 32g | protein: 17g | carbs: 7g | net carbs: 6g | fiber: 1g

Chilled Cilantro and Avocado Soup

Prep time: 10 minutes | Cook time: 7 minutes | Serves 6

2 to 3 tablespoons olive oil	halved, and pitted
1 large white onion, diced	4 cups chicken broth, or
3 garlic cloves, crushed	vegetable broth
1 serrano chile, seeded and diced	2 cups water
	Juice of 1 lemon
Salt and freshly ground black pepper, to taste	¼ cup chopped fresh cilantro, plus more for garnish
4 or 5 ripe avocados, peeled,	½ cup sour cream

1. In a large pan over medium heat, heat the olive oil. 2. Add the onion and garlic. Sauté for 5 to 7 minutes until the onion is softened and translucent. 3. Add the serrano, season with salt and pepper, and remove from the heat. 4. In a blender, combine the avocados, chicken broth, water, lemon juice, cilantro, and onion-garlic-chile mixture. Purée until smooth (you may have to do this in batches), strain through a fine-mesh sieve, and season with more salt and pepper. Refrigerate, covered, for about 3 hours or until chilled through. 5. To serve, top with sour cream and a sprinkle of chopped cilantro. Refrigerate leftovers in an airtight container for up to 1 week.

Per Serving:

calories: 513 | fat: 45g | protein: 7g | carbs: 20g | net carbs: 8g | fiber: 12g

Coconut Curry Broccoli Soup

Prep time: 10 minutes | Cook time: 20 minutes | Serves 4

4 tablespoons butter	1 teaspoon red pepper flakes
1 celery stalk, diced	3 cups chicken broth
1 carrot, diced	2 cups broccoli florets
½ onion, diced	1 cup canned coconut cream
1 garlic clove, minced	Salt and freshly ground black
2 tablespoons curry powder	pepper, to taste

1. In a large saucepan over medium heat, melt the butter. 2. Add the celery, carrot, onion, garlic, curry powder, and red pepper flakes. Stir to combine. Sauté for 5 to 7 minutes until the vegetables soften. 3. Stir in the chicken broth and bring to a simmer. 4. Add the broccoli and simmer for 5 to 7 minutes. 5. Stir in the coconut cream and simmer for 5 to 10 minutes more until the broccoli is cooked. Season well with salt and pepper and serve hot. Refrigerate leftovers in an airtight container for up to 1 week.

Per Serving:

calories: 274 | fat: 25g | protein: 7g | carbs: 11g | net carbs: 8g | fiber: 3g

Cream of Cauliflower Gazpacho

Prep time: 15 minutes | Cook time: 25 minutes | Serves 4 to 6

1 cup raw almonds	2 garlic cloves, finely minced
½ teaspoon salt	2 cups chicken or vegetable
½ cup extra-virgin olive oil,	stock or broth, plus more if
plus 1 tablespoon, divided	needed
1 small white onion, minced	1 tablespoon red wine vinegar
1 small head cauliflower,	¼ teaspoon freshly ground
stalk removed and broken into	black pepper
florets (about 3 cups)	

1. Bring a small pot of water to a boil. Add the almonds to the water and boil for 1 minute, being careful to not boil longer or the almonds will become soggy. Drain in a colander and run under cold water. Pat dry and, using your fingers, squeeze the meat of each almond out of its skin. Discard the skins. 2. In a food processor or blender, blend together the almonds and salt. With the processor running, drizzle in ½ cup extra-virgin olive oil, scraping down the sides as needed. Set the almond paste aside. 3. In a large stockpot, heat the remaining 1 tablespoon olive oil over medium-high heat. Add the onion and sauté until golden, 3 to 4 minutes. Add the cauliflower florets and sauté for another 3 to 4 minutes. Add the garlic and sauté for 1 minute more. 4. Add 2 cups stock and bring to a boil. Cover, reduce the heat to medium-low, and simmer the vegetables until tender, 8 to 10 minutes. Remove from the heat and allow to cool slightly. 5. Add the vinegar and pepper. Using an immersion blender, blend until smooth. Alternatively, you can blend in a stand blender, but you may need to divide the mixture into two or three batches. With the blender running, add the almond paste and blend until smooth, adding extra stock if the soup is too thick. 6. Serve warm, or chill in refrigerator at least 4 to 6 hours to serve a cold gazpacho.

Per Serving:

calories: 562 | fat: 51g | protein: 13g | carbs: 19g | net carbs: 13g | fiber: 6g

Coconut, Green Beans & Shrimp Curry Soup

Prep time: 10 minutes | Cook time: 15 minutes | Serves 4

2 tablespoons ghee	2 tablespoons red curry paste
1 pound jumbo shrimp, peeled	6 ounces coconut milk
and deveined	Salt and chili pepper to taste
2 tablespoons ginger-garlic	1 bunch green beans, halved
puree	

1. Melt ghee in a medium saucepan over medium heat. Add the shrimp, season with salt and black pepper, and cook until they are opaque, 2 to 3 minutes. Remove shrimp to a plate. Add the ginger-garlic puree and red curry paste to the ghee and sauté for 2 minutes until fragrant. 2. Stir in the coconut milk; add the shrimp, salt, chili pepper, and green beans. Cook for 4 minutes. Reduce the heat to a simmer and cook an additional 3 minutes, occasionally stirring. Adjust taste with salt, fetch soup into serving bowls, and serve with cauli rice.

Per Serving:

calories: 138| fat: 1g | protein: 28g | carbs: 4g | net carbs: 3g | fiber: 1g

Blue Cheese Mushroom Soup

Prep time: 15 minutes | Cook time: 20 minutes | Serves 4

2 cups chopped white	1 teaspoon olive oil
mushrooms	½ teaspoon ground cumin
3 tablespoons cream cheese	1 teaspoon salt
4 ounces (113 g) scallions,	2 ounces (57 g) blue cheese,
diced	crumbled
4 cups chicken broth	

1. Combine the mushrooms, cream cheese, scallions, chicken broth, olive oil, and ground cumin in the Instant Pot. 2. Seal the lid. Select Manual mode and set cooking time for 20 minutes on High Pressure. 3. When timer beeps, use a quick pressure release and open the lid. 4. Add the salt and blend the soup with an immersion blender. 5. Ladle the soup in the bowls and top with blue cheese. Serve warm.

Per Serving:

calories: 142 | fat: 9g | protein: 10g | carbs: 5g | net carbs: 4g | fiber: 1g

Beef and Cauliflower Soup

Prep time: 10 minutes | Cook time: 14 minutes | Serves 4

1 cup ground beef	1 teaspoon minced garlic
½ cup cauliflower, shredded	1 teaspoon dried oregano
1 teaspoon unsweetened	½ teaspoon salt
tomato purée	4 cups water
¼ cup coconut milk	

1. Put all ingredients in the Instant Pot and stir well. 2. Close the lid. Select Manual mode and set cooking time for 14 minutes on High Pressure. 3. When timer beeps, make a quick pressure release and open the lid. 4. Blend with an immersion blender until smooth. 5. Serve warm.

Per Serving:

calories: 106 | fat: 8g | protein: 7g | carbs: 2g | net carbs: 1g | fiber: 1g

Pork and Daikon Stew

Prep time: 15 minutes | Cook time: 3 minutes | Serves 6

1 pound (454 g) pork	1 tablespoon heavy cream
tenderloin, chopped	1 tablespoon butter
1 ounce (28 g) green onions,	1 teaspoon ground black
chopped	pepper
½ cup daikon, chopped	3 cups water
1 lemon slice	

1. Put all ingredients in the Instant Pot and stir to mix with a spatula. 2. Seal the lid. Set Manual mode and set cooking time for 20 minutes on High Pressure. 3. When cooking is complete, use a natural pressure release for 15 minutes, then release any remaining pressure. Open the lid. 4. Serve warm.

Per Serving:

calories: 137 | fat: 6g | protein: 20g | carbs: 1g | net carbs: 1g | fiber: 0g

Broccoli and Red Feta Soup

Prep time: 10 minutes | Cook time: 25 minutes | Serves 4

1 cup broccoli, chopped	4 cups beef broth
½ cup coconut cream	1 teaspoon chili flakes
1 teaspoon unsweetened	6 ounces (170 g) feta,
tomato purée	crumbled

1. Put broccoli, coconut cream, tomato purée, and beef broth in the Instant Pot. Sprinkle with chili flakes and stir to mix well. 2. Close the lid and select Manual mode. Set cooking time for 8 minutes on High Pressure. 3. When timer beeps, make a quick pressure release and open the lid. 4. Add the feta cheese and stir the soup on Sauté mode for 5 minutes or until the cheese melt. 5. Serve immediately.

Per Serving:

calories: 229 | fat: 18g | protein: 12g | carbs: 6g | net carbs: 5g | fiber: 1g

Avocado-Lime Soup

Prep time: 5 minutes | Cook time: 20 minutes | serves 8

2 tablespoons cold-pressed	some aside for garnish)
olive oil	½ cup chopped fresh cilantro
½ yellow onion, chopped	½ cup chopped celery
1 teaspoon ground cumin	½ jalapeño pepper, chopped
1 teaspoon ground coriander	8 cups vegetable broth
1 teaspoon chili powder	Juice of 2 limes
¼ cup hemp hearts	1 avocado, peeled, pitted, and
1 medium tomato, chopped	cut into cubes
1 cup chopped cabbage (set	3 flax crackers

1. Heat the olive oil in a large stockpot over medium heat and add the onion, cumin, coriander, and chili powder. Sauté, stirring occasionally, until the onion becomes tender, about 5 minutes. 2. Add the hemp hearts, tomato, cabbage, cilantro, celery, and jalapeño to the pot. Stir to coat the spices and allow to cook for 4 minutes. 3. Pour the broth into the pot and simmer on low for 20 minutes. 4. Remove the pot from the heat and stir in the lime juice. 5. Divide the avocado equally among 4 serving bowls. 6. Pour the soup over the avocado in the bowls and garnish with additional cabbage and cilantro. 7. Break the flax crackers over the top of the soup to create a "tortilla soup" vibe.

Per Serving:

calories: 130 | fat: 9g | protein: 3g | carbs: 9g | net carbs: 5g | fiber: 4g

Beef Reuben Soup

Prep time: 10 minutes | Cook time: 20 minutes | Serves 6

1 onion, diced	1 cup sauerkraut, shredded
6 cups beef stock	1 pound corned beef, chopped
1tsp caraway seeds	3 tablespoons butter
2celery stalks, diced	1 ½ cup swiss cheese,
2 garlic cloves, minced	shredded
2 cups heavy cream	Salt and black pepper, to taste

1. Melt the butter in a large pot. Add onion and celery, and fry for 3 minutes until tender. Add garlic and cook for another minute. 2. Pour the beef stock over and stir in sauerkraut, salt, caraway seeds, and add a pinch of black pepper. Bring to a boil. Reduce the heat to low, and add the corned beef. Cook for about 15 minutes, adjust the seasoning. Stir in heavy cream and cheese and cook for 1 minute.

Per Serving:

calories: 595| fat: 37g | protein: 36g | carbs: 32g | net carbs: 29g | fiber: 3g

Broccoli-Cheese Soup

Prep time: 5 minutes | Cook time: 20 minutes | Serves 4

2 tablespoons butter
1 cup broccoli florets, finely chopped
1 cup heavy (whipping) cream
1 cup chicken or vegetable broth

Pink Himalayan salt
Freshly ground black pepper
1 cup shredded cheese, some reserved for topping (I use sharp Cheddar)

1. In a medium saucepan over medium heat, melt the butter. 2. Add the broccoli and sauté in the butter for about 5 minutes, until tender. 3. Add the cream and the chicken broth, stirring constantly. Season with pink Himalayan salt and pepper. Cook, stirring occasionally, for 10 to 15 minutes, until the soup has thickened. 4. Turn down the heat to low, and begin adding the shredded cheese. Reserve a small handful of cheese for topping the bowls of soup. (Do not add all the cheese at once, or it may clump up.) Add small amounts, slowly, while stirring constantly. 5. Pour the soup into four bowls, top each with half of the reserved cheese, and serve.

Per Serving:

calories: 383 | fat: 37g | protein: 10g | carbs: 4g | net carbs: 4g | fiber: 0g

Broccoli Brie Soup

Prep time: 5 minutes | Cook time: 14 minutes | Serves 6

1 tablespoon coconut oil or unsalted butter
1 cup finely diced onions
1 head broccoli, cut into small florets
2½ cups chicken broth or vegetable broth
8 ounces (227 g) Brie cheese, cut off rind and cut into

chunks
1 cup unsweetened almond milk or heavy cream, plus more for drizzling
Fine sea salt and ground black pepper, to taste
Extra-virgin olive oil, for drizzling
Coarse sea salt, for garnish

1. Place the coconut oil in the Instant Pot and press Sauté. Once hot, add the onions and sauté for 4 minutes, or until soft. Press Cancel to stop the Sauté. 2. Add the broccoli and broth. Seal the lid, press Manual, and set the timer for 10 minutes. Once finished, let the pressure release naturally. 3. Remove the lid and add the Brie and almond milk to the pot. Transfer the soup to a food processor or blender and process until smooth, or purée the soup right in the pot with a stick blender. 4. Season with salt and pepper to taste. Ladle the soup into bowls and drizzle with almond milk and olive oil. Garnish with coarse sea salt and freshly ground pepper.

Per Serving:

calories: 210 | fat: 16g | protein: 9g | carbs: 7g | net carbs: 6g | fiber: 1g

Cauliflower & Blue Cheese Soup

Prep time: 15 minutes | Cook time: 20 minutes | Serves 5

2 tablespoons extra-virgin avocado oil
1 small red onion, diced
1 medium celery stalk, sliced
1 medium cauliflower, cut into small florets
2 cups vegetable or chicken stock
¼ cup goat's cream or heavy

whipping cream
Salt and black pepper, to taste
1 cup crumbled goat's or sheep's blue cheese, such as Roquefort
2 tablespoons chopped fresh chives
5 tablespoons extra-virgin olive oil

1. Heat a medium saucepan greased with the avocado oil over medium heat. Sweat the onion and celery for 3 to 5 minutes, until soft and fragrant. Add the cauliflower florets and cook for 5 minutes. Add the vegetable stock and bring to a boil. Cook for about 10 minutes, or until the cauliflower is tender. Remove from the heat and let cool for a few minutes. 2. Add the cream. Use an immersion blender, or pour into a blender, to process until smooth and creamy. Season with salt and pepper to taste. Divide the soup between serving bowls and top with the crumbled blue cheese, chives, and olive oil. To store, let cool and refrigerate in a sealed container for up to 5 days.

Per Serving:

calories: 367 | fat: 31g | protein: 12g | carbs: 11g | net carbs: 8g | fiber: 3g

Curried Chicken Soup

Prep time: 10 minutes | Cook time: 10 minutes | Serves 6

1 pound (454 g) boneless, skinless chicken thighs
1½ cups unsweetened coconut milk
½ onion, finely diced
3 or 4 garlic cloves, crushed
1 (2-inch) piece ginger, finely chopped

1 cup sliced mushrooms, such as cremini and shiitake
4 ounces (113 g) baby spinach
1 teaspoon salt
½ teaspoon ground turmeric
½ teaspoon cayenne
1 teaspoon garam masala
¼ cup chopped fresh cilantro

1. In the inner cooking pot of your Instant Pot, add the chicken, coconut milk, onion, garlic, ginger, mushrooms, spinach, salt, turmeric, cayenne, garam masala, and cilantro. 2. Lock the lid into place. Select Manual and adjust the pressure to High. Cook for 10 minutes. When the cooking is complete, let the pressure release naturally. Unlock the lid. 3. Use tongs to transfer the chicken to a bowl. Shred the chicken, then stir it back into the soup. 4. Eat and rejoice.

Per Serving:

calories: 378 | fat: 26g | protein: 26g | carbs: 6g | net carbs: 2g | fiber: 4g

Chicken and Vegetable Soup

Prep time: 5 minutes | Cook time: 2 minutes | Serves 4

1 pound (454 g) boneless, skinless chicken thighs, diced small	1 tablespoon powdered chicken broth base
1 (10 ounces / 283 g) bag frozen vegetables	1 teaspoon salt
2 cups water	1 teaspoon freshly ground black pepper
1 teaspoon poultry seasoning	1 cup heavy (whipping) cream

1. Put the chicken, vegetables, water, poultry seasoning, chicken broth base, salt, and pepper in the inner cooking pot of your Instant Pot. 2. Lock the lid into place. Select Manual and adjust the pressure to High. Cook for 2 minutes. When the cooking is complete, quick-release the pressure (you may want to do this in short bursts so the soup doesn't spurt out). Unlock the lid. 3. Add the cream, stir, and serve. Or, if you prefer, you can mash up the chicken with the back of a wooden spoon to break it into shreds before adding the cream.

Per Serving:

calories: 327 | fat: 19g | protein: 26g | carbs: 13g | net carbs: 10g | fiber: 3g

Broccoli Cheddar Pancetta Soup

Prep time: 15 minutes | Cook time: 30 minutes | Serves 6

2 ounces (57 g) pancetta, diced	1 teaspoon onion powder
2 tablespoons butter or ghee	1 teaspoon paprika
¼ medium onion, finely chopped (about ½ cup)	1 teaspoon salt
3 garlic cloves, minced	½ teaspoon freshly ground black pepper
3 cups bone broth	Pinch cayenne pepper
½ cup heavy (whipping) cream	½ tablespoon gelatin (or ½ teaspoon xanthan or guar gum), for thickening
2 cups broccoli florets, chopped into bite-size pieces	2 cups shredded sharp Cheddar cheese
1 teaspoon garlic powder	

1. In a large pot over medium heat, cook the pancetta, stirring often, until crisp. Remove the pancetta pieces to a paper towel using a slotted spoon, leaving as much grease as possible in the pot. 2. Add the butter, onion, and garlic to the pot and sauté for 5 minutes. 3. Add the bone broth, cream, broccoli, garlic, onion, paprika, salt, pepper, and cayenne to the pot and stir well. Sprinkle in the gelatin and stir until well incorporated. Bring to a boil. 4. Once boiling, reduce the heat to low and simmer for 10 to 15 minutes, stirring occasionally. 5. Then, with the heat on low, gradually add the cheese, ½ cup at a time, stirring constantly. Once all of the cheese has been added, remove the pot from the heat. Sprinkle the pancetta pieces over the top and serve. 6. To store, divide the soup into glass jars and freeze for easy meals throughout the coming weeks and months. Make sure to only fill the jars three-quarters full because the liquid will expand as it freezes.

Per Serving:

1½ cups: calories: 311 | fat: 29g | protein: 17g | carbs: 5g | net carbs: 4g | fiber: 1g

Keto Pho with Shirataki Noodles

Prep time: 20 minutes | Cook time: 10 minutes | Makes 4 bowls

8 ounces (227 g) sirloin, very thinly sliced	ground ginger
3 tablespoons coconut oil (or butter or ghee)	8 cups bone broth
2 garlic cloves, minced	4 (7-ounce / 198-g) packages shirataki noodles, drained and rinsed
2 tablespoons liquid or coconut aminos	1 cup bean sprouts
2 tablespoons fish sauce	1 scallion, chopped
1 teaspoon freshly grated or	1 tablespoon toasted sesame seeds (optional)

1. Put the sirloin in the freezer while you prepare the broth and other ingredients (about 15 to 20 minutes). This makes it easier to slice. 2. In a large pot over medium heat, melt the coconut oil. Add the garlic and cook for 3 minutes. Then add the aminos, fish sauce, ginger, and bone broth. Bring to a boil. 3. Remove the beef from the freezer and slice it very thin. 4. Divide the noodles, beef, and bean sprouts evenly among four serving bowls. Carefully ladle 2 cups of broth into each bowl. Cover the bowls with plates and let sit for 3 to 5 minutes to cook the meat. 5. Serve garnished with the chopped scallion and sesame seeds (if using).

Per Serving:

1 bowl: calories: 385 | fat: 29g | protein: 23g | carbs: 8g | net carbs: 4g | fiber: 4g

Parmesan Zucchini Soup

Prep time: 10 minutes | Cook time: 1 minute | Serves 2

1 zucchini, grated	1 cup beef broth
1 teaspoon ground paprika	1 tablespoon dried cilantro
½ teaspoon cayenne pepper	1 ounce (28 g) Parmesan, grated
½ cup coconut milk	

1. Put the grated zucchini, paprika, cayenne pepper, coconut milk, beef broth, and dried cilantro in the instant pot. 2. Close and seal the lid. 3. Cook the soup on Manual (High Pressure) for 1 minute. Make a quick pressure release. 4. Ladle the soup in the serving bowls and top with Parmesan.

Per Serving:

calories: 223 | fat: 18g | protein: 10g | carbs: 8g | net carbs: 5g | fiber: 3g

Salmon and Tomatillos Stew

Prep time: 15 minutes | Cook time: 12 minutes | Serves 2

10 ounces (283 g) salmon fillet, chopped
2 tomatillos, chopped
½ teaspoon ground turmeric
1 cup coconut cream
1 teaspoon ground paprika
½ teaspoon salt

1. Put all ingredients in the Instant Pot. Stir to mix well. 2. Close the lid. Select Manual mode and set cooking time for 12 minutes on Low Pressure. 3. When timer beeps, use a quick pressure release. Open the lid. 4. Serve warm.

Per Serving:

calories: 479 | fat: 38g | protein: 31g | carbs: 10g | net carbs: 6g | fiber: 4g

Chicken Soup

Prep time: 15 minutes | Cook time: 45 minutes | Serves 4

3 tablespoons olive oil
1 (14 ounces / 397 g) bag frozen peppers and onions
1 pound (454 g) chicken thigh meat, diced
1 tablespoon dried thyme
½ tablespoon garlic powder
1 teaspoon salt
1 teaspoon freshly ground black pepper
1 (32 ounces / 907 g) container chicken or vegetable broth, or bone broth
½ pound (227 g) spinach
1 teaspoon dried basil (optional)

1. Heat the oil in a large pot over medium heat. 2. Add the peppers and onions and cook until no longer frozen, 8 to 10 minutes. 3. Add the chicken and cook, stirring occasionally. 4. Stir in the thyme, garlic powder, salt, and pepper. Add the broth and cook for about 25 minutes. 5. Add the spinach and cook for another 5 minutes. 6. Serve the soup in bowls, sprinkled with the basil (if using).

Per Serving:

calories: 323 | fat: 19g | protein: 28g | carbs: 10g | net carbs: 7g | fiber: 3g

Cabbage and Pork Soup

Prep time: 10 minutes | Cook time: 12 minutes | Serves 3

1 teaspoon butter
½ cup shredded white cabbage
½ teaspoon ground coriander
½ teaspoon salt
½ teaspoon chili flakes
2 cups chicken broth
½ cup ground pork

1. Melt the butter in the Instant Pot on Sauté mode. 2. Add cabbage and sprinkle with ground coriander, salt, and chili flakes. 3. Fold in the chicken broth and ground pork. 4. Close the lid and select Manual mode. Set cooking time for 12 minutes on High Pressure. 5. When timer beeps, use a quick pressure release. Open the lid. 6. Ladle the soup and serve warm.

Per Serving:

calories: 350 | fat: 24g | protein: 30g | carbs: 1g | net carbs: 1g | fiber: 0g

Cabbage Soup

Prep time: 20 minutes | Cook time: 30 minutes | Serves 6

1 tablespoon olive oil
3 garlic cloves, minced
1 onion, diced
3 carrots, diced
1 celery stalk, diced
½ green bell pepper, diced
Salt and freshly ground black pepper, to taste
1 cup chopped kale
2 tablespoons tomato paste
2 (32-ounce / 907-g) cartons chicken broth
1 large head cabbage, chopped
1 teaspoon dried oregano
1 teaspoon dried thyme
Grated Parmesan cheese, for topping

1. In a large saucepan over medium heat, heat the olive oil. 2. Add the garlic and onion. Sauté for 5 minutes. 3. Add the carrots and celery. Cook for 5 to 7 minutes until softened. 4. Add the bell pepper and stir well to combine. Cook for 5 to 7 minutes more. Season with salt and pepper and add the kale. 5. Stir in the tomato paste until well combined. 6. Pour in the chicken broth and bring the soup to a gentle boil. 7. Add the cabbage, oregano, and thyme. Season with more salt and pepper. Reduce the heat to low, cover the pan, and simmer for 15 minutes (a little longer if you have the time). Ladle into bowls and top with Parmesan before serving.

Per Serving:

calories: 156 | fat: 5g | protein: 10g | carbs: 23g | net carbs: 16g | fiber: 7g

Mushroom Pizza Soup

Prep time: 10 minutes | Cook time: 22 minutes | Serves 3

1 teaspoon coconut oil
¼ cup cremini mushrooms, sliced
5 ounces (142 g) Italian sausages, chopped
½ jalapeño pepper, sliced
½ teaspoon Italian seasoning
1 teaspoon unsweetened tomato purée
1 cup water
4 ounces (113 g) Mozzarella, shredded

1. Melt the coconut oil in the Instant Pot on Sauté mode. 2. Add the mushrooms and cook for 10 minutes. 3. Add the chopped sausages, sliced jalapeño, Italian seasoning, and unsweetened tomato purée. Pour in the water and stir to mix well. 4. Close the lid and select Manual mode. Set cooking time for 12 minutes on High Pressure. 5. When timer beeps, use a quick pressure release and open the lid. 6. Ladle the soup in the bowls. Top it with Mozzarella. Serve warm.

Per Serving:

calories: 289 | fat: 23g | protein: 18g | carbs: 3g | net carbs: 2g | fiber: 0g

Chapter 11

Desserts

Vanilla Cream Pie

Prep time: 20 minutes | Cook time: 35 minutes | Serves 12

1 cup heavy cream	1 cup coconut flour
3 eggs, beaten	1 tablespoon butter, melted
1 teaspoon vanilla extract	1 cup water, for cooking
¼ cup erythritol	

1. In the mixing bowl, mix up coconut flour, erythritol, vanilla extract, eggs, and heavy cream. 2. Grease the baking pan with melted butter. 3. Pour the coconut mixture in the baking pan. 4. Pour water and insert the steamer rack in the instant pot. 5. Place the pie on the rack. Close and seal the lid. 6. Cook the pie on Manual mode (High Pressure) for 35 minutes. 7. Allow the natural pressure release for 10 minutes.

Per Serving:

calories: 100 | fat: 7g | protein: 3g | carbs: 12g | net carbs: 8g | fiber: 4g

Almond Butter Keto Fat Bombs

Prep time: 3 minutes | Cook time: 3 minutes | Serves 6

¼ cup coconut oil	2 tablespoons cacao powder
¼ cup no-sugar-added almond butter	¼ cup powdered erythritol

1. Press the Sauté button and add coconut oil to Instant Pot. Let coconut oil melt completely and press the Cancel button. Stir in remaining ingredients. Mixture will be liquid. 2. Pour into 6 silicone molds and place into freezer for 30 minutes until set. Store in fridge.

Per Serving:

calories: 142 | fat: 14g | protein: 3g | carbs: 9g | net carbs: 7g | fiber: 2g

Strawberry Panna Cotta

Prep time: 10 minutes | Cook time: 10 minutes | Serves 4

2 tablespoons warm water	sweetener of choice (optional)
2 teaspoons gelatin powder	1½ teaspoons pure vanilla extract
2 cups heavy cream	
1 cup sliced strawberries, plus more for garnish	4 to 6 fresh mint leaves, for garnish (optional)
1 to 2 tablespoons sugar-free	

1. Pour the warm water into a small bowl. Sprinkle the gelatin over the water and stir well to dissolve. Allow the mixture to sit for 10 minutes. 2. In a blender or a large bowl, if using an immersion blender, combine the cream, strawberries, sweetener (if using), and vanilla. Blend until the mixture is smooth and the strawberries are well puréed. 3. Transfer the mixture to a saucepan and heat over medium-low heat until just below a simmer. Remove from the heat and cool for 5 minutes. 4. Whisking constantly, add in the gelatin mixture until smooth. Divide the custard between ramekins or small glass bowls, cover and refrigerate until set, 4 to 6 hours. 5. Serve chilled, garnishing with additional sliced strawberries or mint leaves (if using).

Per Serving:

calories: 540 | fat: 57g | protein: 6g | carbs: 8g | net carbs: 7g | fiber: 1g

Dark-Chocolate Strawberry Bark

Prep time: 10 minutes | Cook time: 1 minutes | Serves 2

½ (2.8 ounces) keto-friendly chocolate bar (I use Lily's)	(whipping) cream
1 tablespoon heavy	2 tablespoons salted almonds
	1 fresh strawberry, sliced

1. Line a baking sheet with parchment paper. 2. Break up the chocolate bar half into small pieces, and put them in a microwave-safe bowl with the cream. 3. Heat in the microwave for 45 seconds at 50 percent power. Stir the chocolate, and cook for 20 seconds more at 50 percent power. Stir again, making sure the mixture is fully melted and combined. If not, microwave for another 20 seconds. 4. Pour the chocolate mixture onto the parchment paper and spread it in a thin, uniform layer. 5. Sprinkle on the almonds, then add the strawberry slices. 6. Refrigerate until hardened, about 2 hours. 7. Once the bark is nice and hard, break it up into smaller pieces to nibble on. Yum! 8. The bark will keep for up to 4 days in a sealed container in the refrigerator.

Per Serving:

calories: 111 | fat: 10g | protein: 3g | carbs: 9g | net carbs: 4g | fiber: 5g

Pecan Brownies

Prep time: 10 minutes | Cook time: 20 minutes | Serves 6

½ cup blanched finely ground almond flour	¼ cup unsalted butter, softened
	1 large egg
½ cup powdered erythritol	¼ cup chopped pecans
2 tablespoons unsweetened cocoa powder	¼ cup low-carb, sugar-free chocolate chips
½ teaspoon baking powder	

In a large bowl, mix almond flour, erythritol, cocoa powder, and baking powder. Stir in butter and egg. 2. Fold in pecans and chocolate chips. Scoop mixture into a round baking pan. Place pan into the air fryer basket. 3. Adjust the temperature to 300°F (149°C) and bake for 20 minutes. 4. When fully cooked a toothpick inserted in center will come out clean. Allow 20 minutes to fully cool and firm up.

Per Serving:

calories: 218 | fat: 20g | protein: 4g | carbs: 10g | net carbs: 4g | fiber: 6g

Chocolate Chip Almond Cookies

Prep time: 15 minutes | Cook time: 10 minutes | Makes 20 cookies

1 cup grass-fed butter, at room temperature	3½ cups almond flour
¾ cup monk fruit sweetener, granulated form	1 teaspoon baking soda
	½ teaspoon sea salt
2 eggs	1½ cups keto-friendly chocolate chips, like Lily's Dark Chocolate Chips
1 tablespoon vanilla extract	

1. Preheat the oven. Set the oven temperature to 350°F. Line a baking sheet with parchment paper and set it aside. 2. Mix the wet ingredients. In a large bowl, cream the butter and sweetener until the mixture is very fluffy, either by hand or with a hand mixer. Add the eggs and vanilla and beat until everything is well blended. 3. Mix the dry ingredients. In a medium bowl, stir together the almond flour, baking soda, and salt until they're well mixed together. 4. Add the dry to the wet ingredients. Stir the dry ingredients into the wet ingredients and mix until everything is well combined. Stir in the chocolate chips. 5. Bake. Drop the batter by tablespoons onto the baking sheet about 2 inches apart and flatten them down slightly. Bake the cookies for 10 minutes, or until they're golden. Repeat with any remaining dough. Transfer the cookies to a wire rack and let them cool. 6. Store. Store the cookies in a sealed container in the refrigerator for up to five days, or in the freezer for up to one month.

Per Serving:

calories: 226 | fat: 27g | protein: 3g | carbs: 1g | net carbs: 0g | fiber: 1g

Lemon Vanilla Cheesecake

Prep time: 15 minutes | Cook time: 20 minutes | Serves 6

2 teaspoons freshly squeezed lemon juice	room temperature
	½ cup plus 2 teaspoons Swerve
2 teaspoons vanilla extract or almond extract	8 ounces (227 g) cream cheese, at room temperature
½ cup sour cream, divided, at	2 eggs, at room temperature

1. Pour 2 cups of water into the inner cooking pot of the Instant Pot, then place a trivet (preferably with handles) in the pot. Line the sides of a 6-inch springform pan with parchment paper. 2. In a food processor, put the lemon juice, vanilla, ¼ cup of sour cream, ½ cup of Swerve, and the cream cheese. 3. Gently but thoroughly blend all the ingredients, scraping down the sides of the bowl as needed. 4. Add the eggs and blend only as long as you need to in order to get them well incorporated, 20 to 30 seconds. Your mixture will be pourable by now. 5. Pour the mixture into the prepared pan. Cover the pan with aluminum foil and place on the trivet. (If your trivet doesn't have handles, you may wish to use a foil sling to make removing the pan easier.) 6. Lock the lid into place. Select Manual and adjust the pressure to High. Cook for 20 minutes. When the cooking is complete, let the pressure release naturally. Unlock the lid. 7. Meanwhile, in a small bowl, mix together the remaining ¼ cup of sour cream and 2 teaspoons of Swerve for the topping. 8. Take out the cheesecake and remove the foil. Spread the topping over the top. Doing this while the cheesecake is still hot helps melt the topping into the cheesecake. 9. Put the cheesecake in the refrigerator and leave it alone. Seriously. Leave it alone and let it chill for at least 6 to 8 hours. It won't taste right hot. 10. When you're ready to serve, open the sides of the pan and peel off the parchment paper. Slice and serve.

Per Serving:

calories: 207 | fat: 19g | protein: 5g | carbs: 4g | net carbs: 4g | fiber: 0g

Chocolate Pecan Clusters

Prep time: 5 minutes | Cook time: 5 minutes | Makes 8 clusters

3 tablespoons butter	1 cup chopped pecans
¼ cup heavy cream	¼ cup low-carb chocolate chips
1 teaspoon vanilla extract	

1. Press the Sauté button and add butter to Instant Pot. Allow butter to melt and begin to turn golden brown. Once it begins to brown, immediately add heavy cream. Press the Cancel button. 2. Add vanilla and chopped pecans to Instant Pot. Allow to cool for 10 minutes, stirring occasionally. Spoon mixture onto parchment-lined baking sheet to form eight clusters, and scatter chocolate chips over clusters. Place in fridge to cool.

Per Serving:

calories: 194 | fat: 18g | protein: 2g | carbs: 7g | net carbs: 6g | fiber: 1g

Blackberry "Cheesecake" Bites

Prep time: 5 minutes | Cook time: 0 minutes | serves 4

1½ cups almonds, soaked overnight	¼ cup full-fat coconut cream
	⅓ cup monk fruit sweetener
1 cup blackberries	¼ cup freshly squeezed lemon juice
⅓ cup coconut oil, melted	

1. Prepare a muffin tin by lining the cups with cupcake liners. Set aside. 2. In a high-powered blender, combine the soaked almonds, blackberries, melted coconut oil, coconut cream, monk fruit sweetener, and lemon juice. 3. Blend on high until the mixture is whipped and fluffy. 4. Divide the mixture equally among the muffin cups. 5. Place the muffin tin in the freezer for 90 minutes to allow the cheesecake bites to set.

Per Serving:

calories: 514 | fat: 48g | protein: 12g | carbs: 18g | net carbs: 9g | fiber: 9g

Lemon Drops

Prep time: 5 minutes | Cook time: 0 minutes | Serves 4

¼ cup (60 ml) melted (but not hot) cacao butter

¼ cup (60 ml) melted (but not hot) coconut oil

1½ teaspoons confectioners'-style erythritol

2 teaspoons lemon-flavored magnesium powder (optional)

1 teaspoon lemon extract

Special Equipment:

Silicone mold(s) with 20 (½-ounce/15-ml) round cavities

1. Set the silicone mold(s) on a baking sheet. 2. Place the cacao butter, coconut oil, and erythritol in a small bowl. Whisk until the erythritol has dissolved. 3. If using magnesium powder, add it to the bowl along with the lemon extract. Whisk to combine. 4. Pour the mixture into the silicone mold(s), filling to the top. Transfer the baking sheet to the fridge to harden for 1 hour. 5. Once hardened, remove the lemon drops from the molds and enjoy! Serve directly from the fridge.

Per Serving:

calories: 258 | fat: 29g | protein: 0g | carbs: 0g | net carbs: 0g | fiber: 0g

Trail Mix with Dried Coconut and Strawberries

Prep time: 15 minutes | Cook time: 3 hours 30 minutes | Makes 7 cups

10 medium strawberries, hulled and halved

2 tablespoons coconut oil

1 teaspoon ground cinnamon

½ teaspoon vanilla extract

Sweetener of choice (optional)

2 cups chopped pecans

2 cups walnut halves, chopped

1 cup unsweetened coconut flakes

½ cup macadamia nuts

½ cup sliced almonds

3 Brazil nuts, chopped

3 tablespoons hulled pumpkin seeds

1. Preheat the oven to 200°F (93°C). Line a baking sheet with parchment paper. 2. Arrange the strawberries cut-side up on the prepared baking sheet and bake for 3 hours, rotating the baking sheet every hour. Remove from the oven and let cool for 30 minutes. If they are still moist, cook for another 30 minutes. 3. While the strawberries are cooling, increase the oven heat to 375°F (190°C). 4. In a microwave-safe bowl, melt the coconut oil in the microwave. Stir in the cinnamon, vanilla, and sweetener (if using). In another bowl, combine the pecans, walnuts, coconut flakes, macadamia nuts, almonds, Brazil nuts, and pumpkin seeds. Drizzle the coconut oil mixture over the nuts until everything is lightly coated but not soaked. 5. Line two more baking sheets with parchment paper and spread the nut mixture over the sheets evenly.

Bake for 15 to 30 minutes until the nuts begin to brown. Remove from the oven and pour onto a paper towel to dry. 6. Once all the ingredients have cooled, toss the nuts and strawberries together and eat right away. 7. If not eating right away, store the strawberries and nuts separately. Both will store safely in an airtight container for 1 week. If moisture develops in your strawberry container, bake for another 30 minutes at 200°F.

Per Serving:

½ cup: calories: 388 | fat: 36g | protein: 7g | carbs: 9g | net carbs: 4g | fiber: 5g

Fudgy Brownies

Prep time: 5 minutes | Cook time: 20 minutes | Makes 16 brownies

½ cup (1 stick) butter

4 ounces (113 g) unsweetened baker's chocolate

1 teaspoon vanilla extract (optional)

¾ cup (3 ounces / 85 g) blanched almond flour

⅔ cup powdered erythritol

2 tablespoons unsweetened cocoa powder

¼ teaspoon sea salt (only if using unsalted butter)

2 large eggs, at room temperature, whisked

¼ cup walnuts, chopped (optional)

1. Preheat the oven to 350°F (180°C). Line an 8-inch square pan with parchment paper, with the edges of the paper over two of the sides. 2. In a double boiler top or heatproof bowl, combine the butter and chocolate. Bring water to a simmer in the bottom part of the double boiler or a saucepan. Place the double boiler top or bowl over the simmering water and heat gently, stirring frequently. 3. Remove the bowl from the pan as soon as the chocolate pieces have all melted and stir in the vanilla, if desired. 4. Add the almond flour, powdered erythritol, cocoa powder, sea salt, and eggs. Stir together until uniform. The batter will be a little grainy looking. 5. Transfer the batter to the lined pan. Smooth the top with a spatula or the back of a spoon. If desired, sprinkle with the chopped walnuts and press into the top. 6. Bake for 15 to 20 minutes, until an inserted toothpick comes out almost clean with just a little batter on it that balls up between your fingers. (Do not wait for it to come out totally clean. Do not wait for the brownies to be totally firm or completely set. Do not pour off any liquid pooled on top.) 7. Cool completely before moving or cutting. (Do not cut while warm.) Use the overhanging pieces of parchment paper to lift the uncut brownies out of the pan and place on a cutting board. Cut into 16 brownies using a straight-down motion, not a seesaw motion, and wipe the knife between cuts if you notice sticking. These brownies are even better the next day!

Per Serving:

calories: 163 | fat: 15g | protein: 2g | carbs: 6g | net carbs: 1g | fiber: 5g

Espresso Cheesecake with Raspberries

Prep time: 5 minutes | Cook time: 35 minutes | Serves 8

1 cup blanched almond flour	16 ounces (454 g) cream
½ cup plus 2 tablespoons	cheese
Swerve	1 cup water
3 tablespoons espresso	6 ounces (170 g) dark
powder, divided	chocolate (at least 80% cacao)
2 tablespoons butter	8 ounces (227 g) full-fat
1 egg	heavy whipping cream
½ cup full-fat heavy cream	2 cups raspberries

1. In a small mixing bowl, combine the almond flour, 2 tablespoons of Swerve, 1 tablespoon of espresso powder and the butter. 2. Line the bottom of a springform pan with parchment paper. Press the almond flour dough flat on the bottom and about 1 inch on the sides. Set aside. 3. In a food processor, mix the egg, heavy cream, cream cheese, remaining Swerve and remaining espresso powder until smooth. 4. Pour the cream cheese mixture into the springform pan. Loosely cover with aluminum foil. 5. Put the water in the Instant Pot and place the trivet inside. 6. Close the lid. Select Manual button and set the timer for 35 minutes on High pressure. 7. When timer beeps, use a natural pressure release for 15 minutes, then release any remaining pressure. Open the lid. 8. Remove the springform pan and place it on a cooling rack for 2 to 3 hours or until it reaches room temperature. Refrigerate overnight. 9. Melt the chocolate and heavy whipping cream in the double boiler. Cool for 15 minutes and drizzle on top of the cheesecake, allowing the chocolate to drip down the sides. 10. Add the raspberries on top of the cheesecake before serving.

Per Serving:
calories: 585 | fat: 54g | protein: 12g | carbs: 15g | net carbs: 11g | fiber: 4g

Traditional Kentucky Butter Cake

Prep time: 5 minutes | Cook time: 35 minutes | Serves 4

2 cups almond flour	1 tablespoon vanilla extract
¾ cup granulated erythritol	½ cup butter, melted
1½ teaspoons baking powder	Cooking spray
4 eggs	½ cup water

1. In a medium bowl, whisk together the almond flour, erythritol, and baking powder. Whisk well to remove any lumps. 2. Add the eggs and vanilla and whisk until combined. 3. Add the butter and whisk until the batter is mostly smooth and well combined. 4. Grease the pan with cooking spray and pour in the batter. Cover tightly with aluminum foil. 5. Add the water to the pot. Place the Bundt pan on the trivet and carefully lower it into the pot using. 6. Set the lid in place. Select the Manual mode and set the cooking time for 35 minutes on High Pressure. When the timer goes off, do a quick pressure release. Carefully open the lid. 7. Remove the

pan from the pot. Let the cake cool in the pan before flipping out onto a plate.

Per Serving:
calories: 179 | fat: 16g | protein: 2g | carbs: 2g | net carbs: 2g | fiber: 0g

Lavender Ice Cream

Prep time: 5 minutes | Cook time: 0 minutes | serves 4

2 (14 ounces) cans full-fat	¼ cup coconut oil, melted
coconut cream	3 tablespoons dried lavender
¾ cup monk fruit sweetener	1 teaspoon vanilla extract
½ cup raw cashews, soaked in	1 teaspoon almond extract
water overnight	Sea salt

1. Combine all the ingredients in a high-powered blender and blend on high for 5 minutes until the mixture grows in volume by about one-third and becomes fluffy. 2. Pour the mixture into a freezer-safe pan and freeze for 2 hours. 3. Remove the mixture from the freezer and break it into chunks. 4. Transfer the mixture to a food processor and blend until a soft-serve consistency is achieved. 5. Spoon the ice cream into a freezer-safe pan and place back in the freezer to set for 3 hours before serving.

Per Serving:
calories: 571 | fat: 60g | protein: 3g | carbs: 10g | net carbs: 9g | fiber: 1g

Orange-Olive Oil Cupcakes

Prep time: 15 minutes | Cook time: 20 minutes | Makes 6 cupcakes

1 large egg	Zest of 1 orange
2 tablespoons powdered	1 cup almond flour
sugar-free sweetener (such as	¾ teaspoon baking powder
stevia or monk fruit extract)	⅛ teaspoon salt
½ cup extra-virgin olive oil	1 tablespoon freshly squeezed
1 teaspoon almond extract	orange juice

1. Preheat the oven to 350°F (180°C). Place muffin liners into 6 cups of a muffin tin. 2. In a large bowl, whisk together the egg and powdered sweetener. Add the olive oil, almond extract, and orange zest and whisk to combine well. 3. In a small bowl, whisk together the almond flour, baking powder, and salt. Add to wet ingredients along with the orange juice and stir until just combined. 4. Divide the batter evenly into 6 muffin cups and bake until a toothpick inserted in the center of the cupcake comes out clean, 15 to 18 minutes. 5. Remove from the oven and cool for 5 minutes in the tin before transferring to a wire rack to cool completely.

Per Serving:
1 cupcake: calories: 305 | fat: 28g | protein: 6g | carbs: 10g | net carbs: 4g | fiber: 6g

Glazed Pumpkin Bundt Cake

Prep time: 7 minutes | Cook time: 35 minutes | Serves 12

Cake:

3 cups blanched almond flour	6 large eggs
1 teaspoon baking soda	2 cups pumpkin purée
½ teaspoon fine sea salt	1 cup Swerve
2 teaspoons ground cinnamon	¼ cup (½ stick) unsalted
1 teaspoon ground nutmeg	butter (or coconut oil for
1 teaspoon ginger powder	dairy-free), softened
¼ teaspoon ground cloves	

Glaze:

1 cup (2 sticks) unsalted butter	melted
(or coconut oil for dairy-free),	½ cup Swerve

1. In a large bowl, stir together the almond flour, baking soda, salt, and spices. In another large bowl, add the eggs, pumpkin, sweetener, and butter and stir until smooth. Pour the wet ingredients into the dry ingredients and stir well. 2. Grease a 6-cup Bundt pan. Pour the batter into the prepared pan and cover with a paper towel and then with aluminum foil. 3. Place a trivet in the bottom of the Instant Pot and pour in 2 cups of cold water. Place the Bundt pan on the trivet. 4. Lock the lid. Select the Manual mode and set the cooking time for 35 minutes at High Pressure. 5. When the timer beeps, use a natural pressure release for 10 minutes. Carefully remove the lid. 6. Let the cake cool in the pot for 10 minutes before removing. 7. While the cake is cooling, make the glaze: In a small bowl, mix the butter and sweetener together. Spoon the glaze over the warm cake. 8. Allow to cool for 5 minutes before slicing and serving.

Per Serving:

calories: 332 | fat: 22g | protein: 7g | carbs: 27g | net carbs: 26g | fiber: 1g

Five-Minute Keto Cookie Dough

Prep time: 5 minutes | Cook time: 0 minutes | Makes 20 dough balls

8 ounces (227 g) cream cheese, at room temperature	½ teaspoon vanilla extract
6 tablespoons butter or ghee, at room temperature	½ to 1 teaspoon monk fruit or stevia, or more (optional)
½ cup peanut butter (or almond butter)	¼ teaspoon sea salt
¼ cup granulated sweetener (such as erythritol)	¼ cup stevia-sweetened chocolate chips (or >90% dark chocolate chunks)

1. In a large bowl, mix together the cream cheese and butter using an electric hand mixer. 2. Add the peanut butter, granulated sweetener, vanilla, monk fruit, and salt and mix again until well combined. Taste and adjust the sweetness to your liking. 3. Fold in the chocolate chips and then use a tablespoon or small scoop to form 20 dough balls. Arrange the dough balls on a plate or baking sheet. 4. Let chill in the refrigerator for 1 hour and store in an airtight container for up to 3 weeks.

Per Serving:

1 dough ball: calories: 123 | fat: 11g | protein: 2g | carbs: 4g | net carbs: 3g | fiber: 1g

Fudge Pops

Prep time: 5 minutes | Cook time: 0 minutes | serves 4

1 (14 ounces) can full-fat coconut cream	5 or 6 drops liquid stevia
3 avocados, peeled, pitted, and chopped	⅓ cup freshly grated orange zest
⅓ cup cacao powder	Sea salt

1. In a high-powered blender, combine the coconut cream with the avocados, cacao powder, and stevia. 2. Whip the mixture in the blender for 5 minutes until it becomes airy. 3. Stir in the orange zest and salt and pour the mixture into popsicle molds. 4. Place the molds in the freezer overnight to set. 5. To serve, run warm water over the popsicle molds to loosen the fudge pops.

Per Serving:

calories: 434 | fat: 40g | protein: 4g | carbs: 21g | net carbs: 9g | fiber: 12g

Espresso Cream

Prep time: 10 minutes | Cook time: 9 minutes | Serves 4

1 cup heavy cream	¼ cup low-carb chocolate chips
½ teaspoon espresso powder	
½ teaspoon vanilla extract	½ cup powdered erythritol
2 teaspoons unsweetened cocoa powder	3 egg yolks
	1 cup water

1. Press the Sauté button and add heavy cream, espresso powder, vanilla, and cocoa powder. Bring mixture to boil and add chocolate chips. Press the Cancel button. Stir quickly until chocolate chips are completely melted. 2. In medium bowl, whisk erythritol and egg yolks. Fold mixture into Instant Pot chocolate mix. Ladle into four (4-inch) ramekins. 3. Rinse inner pot and replace. Pour in 1 cup of water and place steam rack on bottom of pot. Cover ramekins with foil and carefully place on top of steam rack. Click lid closed. 4. Press the Manual button and adjust time for 9 minutes. Allow a full natural release. When the pressure indicator drops, carefully remove ramekins and allow to completely cool, then refrigerate. Serve chilled with whipped topping.

Per Serving:

calories: 320 | fat: 29g | protein: 3g | carbs: 10g | net carbs: 8g | fiber: 2g

Halle Berries-and-Cream Cobbler

Prep time: 10 minutes | Cook time: 25 minutes | Serves 4

12 ounces (340 g) cream cheese (1½ cups), softened
1 large egg
¾ cup Swerve confectioners'-style sweetener or equivalent amount of powdered

sweetener
½ teaspoon vanilla extract
¼ teaspoon fine sea salt
1 cup sliced fresh raspberries or strawberries

Biscuits:

3 large egg whites
¾ cup blanched almond flour
1 teaspoon baking powder

2½ tablespoons very cold unsalted butter, cut into pieces
¼ teaspoon fine sea salt

Frosting:

2 ounces (57 g) cream cheese (¼ cup), softened
1 tablespoon Swerve confectioners'-style sweetener or equivalent amount of powdered or liquid sweetener

1 tablespoon unsweetened, unflavored almond milk or heavy cream
Fresh raspberries or strawberries, for garnish

1. Preheat the air fryer to 400°F (204°C). Grease a pie pan. 2. In a large mixing bowl, use a hand mixer to combine the cream cheese, egg, and sweetener until smooth. Stir in the vanilla and salt. Gently fold in the raspberries with a rubber spatula. Pour the mixture into the prepared pan and set aside. 3. Make the biscuits: Place the egg whites in a medium-sized mixing bowl or the bowl of a stand mixer. Using a hand mixer or stand mixer, whip the egg whites until very fluffy and stiff. 4. In a separate medium-sized bowl, combine the almond flour and baking powder. Cut in the butter and add the salt, stirring gently to keep the butter pieces intact. 5. Gently fold the almond flour mixture into the egg whites. Use a large spoon or ice cream scooper to scoop out the dough and form it into a 2-inch-wide biscuit, making sure the butter stays in separate clumps. Place the biscuit on top of the raspberry mixture in the pan. Repeat with remaining dough to make 4 biscuits. 6. Place the pan in the air fryer and bake for 5 minutes, then lower the temperature to 325°F (163°C) and bake for another 17 to 20 minutes, until the biscuits are golden brown. 7. While the cobbler cooks, make the frosting: Place the cream cheese in a small bowl and stir to break it up. Add the sweetener and stir. Add the almond milk and stir until well combined. If you prefer a thinner frosting, add more almond milk. 8. Remove the cobbler from the air fryer and allow to cool slightly, then drizzle with the frosting. Garnish with fresh raspberries. 9. Store leftovers in an airtight container in the refrigerator for up to 3 days. Reheat the cobbler in a preheated 350°F (177°C) air fryer for 3 minutes, or until warmed through.

Per Serving:

calories: 535 | fat: 14g | protein: 13g | carbs: 14g | net carbs: 10g | fiber: 4g

Cholesterol Caring Nut Clusters

Prep time: 5 minutes | Cook time: 20 minutes | Makes 18 mini clusters

Cluster Base:

1 cup macadamia nuts
1 cup pecan halves
½ cup pistachios
¼ cup tahini or coconut butter

(although tahini is preferable)
1 large egg
1 teaspoon vanilla powder
2 teaspoons cinnamon

Topping:

2 ounces (57 g) dark chocolate
1 tablespoon virgin coconut

oil or cacao butter
Pinch of flaked salt

1. Preheat the oven to 285°F (140°C) fan assisted or 320°F (160°C) conventional. 2. Make the cluster base: Roughly chop the nuts or place in a food processor and pulse until chopped but still chunky. Add the remaining base ingredients. Press the "dough" into 18 mini muffin cups and bake for 15 to 20 minutes, until crispy. Remove from the oven and allow to cool completely. Just before adding the chocolate topping, place them in the freezer for 5 to 10 minutes. 3. Meanwhile, make the topping: Melt the dark chocolate and coconut oil in a double boiler, or use a heatproof bowl placed over a small saucepan filled with 1 cup of water, placed over medium heat. Let cool to room temperature. Alternatively, use a microwave and melt in short 10- to 15-second bursts until melted, stirring in between. 4. Top the cooled clusters with the melted dark chocolate and flaked salt. Store in a sealed container in the fridge for up to 2 weeks or freeze for up to 3 months.

Per Serving:

calories: 149 | fat: 14g | protein: 3g | carbs: 5g | net carbs: 3g | fiber: 2g

Lime Muffins

Prep time: 10 minutes | Cook time: 15 minutes | Serves 6

1 teaspoon lime zest
1 tablespoon lemon juice
1 teaspoon baking powder
1 cup almond flour

2 eggs, beaten
1 tablespoon Swerve
¼ cup heavy cream
1 cup water, for cooking

1. In the mixing bowl, mix up lemon juice, baking powder, almond flour, eggs, Swerve, and heavy cream. 2. When the muffin batter is smooth, add lime zest and mix it up. 3. Fill the muffin molds with batter. 4. Then pour water and insert the rack in the instant pot. 5. Place the muffins on the rack. Close and seal the lid. 6. Cook the muffins on Manual (High Pressure) for 15 minutes. 7. Then allow the natural pressure release.

Per Serving:

calories: 153 | fat: 12g | protein: 6g | carbs: 5g | net carbs: 3g | fiber: 2g

Coconut Almond Cream Cake

Prep time: 10 minutes | Cook time: 40 minutes | Serves 8

Nonstick cooking spray	1 teaspoon apple pie spice
1 cup almond flour	2 eggs, lightly whisked
½ cup unsweetened shredded coconut	¼ cup unsalted butter, melted
⅓ cup Swerve	½ cup heavy (whipping) cream
1 teaspoon baking powder	

1. Grease a 6-inch round cake pan with the cooking spray. 2. In a medium bowl, mix together the almond flour, coconut, Swerve, baking powder, and apple pie spice. 3. Add the eggs, then the butter, then the cream, mixing well after each addition. 4. Pour the batter into the pan and cover with aluminum foil. 5. Pour 2 cups of water into the inner cooking pot of the Instant Pot, then place a trivet in the pot. Place the pan on the trivet. 6. Lock the lid into place. Select Manual and adjust the pressure to High. Cook for 40 minutes. When the cooking is complete, let the pressure release naturally for 10 minutes, then quick-release any remaining pressure. Unlock the lid. 7. Carefully take out the pan and let it cool for 15 to 20 minutes. Invert the cake onto a plate. Sprinkle with shredded coconut, almond slices, or powdered sweetener, if desired, and serve.

Per Serving:

calories: 231 | fat: 19g | protein: 3g | carbs: 12g | net carbs: 10g | fiber: 2g

Fried Cheesecake Bites

Prep time: 30 minutes | Cook time: 2 minutes | Makes 16 bites

8 ounces (227 g) cream cheese, softened	4 tablespoons heavy cream, divided
½ cup plus 2 tablespoons Swerve, divided	½ teaspoon vanilla extract
	½ cup almond flour

In a stand mixer fitted with a paddle attachment, beat the cream cheese, ½ cup of the Swerve, 2 tablespoons of the heavy cream, and the vanilla until smooth. Using a small ice-cream scoop, divide the mixture into 16 balls and arrange them on a rimmed baking sheet lined with parchment paper. Freeze for 45 minutes until firm. 2. Line the air fryer basket with parchment paper and preheat the air fryer to 350°F (177°C). 3. In a small shallow bowl, combine the almond flour with the remaining 2 tablespoons Swerve. 4. In another small shallow bowl, place the remaining 2 tablespoons cream. 5. One at a time, dip the frozen cheesecake balls into the cream and then roll in the almond flour mixture, pressing lightly to form an even coating. Arrange the balls in a single layer in the air fryer basket, leaving room between them. Air fry for 2 minutes until the coating is lightly browned.

Per Serving:

calories: 99 | fat: 9g | protein: 2g | carbs: 3g | net carbs: 2g | fiber: 1g

Almond Butter Cookie Balls

Prep time: 5 minutes | Cook time: 10 minutes | Makes 10 balls

1 cup almond butter	¼ cup shredded unsweetened coconut
1 large egg	¼ cup low-carb, sugar-free chocolate chips
1 teaspoon vanilla extract	½ teaspoon ground cinnamon
¼ cup low-carb protein powder	
¼ cup powdered erythritol	

In a large bowl, mix almond butter and egg. Add in vanilla, protein powder, and erythritol. 2. Fold in coconut, chocolate chips, and cinnamon. Roll into 1-inch balls. Place balls into a round baking pan and put into the air fryer basket. 3. Adjust the temperature to 320°F (160°C) and bake for 10 minutes. 4. Allow to cool completely. Store in an airtight container in the refrigerator up to 4 days.

Per Serving:

calories: 199 | fat: 16g | protein: 7g | carbs: 7g | net carbs: 3g | fiber: 4g

Nutty Shortbread Cookies

Prep time: 10 minutes | Cook time: 10 minutes | Makes 10 cookies

½ cup butter, at room temperature, plus additional for greasing the baking sheet	vanilla extract
	1½ cups almond flour
½ cup granulated sweetener	½ cup ground hazelnuts
1 teaspoon alcohol-free pure	Pinch sea salt

1. In a medium bowl, cream together the butter, sweetener, and vanilla until well blended. 2. Stir in the almond four, ground hazelnuts, and salt until a firm dough is formed. 3. Roll the dough into a 2-inch cylinder and wrap it in plastic wrap. Place the dough in the refrigerator for at least 30 minutes until firm. 4. Preheat the oven to 350°F. Line a baking sheet with parchment paper and lightly grease the paper with butter; set aside. 5. Unwrap the chilled cylinder, slice the dough into 18 cookies, and place the cookies on the baking sheet. 6. Bake the cookies until firm and lightly browned, about 10 minutes. 7. Allow the cookies to cool on the baking sheet for 5 minutes and then transfer them to a wire rack to cool completely.

Per Serving:

1 cookie: calories: 105 | fat: 10g | protein: 3g | carbs: 2g | net carbs: 1g | fiber: 1g

Mixed Berry Cobbler

Prep time: 10 minutes | Cook time: 35 minutes | Serves 4

Filling:

2 cups frozen mixed berries

1 tablespoon granulated erythritol

½ teaspoon water

¼ teaspoon freshly squeezed lemon juice

¼ teaspoon vanilla extract

Crust:

½ cup coconut flour

2 tablespoons granulated erythritol

½ teaspoon xanthan gum

½ teaspoon baking powder

6 tablespoons butter, cold

¼ cup heavy (whipping) cream

Topping:

1 teaspoon granulated erythritol

¼ teaspoon ground cinnamon

1. Preheat the oven to 350°F (180°C). 2. To make the filling: In a 9-inch round pie dish, combine the berries, erythritol, water, lemon juice, and vanilla. 3. To make the crust: In a food processor, pulse to combine the coconut flour, erythritol, xanthan gum, and baking powder. 4. Add the butter and cream, and pulse until pea-sized pieces of dough form. Don't overprocess. 5. Form 5 equal balls of dough, then flatten them to between ¼- and ½-inch thickness. 6. Place the dough rounds on the top of the berries so that they are touching, but not overlapping. 7. To make the topping: In a small bowl, combine the erythritol and cinnamon. Sprinkle the mixture over the dough. 8. Bake for 30 to 35 minutes, until the topping is beginning to brown, then let cool for 10 minutes before serving.

Per Serving:

calories: 317 | fat: 25g | protein: 4g | carbs: 19g | net carbs: 12g | fiber: 7g

Mini Cheesecake

Prep time: 10 minutes | Cook time: 15 minutes | Serves 2

½ cup walnuts

2 tablespoons salted butter

2 tablespoons granular erythritol

4 ounces (113 g) full-fat

cream cheese, softened

1 large egg

½ teaspoon vanilla extract

⅛ cup powdered erythritol

1. Place walnuts, butter, and granular erythritol in a food processor. Pulse until ingredients stick together and a dough forms. 2. Press dough into a springform pan then place the pan into the air fryer basket. 3. Adjust the temperature to 400°F (204°C) and bake for 5 minutes. 4. When done, remove the crust and let cool. 5. In a medium bowl, mix cream cheese with egg, vanilla extract, and powdered erythritol until smooth. 6. Spoon mixture on top of baked walnut crust and place into the air fryer basket. 7. Adjust the temperature to 300°F (149°C) and bake for 10 minutes. 8. Once done, chill for 2 hours before serving.

Per Serving:

calories: 699 | fat: 68g | protein: 15g | carbs: 12g | net carbs: 6g | fiber: 3g

Coconut–White Chocolate Fudge

Prep time: 10 minutes | Cook time: 0 minutes | Makes 16 squares

Coconut oil for greasing

1 cup full-fat unsweetened coconut milk

4 ounces (113 g) unsweetened cacao/cocoa butter, chopped

½ cup coconut butter/manna

⅓ cup vanilla-flavored

collagen powder

1 teaspoon vanilla extract

¼ teaspoon sea salt

⅛ teaspoon ground cinnamon (optional)

½ teaspoon sweetener of choice (optional)

1. Grease an 8-inch square pan with oil and then line it with a piece of parchment paper, pressing down so that it sticks and evenly covers the pan. 2. In a medium saucepan over low heat, melt together the coconut milk, cacao butter, and coconut butter, stirring occasionally, until smooth. Remove from the heat and whisk in the collagen powder, vanilla, salt, and cinnamon (if using). Taste the mixture and then add the sweetener (if using), adjusting the sweetness to your liking. 3. Pour the mixture into the prepared pan and spread evenly. Refrigerate overnight. 4. Cut into 16 squares and store in an airtight container in the refrigerator for up to 2 weeks.

Per Serving:

1 square: calories: 148 | fat: 15g | protein: 2g | carbs: 2g | net carbs: 1g | fiber: 1g

Almond Pie with Coconut

Prep time: 5 minutes | Cook time: 41 minutes | Serves 8

1 cup almond flour

½ cup coconut milk

1 teaspoon vanilla extract

2 tablespoons butter, softened

1 tablespoon Truvia

¼ cup shredded coconut

1 cup water

1. In the mixing bowl, mix up almond flour, coconut milk, vanilla extract, butter, Truvia, and shredded coconut. 2. When the mixture is smooth, transfer it in the baking pan and flatten. 3. Pour water and insert the trivet in the instant pot. 4. Put the baking pan with cake on the trivet. 5. Lock the lid. Select the Manual mode and set the cooking time for 41 minutes on High Pressure. Once the timer goes off, perform a natural pressure release for 10 minutes, then release any remaining pressure. Carefully open the lid. 6. Serve immediately.

Per Serving:

calories: 89 | fat: 9g | protein: 1g | carbs: 3g | net carbs: 2g | fiber: 1g

Lemon Berry Cream Pops

Prep time: 10 minutes | Cook time: 5 minutes | Makes 8 ice pops

Cream Pops:

2 cups coconut cream

1 tablespoon unsweetened vanilla extract

Optional: low-carb sweetener,

to taste

2 cups raspberries, fresh or frozen and defrosted

Coating:

1⅓ cups coconut butter

¼ cup virgin coconut oil

Zest from 2 lemons, about 2

tablespoons

1 teaspoon unsweetened vanilla extract

1. To make the cream pops: In a bowl, whisk the coconut cream with the vanilla and optional sweetener until smooth and creamy. In another bowl, crush the raspberries using a fork, then add them to the bowl with the coconut cream and mix to combine. 2. Divide the mixture among eight ⅓-cup ice pop molds. Freeze until solid for 3 hours, or until set. 3. To easily remove the ice pops from the molds, fill a pot as tall as the ice pops with warm (not hot) water and dip the ice pop molds in for 15 to 20 seconds. Remove the ice pops from the molds and then freeze again. 4. Meanwhile, prepare the coating: Place the coconut butter and coconut oil in a small saucepan over low heat. Stir until smooth, remove from the heat, and add the lemon zest and vanilla. Let cool to room temperature. 5. Remove the ice pops from the freezer, two at a time, and, holding the ice pops over the saucepan, use a spoon to drizzle the coating all over. Return to the freezer until fully set, about 10 minutes. Store in the freezer in a resealable bag for up to 3 months.

Per Serving:

calories: 533 | fat: 54g | protein: 3g | carbs: 13g | net carbs: 9g | fiber: 4g

Lemon Poppy Seed Macaroons

Prep time: 10 minutes | Cook time: 14 minutes | Makes 1 dozen cookies

2 large egg whites, room temperature

⅓ cup Swerve confectioners'-style sweetener or equivalent amount of powdered sweetener

2 tablespoons grated lemon zest, plus more for garnish if desired

2 teaspoons poppy seeds

1 teaspoon lemon extract

¼ teaspoon fine sea salt

2 cups unsweetened shredded coconut

Lemon Icing:

¼ cup Swerve confectioners'-style sweetener or equivalent amount of powdered sweetener

1 tablespoon lemon juice

Preheat the air fryer to 325°F (163°C). Line a pie pan or a casserole dish that will fit inside your air fryer with parchment paper. 2. Place the egg whites in a medium-sized bowl and use a hand mixer on high to beat the whites until stiff peaks form. Add the sweetener, lemon zest, poppy seeds, lemon extract, and salt. Mix on low until combined. Gently fold in the coconut with a rubber spatula. 3. Use a 1-inch cookie scoop to place the cookies on the parchment, spacing them about ¼ inch apart. Place the pan in the air fryer and bake for 12 to 14 minutes, until the cookies are golden and a toothpick inserted into the center comes out clean. 4. While the cookies bake, make the lemon icing: Place the sweetener in a small bowl. Add the lemon juice and stir well. If the icing is too thin, add a little more sweetener. If the icing is too thick, add a little more lemon juice. 5. Remove the cookies from the air fryer and allow to cool for about 10 minutes, then drizzle with the icing. Garnish with lemon zest, if desired. Store leftovers in an airtight container in the fridge for up to 5 days or in the freezer for up to a month.

Per Serving:

calories: 86 | fat: 7g | protein: 2g | carbs: 5g | net carbs: 2g | fiber: 3g

Angel Food Mug Cake with Strawberries

Prep time: 5 minutes | Cook time: 15 minutes | Serves 2

¼ cup egg whites

Pinch of cream of tartar

¼ teaspoon vanilla extract

1/16 teaspoon almond extract (optional)

¼ cup (1 ounce / 28 g) blanched almond flour

2 tablespoons erythritol

⅛ teaspoon sea salt

Whipped cream or whipped coconut cream, for serving (optional)

¼ cup (1½ ounces / 43 g) strawberries, sliced

1. If using the oven method, preheat the oven to 350°F (180°C). 2. In a medium bowl, with an electric hand mixer, beat the egg whites with the cream of tartar for a couple of minutes at high speed, until stiff peaks form. Beat in the vanilla and almond extract. 3. In another medium bowl, stir together the almond flour, erythritol, and sea salt. Gently fold the flour mixture into the egg whites, being careful not to break them down. 4. Divide the batter between two 4 ounces / 113 g ramekins or two small mugs. 5. Oven method: Place the ramekins in the oven and bake for about 15 minutes, until the tops of the cakes are firm and an inserted toothpick comes out mostly clean (a few crumbs are fine). Microwave method: Place the ramekins in the microwave for 70 to 90 seconds, until the tops of the cakes are firm and an inserted toothpick comes out mostly clean (a few crumbs are fine). 6. If desired, garnish with whipped cream (or whipped coconut cream for a dairy-free version). Serve with the sliced strawberries on top.

Per Serving:

calories: 104 | fat: 7g | protein: 6g | carbs: 8g | net carbs: 3g | fiber: 5g

Chapter 12

Vegetarian Main

Zucchini and Spinach Croquettes

Prep time: 9 minutes | Cook time: 7 minutes | Serves 6

4 eggs, slightly beaten
½ cup almond flour
½ cup goat cheese, crumbled
1 teaspoon fine sea salt
4 garlic cloves, minced
1 cup baby spinach

½ cup Parmesan cheese, grated
⅓ teaspoon red pepper flakes
1 pound (454 g) zucchini, peeled and grated
⅓ teaspoon dried dill weed

Thoroughly combine all ingredients in a bowl. Now, roll the mixture to form small croquettes. Air fry at 340ºF (171ºC) for 7 minutes or until golden. Tate, adjust for seasonings and serve warm.

Per Serving:
calories: 179 | fat: 12g | protein: 11g | carbs: 6g | net carbs: 3g | fiber: 3g

Sweet Pepper Nachos

Prep time: 10 minutes | Cook time: 5 minutes | Serves 2

6 mini sweet peppers, seeded and sliced in half
¾ cup shredded Colby jack cheese

¼ cup sliced pickled jalapeños
½ medium avocado, peeled, pitted, and diced
2 tablespoons sour cream

1. Place peppers into an ungreased round nonstick baking dish. Sprinkle with Colby and top with jalapeños. 2. Place dish into air fryer basket. Adjust the temperature to 350ºF (177ºC) and bake for 5 minutes. Cheese will be melted and bubbly when done. 3. Remove dish from air fryer and top with avocado. Drizzle with sour cream. Serve warm.

Per Serving:
calories: 255 | fat: 21g | protein: 11g | carbs: 9g | net carbs: 5g | fiber: 4g

Broccoli-Cheese Fritters

Prep time: 5 minutes | Cook time: 20 to 25 minutes | Serves 4

1 cup broccoli florets
1 cup shredded Mozzarella cheese
¾ cup almond flour
½ cup flaxseed meal, divided
2 teaspoons baking powder

1 teaspoon garlic powder
Salt and freshly ground black pepper, to taste
2 eggs, lightly beaten
½ cup ranch dressing

1. Preheat the air fryer to 400ºF (204ºC). 2. In a food processor fitted with a metal blade, pulse the broccoli until very finely chopped. 3. Transfer the broccoli to a large bowl and add the Mozzarella, almond flour, ¼ cup of the flaxseed meal, baking powder, and garlic powder. Stir until thoroughly combined. Season to taste

with salt and black pepper. Add the eggs and stir again to form a sticky dough. Shape the dough into 1¼-inch fritters. 4. Place the remaining ¼ cup flaxseed meal in a shallow bowl and roll the fritters in the meal to form an even coating. 5. Working in batches if necessary, arrange the fritters in a single layer in the basket of the air fryer and spray generously with olive oil. Pausing halfway through the cooking time to shake the basket, air fry for 20 to 25 minutes until the fritters are golden brown and crispy. Serve with the ranch dressing for dipping.

Per Serving:
calories: 638 | fat: 54g | protein: 28g | carbs: 16g | net carbs: 9g | fiber: 7g

Whole Roasted Lemon Cauliflower

Prep time: 5 minutes | Cook time: 15 minutes | Serves 4

1 medium head cauliflower
2 tablespoons salted butter, melted

1 medium lemon
½ teaspoon garlic powder
1 teaspoon dried parsley

1. Remove the leaves from the head of cauliflower and brush it with melted butter. Cut the lemon in half and zest one half onto the cauliflower. Squeeze the juice of the zested lemon half and pour it over the cauliflower. 2. Sprinkle with garlic powder and parsley. Place cauliflower head into the air fryer basket. 3. Adjust the temperature to 350ºF (177ºC) and air fry for 15 minutes. 4. Check cauliflower every 5 minutes to avoid overcooking. It should be fork tender. 5. To serve, squeeze juice from other lemon half over cauliflower. Serve immediately.

Per Serving:
calories: 90 | fat: 7g | protein: 3g | carbs: 6g | net carbs: 4g | fiber: 2g

Stuffed Portobellos

Prep time: 10 minutes | Cook time: 8 minutes | Serves 4

3 ounces (85 g) cream cheese, softened
½ medium zucchini, trimmed and chopped
¼ cup seeded and chopped red bell pepper
1½ cups chopped fresh

spinach leaves
4 large portobello mushrooms, stems removed
2 tablespoons coconut oil, melted
½ teaspoon salt

1. In a medium bowl, mix cream cheese, zucchini, pepper, and spinach. 2. Drizzle mushrooms with coconut oil and sprinkle with salt. Scoop ¼ zucchini mixture into each mushroom. 3. Place mushrooms into ungreased air fryer basket. Adjust the temperature to 400ºF (204ºC) and air fry for 8 minutes. Portobellos will be tender and tops will be browned when done. Serve warm.

Per Serving:
calories: 157 | fat: 14g | protein: 4g | carbs: 5g | net carbs: 3g | fiber: 2g

Zucchini Roll Manicotti

Prep time: 15 minutes | Cook time: 30 minutes | Serves 4

Olive oil cooking spray	cheese
4 zucchini	1 tablespoon chopped fresh
2 tablespoons good-quality	oregano
olive oil	Sea salt, for seasoning
1 red bell pepper, diced	Freshly ground black pepper,
½ onion, minced	for seasoning
2 teaspoons minced garlic	2 cups low-carb marinara
1 cup goat cheese	sauce, divided
1 cup shredded mozzarella	½ cup grated Parmesan cheese

1. Preheat the oven. Set the oven temperature to 375°F. Lightly grease a 9-by-13-inch baking dish with olive oil cooking spray. 2. Prepare the zucchini. Cut the zucchini lengthwise into ⅛-inch-thick slices and set them aside. 3. Make the filling. In a medium skillet over medium-high heat, warm the olive oil. Add the red bell pepper, onion, and garlic and sauté until they've softened, about 4 minutes. Remove the skillet from the heat and transfer the vegetables to a medium bowl. Stir the goat cheese, mozzarella, and oregano into the vegetables. Season it all with salt and pepper. 4. Assemble the manicotti. Spread 1 cup of the marinara sauce in the bottom of the baking dish. Lay a zucchini slice on a clean cutting board and place a couple tablespoons of filling at one end. Roll the slice up and place it in the baking dish, seam-side down. Repeat with the remaining zucchini slices. Spoon the remaining sauce over the rolls and top with the Parmesan. 5. Bake. Bake the rolls for 30 to 35 minutes until the zucchini is tender and the cheese is golden. 6. Serve. Spoon the rolls onto four plates and serve them hot.

Per Serving:
calories: 342 | fat: 24g | protein: 20g | carbs: 14g | net carbs: 11g | fiber: 3g

Cheesy Broccoli Casserole

Prep time: 10 minutes | Cook time: 35 minutes | Serves 4

2 tablespoons butter	4 ounces (113 g) cream
¼ white onion, diced	cheese, at room temperature
1 garlic clove, minced	1 cup shredded Cheddar
1 pound (454 g) broccoli	cheese, divided
florets, roughly chopped	½ cup heavy (whipping)
Salt, to taste	cream
Freshly ground black pepper,	2 eggs
to taste	

1. Preheat the oven to 350ºF (180ºC). 2. In a large skillet over medium heat, melt the butter. 3. Add the onion and garlic. Sauté for 5 to 7 minutes until the onion is softened and translucent. 4. Add the broccoli. Season with salt and pepper. Cook for 4 to 5 minutes until just softened. Transfer to a 7-by-11-inch baking dish. 5. In a medium bowl, stir together the cream cheese, ½ cup of Cheddar, the cream, and eggs. Pour over the broccoli. Season with more salt and pepper, and top with the remaining ½ cup of Cheddar. Bake for 20 minutes. Refrigerate leftovers in an airtight container for up to 1 week.

Per Serving:
calories: 440 | fat: 39g | protein: 16g | carbs: 11g | net carbs: 8g | fiber: 3g

Cheese Stuffed Peppers

Prep time: 20 minutes | Cook time: 15 minutes | Serves 2

1 red bell pepper, top and	Salt and pepper, to taste
seeds removed	1 cup Cottage cheese
1 yellow bell pepper, top and	4 tablespoons mayonnaise
seeds removed	2 pickles, chopped

1. Arrange the peppers in the lightly greased air fryer basket. Cook in the preheated air fryer at 400ºF (204ºC) for 15 minutes, turning them over halfway through the cooking time. 2. Season with salt and pepper. Then, in a mixing bowl, combine the cream cheese with the mayonnaise and chopped pickles. Stuff the pepper with the cream cheese mixture and serve. Enjoy!

Per Serving:
calories: 250 | fat: 20g | protein: 11g | carbs: 8g | net carbs: 6g | fiber: 2g

Spinach-Artichoke Stuffed Mushrooms

Prep time: 10 minutes | Cook time: 10 to 14 minutes | Serves 4

2 tablespoons olive oil	crumbled
4 large portobello mushrooms,	½ cup chopped marinated
stems removed and gills	artichoke hearts
scraped out	1 cup frozen spinach, thawed
½ teaspoon salt	and squeezed dry
¼ teaspoon freshly ground	½ cup grated Parmesan cheese
pepper	2 tablespoons chopped fresh
4 ounces (113 g) goat cheese,	parsley

1. Preheat the air fryer to 400ºF (204ºC). 2. Rub the olive oil over the portobello mushrooms until thoroughly coated. Sprinkle both sides with the salt and black pepper. Place top-side down on a clean work surface. 3. In a small bowl, combine the goat cheese, artichoke hearts, and spinach. Mash with the back of a fork until thoroughly combined. Divide the cheese mixture among the mushrooms and sprinkle with the Parmesan cheese. 4. Air fry for 10 to 14 minutes until the mushrooms are tender and the cheese has begun to brown. Top with the fresh parsley just before serving.

Per Serving:
calories: 255 | fat: 20g | protein: 13g | carbs: 7g | net carbs: 4g | fiber: 3g

Loaded Cauliflower Steak

Prep time: 5 minutes | Cook time: 7 minutes | Serves 4

1 medium head cauliflower	melted
¼ cup hot sauce	¼ cup blue cheese crumbles
2 tablespoons salted butter,	¼ cup full-fat ranch dressing

1. Remove cauliflower leaves. Slice the head in ½-inch-thick slices. 2. In a small bowl, mix hot sauce and butter. Brush the mixture over the cauliflower. 3. Place each cauliflower steak into the air fryer, working in batches if necessary. 4. Adjust the temperature to 400°F (204°C) and air fry for 7 minutes. 5. When cooked, edges will begin turning dark and caramelized. 6. To serve, sprinkle steaks with crumbled blue cheese. Drizzle with ranch dressing.

Per Serving:

calories: 140 | fat: 12g | protein: 5g | carbs: 6g | net carbs: 5g | fiber: 1g

Vegetable Burgers

Prep time: 10 minutes | Cook time: 12 minutes | Serves 4

8 ounces (227 g) cremini mushrooms	yellow onion
2 large egg yolks	1 clove garlic, peeled and finely minced
½ medium zucchini, trimmed and chopped	½ teaspoon salt
¼ cup peeled and chopped	¼ teaspoon ground black pepper

1. Place all ingredients into a food processor and pulse twenty times until finely chopped and combined. 2. Separate mixture into four equal sections and press each into a burger shape. Place burgers into ungreased air fryer basket. Adjust the temperature to 375°F (191°C) and air fry for 12 minutes, turning burgers halfway through cooking. Burgers will be browned and firm when done. 3. Place burgers on a large plate and let cool 5 minutes before serving.

Per Serving:

calories: 62 | fat: 3g | protein: 3g | carbs: 6g | net carbs: 4g | fiber: 2g

Three-Cheese Zucchini Boats

Prep time: 15 minutes | Cook time: 20 minutes | Serves 2

2 medium zucchini	cheese
1 tablespoon avocado oil	¼ teaspoon dried oregano
¼ cup low-carb, no-sugar-added pasta sauce	¼ teaspoon garlic powder
¼ cup full-fat ricotta cheese	½ teaspoon dried parsley
¼ cup shredded Mozzarella	2 tablespoons grated vegetarian Parmesan cheese

1. Cut off 1 inch from the top and bottom of each zucchini. Slice zucchini in half lengthwise and use a spoon to scoop out a bit of the inside, making room for filling. Brush with oil and spoon 2 tablespoons pasta sauce into each shell. 2. In a medium bowl, mix ricotta, Mozzarella, oregano, garlic powder, and parsley. Spoon the mixture into each zucchini shell. Place stuffed zucchini shells into the air fryer basket. 3. Adjust the temperature to 350°F (177°C) and air fry for 20 minutes. 4. To remove from the basket, use tongs or a spatula and carefully lift out. Top with Parmesan. Serve immediately.

Per Serving:

calories: 245 | fat: 18g | protein: 12g | carbs: 9g | net carbs: 7g | fiber: 2g

Eggplant and Zucchini Bites

Prep time: 30 minutes | Cook time: 30 minutes | Serves 8

2 teaspoons fresh mint leaves, chopped	1 pound (454 g) eggplant, peeled and cubed
1½ teaspoons red pepper chili flakes	1 pound (454 g) zucchini, peeled and cubed
2 tablespoons melted butter	3 tablespoons olive oil

1. Toss all the above ingredients in a large-sized mixing dish. 2. Roast the eggplant and zucchini bites for 30 minutes at 325°F (163°C) in your air fryer, turning once or twice. 3. Serve with a homemade dipping sauce.

Per Serving:

calories: 140 | fat: 12g | protein: 2g | carbs: 8g | net carbs: 6g | fiber: 2g

Broccoli Crust Pizza

Prep time: 15 minutes | Cook time: 12 minutes | Serves 4

3 cups riced broccoli, steamed and drained well	3 tablespoons low-carb Alfredo sauce
1 large egg	½ cup shredded Mozzarella cheese
½ cup grated vegetarian Parmesan cheese	

1. In a large bowl, mix broccoli, egg, and Parmesan. 2. Cut a piece of parchment to fit your air fryer basket. Press out the pizza mixture to fit on the parchment, working in two batches if necessary. Place into the air fryer basket. 3. Adjust the temperature to 370°F (188°C) and air fry for 5 minutes. 4. The crust should be firm enough to flip. If not, add 2 additional minutes. Flip crust. 5. Top with Alfredo sauce and Mozzarella. Return to the air fryer basket and cook an additional 7 minutes or until cheese is golden and bubbling. Serve warm.

Per Serving:

calories: 178 | fat: 11g | protein: 15g | carbs: 10g | net carbs: 4g | fiber: 6g

White Cheddar and Mushroom Soufflés

Prep time: 15 minutes | Cook time: 12 minutes | Serves 4

3 large eggs, whites and yolks separated	¼ teaspoon cream of tartar
½ cup sharp white Cheddar cheese	¼ teaspoon salt
3 ounces (85 g) cream cheese, softened	¼ teaspoon ground black pepper
	½ cup cremini mushrooms, sliced

In a large bowl, whip egg whites until stiff peaks form, about 2 minutes. In a separate large bowl, beat Cheddar, egg yolks, cream cheese, cream of tartar, salt, and pepper together until combined. 2. Fold egg whites into cheese mixture, being careful not to stir. Fold in mushrooms, then pour mixture evenly into four ungreased ramekins. Place ramekins into air fryer basket. Adjust the temperature to 350°F (177°C) and bake for 12 minutes. Eggs will be browned on the top and firm in the center when done. Serve warm.

Per Serving:

calories: 228 | fat: 19g | protein: 13g | carbs: 2g | net carbs: 2g | fiber: 0g

Garlic White Zucchini Rolls

Prep time: 20 minutes | Cook time: 20 minutes | Serves 4

2 medium zucchini	½ cup full-fat ricotta cheese
2 tablespoons unsalted butter	¼ teaspoon salt
¼ white onion, peeled and diced	½ teaspoon garlic powder
½ teaspoon finely minced roasted garlic	¼ teaspoon dried oregano
¼ cup heavy cream	2 cups spinach, chopped
2 tablespoons vegetable broth	½ cup sliced baby portobello mushrooms
⅛ teaspoon xanthan gum	¾ cup shredded Mozzarella cheese, divided

1. Using a mandoline or sharp knife, slice zucchini into long strips lengthwise. Place strips between paper towels to absorb moisture. Set aside. 2. In a medium saucepan over medium heat, melt butter. Add onion and sauté until fragrant. Add garlic and sauté 30 seconds. 3. Pour in heavy cream, broth, and xanthan gum. Turn off heat and whisk mixture until it begins to thicken, about 3 minutes. 4. In a medium bowl, add ricotta, salt, garlic powder, and oregano and mix well. Fold in spinach, mushrooms, and ½ cup Mozzarella. 5. Pour half of the sauce into a round baking pan. To assemble the rolls, place two strips of zucchini on a work surface. Spoon 2 tablespoons of ricotta mixture onto the slices and roll up. Place seam side down on top of sauce. Repeat with remaining ingredients. 6. Pour remaining sauce over the rolls and sprinkle with remaining Mozzarella. Cover with foil and place into the air fryer basket. 7. Adjust the temperature to 350°F (177°C) and bake for 20 minutes. 8. In the last 5 minutes, remove the foil to brown the cheese. Serve immediately.

Per Serving:

calories: 270 | fat: 21g | protein: 14g | carbs: 7g | net carbs: 5g | fiber: 2g

Roasted Veggie Bowl

Prep time: 10 minutes | Cook time: 15 minutes | Serves 2

1 cup broccoli florets	½ medium green bell pepper, seeded and sliced ¼ inch thick
1 cup quartered Brussels sprouts	1 tablespoon coconut oil
½ cup cauliflower florets	2 teaspoons chili powder
¼ medium white onion, peeled and sliced ¼ inch thick	½ teaspoon garlic powder
	½ teaspoon cumin

1. Toss all ingredients together in a large bowl until vegetables are fully coated with oil and seasoning. 2. Pour vegetables into the air fryer basket. 3. Adjust the temperature to 360°F (182°C) and roast for 15 minutes. 4. Shake two or three times during cooking. Serve warm.

Per Serving:

calories: 168 | fat: 11g | protein: 4g | carbs: 15g | net carbs: 9g | fiber: 6g

Almond-Cauliflower Gnocchi

Prep time: 5 minutes | Cook time: 25 to 30 minutes | Serves 4

5 cups cauliflower florets	¼ cup unsalted butter, melted
⅔ cup almond flour	¼ cup grated Parmesan cheese
½ teaspoon salt	

1. In a food processor fitted with a metal blade, pulse the cauliflower until finely chopped. Transfer the cauliflower to a large microwave-safe bowl and cover it with a paper towel. Microwave for 5 minutes. Spread the cauliflower on a towel to cool. 2. When cool enough to handle, draw up the sides of the towel and squeeze tightly over a sink to remove the excess moisture. Return the cauliflower to the food processor and whirl until creamy. Sprinkle in the flour and salt and pulse until a sticky dough comes together. 3. Transfer the dough to a workspace lightly floured with almond flour. Shape the dough into a ball and divide into 4 equal sections. Roll each section into a rope 1 inch thick. Slice the dough into squares with a sharp knife. 4. Preheat the air fryer to 400°F (204°C). 5. Working in batches if necessary, place the gnocchi in a single layer in the basket of the air fryer and spray generously with olive oil. Pausing halfway through the cooking time to turn the gnocchi, air fry for 25 to 30 minutes until golden brown and crispy on the edges. Transfer to a large bowl and toss with the melted butter and Parmesan cheese.

Per Serving:

calories: 220 | fat: 20g | protein: 7g | carbs: 8g | net carbs: 5g | fiber: 3g

Crustless Spanakopita

Prep time: 15 minutes | Cook time: 45 minutes | Serves 6

12 tablespoons extra-virgin olive oil, divided
1 small yellow onion, diced
1 (32-ounce / 907-g) bag frozen chopped spinach, thawed, fully drained, and patted dry (about 4 cups)
4 garlic cloves, minced
½ teaspoon salt
½ teaspoon freshly ground black pepper
1 cup whole-milk ricotta cheese
4 large eggs
¾ cup crumbled traditional feta cheese
¼ cup pine nuts

1. Preheat the oven to 375°F (190°C). 2. In a large skillet, heat 4 tablespoons olive oil over medium-high heat. Add the onion and sauté until softened, 6 to 8 minutes. 3. Add the spinach, garlic, salt, and pepper and sauté another 5 minutes. Remove from the heat and allow to cool slightly. 4. In a medium bowl, whisk together the ricotta and eggs. Add to the cooled spinach and stir to combine. 5. Pour 4 tablespoons olive oil in the bottom of a 9-by-13-inch glass baking dish and swirl to coat the bottom and sides. Add the spinach-ricotta mixture and spread into an even layer. 6. Bake for 20 minutes or until the mixture begins to set. Remove from the oven and crumble the feta evenly across the top of the spinach. Add the pine nuts and drizzle with the remaining 4 tablespoons olive oil. Return to the oven and bake for an additional 15 to 20 minutes, or until the spinach is fully set and the top is starting to turn golden brown. Allow to cool slightly before cutting to serve.

Per Serving:

calories: 440 | fat: 38g | protein: 17g | carbs: 9g | net carbs: 8g | fiber: 1g

Crispy Tofu

Prep time: 30 minutes | Cook time: 15 to 20 minutes | Serves 4

1 (16 ounces / 454 g) block extra-firm tofu
2 tablespoons coconut aminos
1 tablespoon toasted sesame oil
1 tablespoon olive oil
1 tablespoon chili-garlic sauce
1½ teaspoons black sesame seeds
1 scallion, thinly sliced

1. Press the tofu for at least 15 minutes by wrapping it in paper towels and setting a heavy pan on top so that the moisture drains. 2. Slice the tofu into bite-size cubes and transfer to a bowl. Drizzle with the coconut aminos, sesame oil, olive oil, and chili-garlic sauce. Cover and refrigerate for 1 hour or up to overnight. 3. Preheat the air fryer to 400°F (204°C). 4. Arrange the tofu in a single layer in the air fryer basket. Pausing to shake the pan halfway through the cooking time, air fry for 15 to 20 minutes until crisp. Serve with any juices that accumulate in the bottom of the air fryer, sprinkled with the sesame seeds and sliced scallion.

Per Serving:

calories: 186 | fat: 14g | protein: 12g | carbs: 4g | net carbs: 3g | fiber: 1g

Pesto Vegetable Skewers

Prep time: 30 minutes | Cook time: 8 minutes | Makes 8 skewers

1 medium zucchini, trimmed and cut into ½-inch slices
½ medium yellow onion, peeled and cut into 1-inch squares
1 medium red bell pepper, seeded and cut into 1-inch
squares
16 whole cremini mushrooms
⅓ cup basil pesto
½ teaspoon salt
¼ teaspoon ground black pepper

1. Divide zucchini slices, onion, and bell pepper into eight even portions. Place on 6-inch skewers for a total of eight kebabs. Add 2 mushrooms to each skewer and brush kebabs generously with pesto. 2. Sprinkle each kebab with salt and black pepper on all sides, then place into ungreased air fryer basket. Adjust the temperature to 375°F (191°C) and air fry for 8 minutes, turning kebabs halfway through cooking. Vegetables will be browned at the edges and tender-crisp when done. Serve warm.

Per Serving:

calories: 50 | fat: 4g | protein: 2g | carbs: 4g | net carbs: 3g | fiber: 1g

Broccoli with Garlic Sauce

Prep time: 19 minutes | Cook time: 15 minutes | Serves 4

2 tablespoons olive oil
Kosher salt and freshly ground black pepper, to taste
Dipping Sauce:
2 teaspoons dried rosemary, crushed
3 garlic cloves, minced
⅓ teaspoon dried marjoram,
1 pound (454 g) broccoli florets

crushed
¼ cup sour cream
⅓ cup mayonnaise

1. Lightly grease your broccoli with a thin layer of olive oil. Season with salt and ground black pepper. 2. Arrange the seasoned broccoli in the air fryer basket. Bake at 395°F (202°C) for 15 minutes, shaking once or twice. In the meantime, prepare the dipping sauce by mixing all the sauce ingredients. Serve warm broccoli with the dipping sauce and enjoy!

Per Serving:

calories: 250 | fat: 23g | protein: 3g | carbs: 10g | net carbs: 9g | fiber: 1g

Quiche-Stuffed Peppers

Prep time: 5 minutes | Cook time: 15 minutes | Serves 2

2 medium green bell peppers	½ cup chopped broccoli
3 large eggs	½ cup shredded medium
¼ cup full-fat ricotta cheese	Cheddar cheese
¼ cup diced yellow onion	

Cut the tops off of the peppers and remove the seeds and white membranes with a small knife. 2. In a medium bowl, whisk eggs and ricotta. 3. Add onion and broccoli. Pour the egg and vegetable mixture evenly into each pepper. Top with Cheddar. Place peppers into a 4-cup round baking dish and place into the air fryer basket. 4. Adjust the temperature to 350°F (177°C) and bake for 15 minutes. 5. Eggs will be mostly firm and peppers tender when fully cooked. Serve immediately.

Per Serving:

calories: 382 | fat: 27g | protein: 24g | carbs: 11g | net carbs: 7g | fiber: 4g

Italian Baked Egg and Veggies

Prep time: 10 minutes | Cook time: 10 minutes | Serves 2

2 tablespoons salted butter	diced
1 small zucchini, sliced	2 large eggs
lengthwise and quartered	¼ teaspoon onion powder
½ medium green bell pepper,	¼ teaspoon garlic powder
seeded and diced	½ teaspoon dried basil
1 cup fresh spinach, chopped	¼ teaspoon dried oregano
1 medium Roma tomato,	

1. Grease two ramekins with 1 tablespoon butter each. 2. In a large bowl, toss zucchini, bell pepper, spinach, and tomatoes. Divide the mixture in two and place half in each ramekin. 3. Crack an egg on top of each ramekin and sprinkle with onion powder, garlic powder, basil, and oregano. Place into the air fryer basket. 4. Adjust the temperature to 330°F (166°C) and bake for 10 minutes. 5. Serve immediately.

Per Serving:

calories: 260 | fat: 21g | protein: 10g | carbs: 8g | net carbs: 5g | fiber: 3g

Parmesan Artichokes

Prep time: 10 minutes | Cook time: 10 minutes | Serves 4

2 medium artichokes, trimmed	Parmesan cheese
and quartered, center removed	¼ cup blanched finely ground
2 tablespoons coconut oil	almond flour
1 large egg, beaten	½ teaspoon crushed red
½ cup grated vegetarian	pepper flakes

1. In a large bowl, toss artichokes in coconut oil and then dip each piece into the egg. 2. Mix the Parmesan and almond flour in a large bowl. Add artichoke pieces and toss to cover as completely as possible, sprinkle with pepper flakes. Place into the air fryer basket. 3. Adjust the temperature to 400°F (204°C) and air fry for 10 minutes. 4. Toss the basket two times during cooking. Serve warm.

Per Serving:

calories: 220 | fat: 18g | protein: 10g | carbs: 9g | net carbs: 4g | fiber: 5g

Spinach Cheese Casserole

Prep time: 15 minutes | Cook time: 15 minutes | Serves 4

1 tablespoon salted butter,	¼ cup chopped pickled
melted	jalapeños
¼ cup diced yellow onion	2 cups fresh spinach, chopped
8 ounces (227 g) full-fat	2 cups cauliflower florets,
cream cheese, softened	chopped
⅓ cup full-fat mayonnaise	1 cup artichoke hearts,
⅓ cup full-fat sour cream	chopped

1. In a large bowl, mix butter, onion, cream cheese, mayonnaise, and sour cream. Fold in jalapeños, spinach, cauliflower, and artichokes. 2. Pour the mixture into a round baking dish. Cover with foil and place into the air fryer basket. 3. Adjust the temperature to 370°F (188°C) and set the timer for 15 minutes. In the last 2 minutes of cooking, remove the foil to brown the top. Serve warm.

Per Serving:

calories: 490 | fat: 46g | protein: 9g | carbs: 12g | net carbs: 8g | fiber: 4g

Spaghetti Squash Alfredo

Prep time: 10 minutes | Cook time: 15 minutes | Serves 2

½ large cooked spaghetti	½ teaspoon garlic powder
squash	1 teaspoon dried parsley
2 tablespoons salted butter,	¼ teaspoon ground
melted	peppercorn
½ cup low-carb Alfredo sauce	½ cup shredded Italian blend
¼ cup grated vegetarian	cheese
Parmesan cheese	

Using a fork, remove the strands of spaghetti squash from the shell. Place into a large bowl with butter and Alfredo sauce. Sprinkle with Parmesan, garlic powder, parsley, and peppercorn. 2. Pour into a 4-cup round baking dish and top with shredded cheese. Place dish into the air fryer basket. 3. Adjust the temperature to 320°F (160°C) and bake for 15 minutes. When finished, cheese will be golden and bubbling. Serve immediately.

Per Serving:

calories: 383 | fat: 30g | protein: 14g | carbs: 14g | net carbs: 11g | fiber: 3g

Eggplant Parmesan

Prep time: 15 minutes | Cook time: 17 minutes | Serves 4

1 medium eggplant, ends trimmed, sliced into ½-inch rounds

¼ teaspoon salt

2 tablespoons coconut oil

½ cup grated Parmesan cheese

1 ounce (28 g) 100% cheese crisps, finely crushed

½ cup low-carb marinara sauce

½ cup shredded Mozzarella cheese

1. Sprinkle eggplant rounds with salt on both sides and wrap in a kitchen towel for 30 minutes. Press to remove excess water, then drizzle rounds with coconut oil on both sides. 2. In a medium bowl, mix Parmesan and cheese crisps. Press each eggplant slice into mixture to coat both sides. 3. Place rounds into ungreased air fryer basket. Adjust the temperature to 350°F (177°C) and air fry for 15 minutes, turning rounds halfway through cooking. They will be crispy around the edges when done. 4. Spoon marinara over rounds and sprinkle with Mozzarella. Continue cooking an additional 2 minutes at 350°F (177°C) until cheese is melted. Serve warm.

Per Serving:

calories: 330 | fat: 24g | protein: 18g | carbs: 13g | net carbs: 9g | fiber: 4g

Crustless Spinach Cheese Pie

Prep time: 10 minutes | Cook time: 20 minutes | Serves 4

6 large eggs

¼ cup heavy whipping cream

1 cup frozen chopped spinach,

¼ cup diced yellow onion

drained

1 cup shredded sharp Cheddar cheese

1. In a medium bowl, whisk eggs and add cream. Add remaining ingredients to bowl. 2. Pour into a round baking dish. Place into the air fryer basket. 3. Adjust the temperature to 320°F (160°C) and bake for 20 minutes. 4. Eggs will be firm and slightly browned when cooked. Serve immediately.

Per Serving:

calories: 317 | fat: 24g | protein: 21g | carbs: 4g | net carbs: 3g | fiber: 1g

Cauliflower Tikka Masala

Prep time: 10 minutes | Cook time: 20 minutes | Serves 4

For The Cauliflower

1 head cauliflower, cut into small florets

1 tablespoon coconut oil,

For The Sauce

2 tablespoons coconut oil

½ onion, chopped

1 tablespoon minced garlic

1 tablespoon grated ginger

2 tablespoons garam masala

1 tablespoon tomato paste

melted

1 teaspoon ground cumin

½ teaspoon ground coriander

½ teaspoon salt

1 cup crushed tomatoes

1 cup heavy (whipping) cream

1 tablespoon chopped fresh cilantro

Make The Cauliflower: 1. Preheat the oven. Set the oven temperature to 425°F. Line a baking sheet with aluminum foil. 2. Prepare the cauliflower. In a large bowl, toss the cauliflower with the coconut oil, cumin, and coriander. Spread the cauliflower on the baking sheet in a single layer and bake it for 20 minutes, until the cauliflower is tender. Make The Sauce: 1. Sauté the vegetables. While the cauliflower is baking, in a large skillet over medium-high heat, warm the coconut oil. Add the onion, garlic, and ginger and sauté until they've softened, about 3 minutes. 2. Finish the sauce. Stir in the garam masala, tomato paste, and salt until the vegetables are coated. Stir in the crushed tomatoes and bring to a boil, then reduce the heat to low and simmer the sauce for 10 minutes, stirring it often. Remove the skillet from the heat and stir in the cream and cilantro. 3. Assemble and serve. Add the cauliflower to the sauce, stirring to combine everything. Divide the mixture between four bowls and serve it hot.

Per Serving:

calories: 372 | fat: 32g | protein: 8g | carbs: 17g | net carbs: 10g | fiber: 7g

Appendix 1: Measurement Conversion Chart

MEASUREMENT CONVERSION CHART

VOLUME EQUIVALENTS(DRY)

US STANDARD	METRIC (APPROXIMATE)
1/8 teaspoon	0.5 mL
1/4 teaspoon	1 mL
1/2 teaspoon	2 mL
3/4 teaspoon	4 mL
1 teaspoon	5 mL
1 tablespoon	15 mL
1/4 cup	59 mL
1/2 cup	118 mL
3/4 cup	177 mL
1 cup	235 mL
2 cups	475 mL
3 cups	700 mL
4 cups	1 L

VOLUME EQUIVALENTS(LIQUID)

US STANDARD	US STANDARD (OUNCES)	METRIC (APPROXIMATE)
2 tablespoons	1 fl.oz.	30 mL
1/4 cup	2 fl.oz.	60 mL
1/2 cup	4 fl.oz.	120 mL
1 cup	8 fl.oz.	240 mL
1 1/2 cup	12 fl.oz.	355 mL
2 cups or 1 pint	16 fl.oz.	475 mL
4 cups or 1 quart	32 fl.oz.	1 L
1 gallon	128 fl.oz.	4 L

TEMPERATURES EQUIVALENTS

FAHRENHEIT(F)	CELSIUS(C) (APPROXIMATE)
225 °F	107 °C
250 °F	120 °C
275 °F	135 °C
300 °F	150 °C
325 °F	160 °C
350 °F	180 °C
375 °F	190 °C
400 °F	205 °C
425 °F	220 °C
450 °F	235 °C
475 °F	245 °C
500 °F	260 °C

WEIGHT EQUIVALENTS

US STANDARD	METRIC (APPROXIMATE)
1 ounce	28 g
2 ounces	57 g
5 ounces	142 g
10 ounces	284 g
15 ounces	425 g
16 ounces (1 pound)	455 g
1.5 pounds	680 g
2 pounds	907 g

Appendix 2: The Dirty Dozen and Clean Fifteen

The Dirty Dozen and Clean Fifteen

The Environmental Working Group (EWG) is a nonprofit, nonpartisan organization dedicated to protecting human health and the environment Its mission is to empower people to live healthier lives in a healthier environment. This organization publishes an annual list of the twelve kinds of produce, in sequence, that have the highest amount of pesticide residue-the Dirty Dozen-as well as a list of the fifteen kinds ofproduce that have the least amount of pesticide residue-the Clean Fifteen.

THE DIRTY DOZEN	THE CLEAN FIFTEEN
• The 2016 Dirty Dozen includes the following produce. These are considered among the year's most important produce to buy organic:	• The least critical to buy organically are the Clean Fifteen list. The following are on the 2016 list:

THE DIRTY DOZEN

Strawberries	Spinach
Apples	Tomatoes
Nectarines	Bell peppers
Peaches	Cherry tomatoes
Celery	Cucumbers
Grapes	Kale/collard greens
Cherries	Hot peppers

• *The Dirty Dozen list contains two additional itemskale/collard greens and hot peppers-because they tend to contain trace levels of highly hazardous pesticides.*

THE CLEAN FIFTEEN

Avocados	Papayas
Corn	Kiw
Pineapples	Eggplant
Cabbage	Honeydew
Sweet peas	Grapefruit
Onions	Cantaloupe
Asparagus	Cauliflower
Mangos	

• *Some of the sweet corn sold in the United States are made from genetically engineered (GE) seedstock. Buy organic varieties of these crops to avoid GE produce.*

Appendix 3: Recipe Index

Made in the USA
Las Vegas, NV
27 August 2023